THE WORLD OF THE TAVERN

The World of the Tavern
Public Houses in Early Modern Europe

Edited by
Beat Kümin and B. Ann Tlusty

ASHGATE

Published by
Ashgate Publishing Limited
Gower House
Croft Road
Aldershot
Hampshire GU11 3HR
England

Ashgate Publishing Company
131 Main Street
Burlington, VT 05401-5600, USA

Ashgate website: http//www.ashgate.com

British Library Cataloguing in Publication Data
The world of the tavern : public houses in early modern
    Europe
    1.Taverns (Inns) - Europe - History 2.Bars (Drinking
    establishments) - Europe - History
    I. Kümin, Beat A. II.Tlusty, B. Ann, 1954-
    647.9'5'4'0903

Library of Congress Cataloging in Publication Data
The world of the tavern : public houses in early modern Europe / edited by Beat Kümin and B. Ann Tlusty.
        p. cm.
    Includes bibliographical references and index.
    ISBN 0-7546-0341-5
    1. Bars (Drinking establishments)--Europe--History. I. Kümin, Beat A. II. Tlusty, B. Ann.

    TX950.59.E85 W67 2002
    647.954--dc21

                                                        2002022346
    ISBN 0 7546 0341 5

Printed and bound in Great Britain by MPG Books Ltd, Bodmin, Cornwall

Contents

I. Introductions

II. Thematic Approaches

III. Regional Studies

List of Figures, Graphs and Tables

List of Contributors

Fabian Brändle is an assistant researcher at the University of Basel. His recent publications include 'Toggenburger Wirtshäuser und Wirte im 17. und 18. Jahrhundert', in Fabian Brändle et al. (eds), *Obrigkeit und Opposition. Drei Beiträge zur Kulturgeschichte des Toggenburgs aus dem 17./18. Jahrhundert* (Wattwil, 1999); and *'Biechlin von meinem ganzen Leben'. Die Autobiographie des Calvinistischen Colmarer Kannengiessers Augustin Güntzer (1596–1657?)*, co-edited with Dominik Sieber (Cologne and Vienna, forthcoming). He is currently working on a Ph.D. thesis concerning the 'Political Culture of the Swiss *Landsgemeindeorte* in the Eighteenth Century'.

John Chartres is Professor of Social & Economic History at the University of Leeds and former Editor of the *Agricultural History Review*. Among recent publications have been 'Country Trades, Crafts and Professions' and 'Industries in the Countryside' in the *Agrarian History of England and Wales*, VII, 1850–1914 (Cambridge, 2000); and 'Leeds, Regional Distributive Centre of Luxuries in the Eighteenth Century', *Northern History* 36 (2000).

Michael Frank was *wissenschaftlicher Assistent* for history at the Ruhr-University Bochum from 1996 until 2001. His publications include: *Dörfliche Gesellschaft und Kriminalität. Das Fallbeispiel Lippe (1650–1800)* (Paderborn, 1995); 'Die fehlende Geduld Hiobs. Suizid und Gesellschaft in der Grafschaft Lippe (1600–1800)', in Gabriela Signori (ed.), *Trauer, Verzweiflung und Anfechtung. Selbstmörder in spätmittelalterlichen und frühneuzeitlichen Gesellschaften* (Tübingen, 1994) 152–88; 'Trunkene Männer und nüchterne Frauen. Zur Gefährdung von Geschlechterrollen durch Alkohol in der Frühen Neuzeit', in Martin Dinges (ed.), *Hausväter, Priester, Kastraten. Zur Konstruktion von Männlichkeit in Spätmittelalter und Früher Neuzeit* (Göttingen, 1998), 187–212.

Hans Heiss is Deputy Director of the State Archives of South Tyrol in Bozen/Bolzano (Italy) and Lecturer at the University of Innsbruck. He is author of *Am Rand der Revolution. Tirol 1848/49* (with Thomas Götz, 1998) and has published essays on the social history of tourism in Tyrol and Austria, most recently 'Tourismus und Urbanisierung. Fremdenverkehr und Stadtentwicklung in den österreichischen Alpenländern bis 1914', in *Stadt. Strom-Strasse-Schiene* (2001).

Judith Hunter, until October 2000 the curator of the Royal Borough Museum Collection at Windsor, is the vice president of the Berkshire Local History Association and founding member of two history societies. Her thesis investigated the legislation imposed and touching upon English inns, taverns, alehouses and other retail outlets concerned with the liquor trade for the two hundred years following the first licensing Act of 1552. As author and co-author she has written eighteen books and booklets, including five on inns and alehouses. The latest of these is *Victuallers' Licences: Records for Family and Local Historians*. Other recent books include *A History of Berkshire* and *A History of the Windsor Guildhall*.

Beat Kümin, formerly a Research Fellow of the Swiss National Science Foundation, is Lecturer in Early Modern European History at the University of Warwick. His publications include *The Shaping of a Community: The Rise and Reformation of the English Parish c. 1400-1560* (Aldershot, 1996) and 'Useful to have, but difficult to govern: Inns and taverns in early modern Bern and Vaud', *Journal of Early Modern History* 3 (1999).

Felix Müller studied history at the Universities of Zurich (*Lizentiat*) and Bern, where he wrote his dissertation, *Aussterben oder verarmen? Die Effinger von Wildegg. Eine Berner Patrizierfamilie während Aufklärung und Revolution* (Baden, 2000). He now works as a librarian and freelance historian. His research concentrates on the Aargau and on inns and taverns. His next publication project is a contribution to the history of Brugg in the Aargau (publication planned in 2005).

Janet Pennington is completing a Ph.D. on inn history at Chichester College of Southampton University under the supervision of Dr. Andrew Foster. She is the archivist at Lancing College in West Sussex, an active member of the Wealden Buildings Study Group and the Vernacular Architecture Group, and the author of various articles in *Sussex Archaeological Collections*, *West Sussex History*, and elsewhere. Among her recent publications is 'Inns and Alehouses of Sussex, 1686', in K. Leslie and B. Short (eds), *An Historical Atlas of Sussex* (Chichester, 1999). She also teaches for the Centre of Continuing Education at the University of Sussex.

George E. Snow is Professor of History at Shippensburg University of Pennsylvania. His areas of research and teaching are the Imperial Russian and Soviet Eras. His publications include 'Socialism, Alcoholism and the Russian Working Class before 1917', in S. Barrows and R. Room (eds), *Drinking: Behavior and Belief in Modern History* (1991); 'Archival Sources: Temperance

Materials in Russian Archives', in *Social History of Alcohol Review* (30/31, 1995); 'Alcoholism in Imperial Russia' and 'Alcohol Production in Russia', in *Supplement to the Modern Encyclopedia of Russian, Soviet and Eurasian History* I (1995); and 'Alcoholism in the Russian Military: The Public Sphere and the Temperance Discourse, 1883–1917', *Jahrbücher für Geschichte Osteuropas* 45/3 (1997).

Alison Stewart's research has emphasized secular and printed art in the Northern Renaissance and Reformation periods. An Associate Professor of Art History at the University of Nebraska-Lincoln, her recent publications include *Saints, Sinners and Sisters. Gender and Visual Art in Medieval and Early Modern Northern Europe*, co-edited with Jane Carroll (Aldershot, expected 2002), and her essay in that volume, 'Distaffs and Spindles. Sexual Misbehavior in Sebald Beham's *Spinning Bee*'.

B. Ann Tlusty is Associate Professor of History at Bucknell University in Pennsylvania. She is the author of *Bacchus and Civic Order: The Culture of Drink in Early Modern Germany* (Charlottesville, VA, 2001) and co-editor of *Ehrkonzepte in der Frühen Neuzeit: Identitäten und Abgrenzungen* (1998). Her further publications include essays on the cultural use of alcohol in early modern Germany in *Central European History, Social History/Histoire Social, Contemporary Drug Problems,* and other English- and German-language publications.

Preface

As much as we would like to claim that the idea for this collection emerged while drinking in a historic public house, it actually originated like most academic projects these days: through electronic contact of two historians working on related themes. When the editors finally met in person, however, it was in the congenial environment of a Munich beer garden. We are grateful to all contributors for responding to our invitation and for their patience in dealing with our enquiries. We would also like to thank the staffs of all the record repositories and institutions that provided assistance and granted copyright clearance for the reproductions in this volume.

Warwick and Lewisburg,
Spring 2002

B. K. AND A. T.

PART ONE

Introductions

The World of the Tavern:
An Introduction

Beat Kümin and B. Ann Tlusty

From the earliest studies of the topic right through to the essays featured in this volume, scholars have acknowledged the multifunctionality of public houses and their importance as social centres. Innumerable authors refer to the phenomenon in more or less detail, from Antiquity and the Middle Ages to modern times,[1] in areas ranging from the Indian subcontinent to the American frontier.[2] As yet, however, there has been no attempt at a synthesis for early modern Europe. This is in spite of the fact that the subject of drink received a great deal of attention from early modern writers, who left the modern scholar with a wealth of sources for exploitation.

The very versatility of this ubiquitous institution may have discouraged comparative approaches, not least because it straddles many different disciplines. Should public houses be discussed by economic historians? Obviously, but in fact they make only scant appearances in specialized textbooks, not fully belonging to any of the pre-modern economic sectors and often combining farming, trading and catering services all under one roof.[3] Could the topic be suitably examined from a social perspective? Yes, but the publican's profession rarely dominates the social landscape sufficiently to stand out in general quantitative analyses. Recent endeavours to develop a 'new' cultural history, perhaps, offer the best prospects of tackling such a heterogeneous and multidimensional topic. According to its ambitious remit, aspects as diverse as

---

[1]   W. C. Firebaugh, *The Inns of Greece & Rome and a History of Hospitality from the Dawn of Time to the Middle Ages* (Chicago, 1928); H. C. Peyer (ed.), *Gastfreundschaft, Taverne und Gasthaus im Mittelalter* (Munich, 1983); a range of case studies in north-eastern Italy and Austria around 1900 in the special issue of *Movimento Operaio e Socialista* 8 (1985).

[2]   A. I. Khan, 'The karawansarays of Mughal India. A study of surviving structures', in *Indian Historical Review* 14 (1987–88), 111–37; R. W. Slatta, 'Comparative frontier social life: Western saloons and Argentine pulperias', in *Great Plains Quarterly* 7 (1987), 155–65.

[3]   See the essay by Pennington; in what follows, contributions to this volume are referred to by their authors' surnames.

political contexts and individual mentalities need to be integrated into a comprehensive picture.[4]

As it happens, we owe the first long-term surveys of commercial hospitality and drinking customs to the more anecdotal and less theoretically charged 'old' cultural history, which flourished in German-speaking Europe in the late nineteenth and early twentieth century.[5] There was at that time also plenty of interest in individual establishments, normative frameworks and inn signs imagery.[6] Architectural historians then pointed to the potential of material evidence,[7] followed by the ascent of social and economic approaches from the 1970s, with English scholars like Alan Everitt and Peter Clark making influential contributions.[8] In Continental Europe, public houses featured in the debate on popular culture and Robert Muchembled's acculturation thesis,[9] and recent years saw a fresh series of comprehensive local and regional studies of the trade in Central Europe.[10] Comparative analysis of this vastly heterogeneous

---

[4] L. Hunt (ed.), *The New Cultural History* (Berkeley, 1989); H.-U. Wehler (ed.), *Die Herausforderung der Kulturgeschichte* (Munich, 1998).

[5] Some of the better major works in this genre include T. von Liebenau, *Das Gasthof- und Wirtshauswesen der Schweiz in älterer Zeit* (Zurich, 1891); F. von Bassermann-Jordan, *Geschichte des Weinbaus* (2 vols, Frankfurt a. M., 1923); O. D. Potthoff and G. Kossenhaschen, *Kulturgeschichte der deutschen Gaststätte, umfassend Deutschland, Österreich, die Schweiz und Deutschböhmen* (Berlin, 1933; reprint Hildesheim, 1996); F. Rauers, *Kulturgeschichte der Gaststätte* (2 vols, Berlin, 1941); G. Schreiber, *Deutsche Weingeschichte: Der Wein in Volksleben, Kult und Wirtschaft* (Cologne, 1980) (this posthumous publication was actually written during the decade preceding Schreiber's death in 1962, and was grounded in the folklorist tradition of the pre-war years; see Gabriel Simons, 'Vorwort des Herausgebers,' in ibid., v–vi). For a recent assessment of German folkloric studies on drinking see G. Hirschfelder, 'Bemerkungen zu Stand und Aufgaben volkskundlich-historischer Alkoholforschung der Neuzeit,' in *Rheinisch-westfälische Zeitschrift für Volkskunde* 39 (1994), 87–127.

[6] A model examination of legal aspects in J. Kachel, *Herberge und Gastwirtschaft in Deutschland bis zum 17. Jahrhundert* (Stuttgart, 1924); enormous amount of antiquarian information e.g. in J. Larwood and J. C. Hotten, *English Inn Signs* (London, 1951).

[7] W. A. Pantin, 'Medieval inns', in E. M. Jope (ed.), *Studies in Building History* (London, 1961), 166–91; M. W. Barley, 'Rural Building in England', in J. Thirsk (ed.), *Agrarian History of England and Wales* (vol. v/2, Cambridge, 1985), 590–685, esp. 682–5.

[8] A. Everitt, 'The English urban inn 1560–1760', in his *Perspectives in English Urban History* (London, 1973), 91–137; K. Wrightson, 'Alehouses, order and reformation in rural England 1590–1660', in S. and E. Yeo (eds), *Popular Culture and Class Conflict 1590–1914* (Brighton, 1981), 1–27; P. Clark, *The English Alehouse: A Social History 1200–1830* (London, 1983).

[9] *Popular Culture and Elite Culture in Early Modern France* (Baton Rouge, 1985; French original Paris, 1978).

[10] R. Linde, 'Ländliche Krüge. Wirtshauskultur in der Grafschaft Lippe im 18. Jahrhundert', in S. Baumeier and J. Carstensen (eds), *Beiträge zur Volkskunde und Hausforschung* 7 (Detmold, 1995), 7–50; F. Brändle, 'Toggenburger Wirtshäuser und Wirte im 17. und 18. Jahrhundert', in *Toggenburgerblätter für Heimatkunde* 41 (1999), 7–51; B. Kümin,

work was pioneered by the Swiss medievalist Hans Conrad Peyer in his examination of the origins of the trade.[11] Over the last two decades, hand in hand with the differentiation of historical sub-disciplines, scholarship on public houses has proliferated, albeit in a fractionalized and scattered manner. Among the most productive fields are studies on travel and trade infrastructure,[12] sociability and communication,[13] the social and cultural history of alcohol,[14] early modern crime,[15] gender,[16] and even popular religion.[17]

By the final decade of the twentieth century, then, the study of inns and taverns had moved beyond the history of 'daily life' and begun to challenge aspects of the major historical debates that define early modern Europe as a field. Public houses, drinking practices, and the controls placed upon them are

---

'Useful to have, but difficult to govern: Inns and taverns in early modern Bern and Vaud', in *Journal of Early Modern History* 3 (1999), 153–75.

[11] Peyer (ed.), *Gastfreundschaft* and his monograph *Von der Gastfreundschaft zum Gasthaus. Studien zur Gastlichkeit im Mittelalter* (Hannover, 1987).

[12] A. Mączak, *Travel in Early Modern Europe* (Cambridge, 1995; Polish original Warsaw, 1980), esp. ch. 2 ('Inns and their hospitality'); H. T. Gräf and R. Pröve, *Wege ins Ungewisse. Reisen in der frühen Neuzeit 1500–1800* (Frankfurt, 1997) [a reader of sources]; B. Kümin and A. Radeff, 'Markt-Wirtschaft. Handelsinfrastruktur und Gastgewerbe im alten Bern', in *Schweizerische Zeitschrift für Geschichte* 50 (2000), 1–19.

[13] D. Freist, *Governed by Opinion: Politics, Religion and the Dynamics of Communication in Stuart London 1637–45* (London, 1997); K. Hürlimann, *Soziale Beziehungen im Dorf. Aspekte dörflicher Sozialität in den Landvogteien Greifensee und Kyburg um 1500* (Zurich, 2000).

[14] T. Brennan, *Public Drinking and Popular Culture in Eighteenth-Century Paris* (Princeton, 1988); K. Simon-Muscheid, 'Formen der Soziabilität und Kriminalisierung der Trunkenheit (13.–17. Jahrhundert)', in J. Küchenhoff (ed.), *Selbstzerstörung und Selbstfürsorge* (Giessen, 1999), 44–53; B. A. Tlusty, *Bacchus and Civic Order: The Culture of Drink in Early Modern Germany* (Charlottesville, 2001).

[15] B. Müller-Wirthmann, 'Raufhändel. Gewalt und Ehre im Dorf', in R. van Dülmen (ed.), *Kultur der einfachen Leute* (Munich, 1983), 79–111; R. Shoemaker, *Prosecution and Punishment. Petty Crime and the Law in London and Rural Middlesex 1660–1725* (Cambridge, 1991); M. Frank, *Dörfliche Gesellschaft und Kriminalität. Das Fallbeispiel Lippe 1650–1800* (Paderborn, 1995); G. Schwerhoff, *Aktenkundig und gerichtsnotorisch: Einführung in die Historische Kriminalitätsforschung* (Tübingen, 1999).

[16] B. A. Tlusty, 'Gender and alcohol use', in *Social History/Histoire Sociale* 27/54 (November, 1994), 241–59; B. Beneder, *Männerort Gasthaus? Öffentlichkeit als sexualisierter Raum* (Frankfurt, 1997); B. A. Hanawalt, 'The host, the law, and the ambiguous space of medieval London taverns', in her *Of Good and Ill Repute. Gender and Social Control in Medieval England* (Oxford, 1998), 104–23; B. A. Tlusty, 'Crossing gender boundaries. Women as drunkards in early modern Augsburg', in S. Backmann et al. (eds), *Ehrkonzepte in der frühen Neuzeit* (Berlin, 1998), 185–98; A. L. Martin, *Alcohol, Sex and Gender in Late Medieval and Early Modern Europe* (Basingstoke, 2001).

[17] G. Maistre, 'La lutte du clergé contre les cabarets du XVIIe au XIX siècle', in *Vie religieuse en Savoie. Mentalités – Associations* (Annecy, 1988), 307–31; P. Hersche, 'Die Lustreise der kleinen Leute – zur geselligen Funktion der barocken Wallfahrt', in W. Adam (ed.), *Geselligkeit und Gesellschaft im Barockzeitalter* (Wiesbaden, 1997), 321–32.

related to the centralizing of government attending the rise of absolutism; con-fessionalization and social disciplining; modes of suppression of the body; and delineation of public and private realms. Most of the scholars currently examining early modern inns and taverns, however, are involved in in-depth local studies that make the best use of archival evidence. This fact has often left researchers working in isolation, with little opportunity for either regional or topical comparisons. The desire to offer a first survey of the state of research and to provide a forum for comparative approaches to the topic prompted the compilation of this collection.

Not surprisingly, problems of terminology became apparent from early on. All contributors used vastly heterogeneous definitions for their establishments, reflecting very real legal, regional and linguistic varieties. In German, for instance, sources refer to hosts as *Wirte, Gastgeben, Brauer, Zäpfler, Bier-* or *Weinschenke*, often without clear demarcations. In order to enable comparative analysis, some common frame of reference was needed. Given the language of this collection, British conventions have been adopted. 'Public house' thus serves as the umbrella term for all relevant establishments (corresponding to the German *Wirtshäuser*), while 'publican' provides the general expression for all hosts. As for common subcategories, 'inn' refers to a fully privileged house entitled to offer alcoholic drinks, hot food, accommodation, stables and cater-ing for large parties, while 'tavern' designates an establishment with more limited rights, selling mainly wine and cold food, but not normally providing hot meals or accommodation. 'Ale'-, 'beer'-, 'brandy'- and 'ginhouse' are used for outlets with similar restrictions, but specializing in particular drinks.[18] In essence, the common denominator of all these institutions is the regular sale of alcohol for consumption on publicly accessible premises, which means that coffee houses and salons remain largely outside the scope of this definition.[19] Establishments not adequately covered by any of these categories are intro-duced with the local vernacular term, defined with a view to the range of services on offer and then referred to by the vernacular throughout the respec-tive essay.

---

[18] In most places, typological differences seem to have centred on whether hot food was available at a drinking establishment. If so, accommodation usually came with it.

[19] Alcohol may have been available in many coffee houses, but the main attractions were other drinks. Furthermore, they emerged only from the mid seventeenth century and were initially quite exclusive, as suggested by their role in the debate on the emerging public sphere. Yet more removed from the 'classic' public house was the private salon. J. Habermas, *The Structural Transformation of the Public Sphere: An Inquiry into a Category of Bourgeois Society* (Cambridge, 1989; German original Neuwied, 1962); B. Lillywhite, *London Coffee Houses* (London, 1963); K. Teply, *Die Einführung des Kaffees in Wien. Georg Franz Koltschitzky, Johannes Diodato, Isaak de Luca* (Wien, 1980); J. C. Bologne, *Histoire des cafés et cafetiers* (Paris, 1993).

The early modern period provides a distinct and coherent time span for the study of public houses. By the late Middle Ages, a dense network of inns and taverns had come into existence, which continued to operate under parameters not fundamentally altered until the revolutions of the late eighteenth century. The essays in this volume thus range from the late Middle Ages – Heiss and Pennington finding thirteenth-century evidence – to the period around 1800 – the time of industrialization and early tourism featured, for example, in Chartres and Kümin. As for geographical scope, 'Europe' cannot be comprehensively covered by a limited number of studies. The focus of the present volume lies on three main regions: German-speaking areas, including present-day Austria, Germany and Switzerland; England; and Russia. France has attracted a fair amount of attention elsewhere,[20] while eastern, northern,[21] and particularly southern Europe remain darker corners, not least due to practical barriers for scholars unfamiliar with the local languages. Contemporaries, at least, saw Spain and Italy as lagging behind Central and Northern Europe with regard to density and quality of provision.[22]

The essays in this volume are arranged in three parts. The first, introductory section begins with general examinations of conflicting pressures affecting publicans (Michael Frank) and the social and gender profile of patrons (Beat Kümin). Part Two is dedicated to thematic approaches, including the legal framework (Judith Hunter for England), confessional tensions (Fabian Brändle with reference to the Swiss region of Toggenburg), visual sources (Alison Stewart on works by the Beham brothers), record linkage (Janet Pennington for the English county of West Sussex) and military aspects (Ann Tlusty with regard to the free imperial city of Augsburg). The third and final part offers a range of local, regional and national case studies, each with a distinct profile: the transit region of Tyrol in Austria (Hans Heiss), noble estates in a rural area

---

[20] Muchembled, *Popular Culture*; J. Nicolas, 'Le tavernier, le juge et le curé', in *Histoire* 25 (1980), 20–28; Brennan, *Public Drinking*; R. L. Spang, *The Invention of the Restaurant. Paris and Modern Gastronomic Culture* (Cambridge/Mass., 2000).

[21] G. Ränk, 'Der Krug in Alt-Livland und im späteren Estland', in *Eesti Teadusliku Seltsi Rootsis. Aastaraamat* 7 (1974–76), 9–88; A. M. Smith, 'Two Highland inns', in *Scottish Historical Review* 56 (1977), 184–8.

[22] H. Kellenbenz, 'Pilgerhospitäler, Albergues und Ventas in Spanien', in Peyer (ed.), *Gastfreundschaft*, 137–52; see also E. Motta, 'Albergatori milanesi nei secoli XIV e XV', in *Archivio storico lombardo* 25 (1898), 366–77; M. G. de la Torre, 'Las ventas en la España del antiguo regimen', in *Hispania* 39 (1979), 397–453; M. Santamaria Arnaiz, 'La invencion de las tabernas', in *Historia y Vida* 21 (1988), 86–98; G. Ortalli, 'Il giudice e la taverna. Momenti ludici in una piccola communità lagunare (Lio Maggiore nel secolo XIV)', in his (ed.), *Gioco e giustizia nell'Italia di Commune* (Treviso, 1993), 49–70; T. J. Dadson, 'El viajar en el siglo de oro: analisis comparativo de gastos de comida y posada', in *Boletin de la Real Academia de la Historia* 191 (1994), 437–54.

of the Swiss Confederation (Felix Müller), the highly centralized state of
Muscovy (George E. Snow), and England during a phase of rapid economic
change (John Chartres).

A first point to note is the multiplicity of sources, each posing peculiar
methodical challenges. On top of numerous types of written evidence – which
include acts and statutes, official registers of public houses and licensees, tax
lists, leases, craft and guild documents, court records, petitions, chronicles,
sermons, church protocols, military records, inventories and insurance papers –
there are countless literary, visual and material sources. Travel reports offer
welcome, if highly subjective glimpses into daily routine; woodcuts, engravings and paintings invite decoding of ambiguous imagery; while the physical
examination of surviving buildings uncovers the 'heritage' dimension of public
houses and points to the existence of extensive supporting infrastructure like
barns, stables and sometimes baking, slaughter, and bathing facilities.

In terms of subject matter, the essays inevitably produce a complex blend of
similarities and contrasts. Only a few general impressions will be highlighted
here. Among common themes, perhaps the most startling insight is the enormous economic importance of public houses. Not only did they provide
livelihoods for publicans and employees, but inns and taverns contributed
massive financial rewards to lords, cities and princes. At the same time, public
houses were indispensable facilitators of economic exchange, by offering mar-
ket- and meeting-places, storage space, auctioning facilities and transport
infrastructure.[23]

A second shared feature of many essays is attention to the early and comprehensive legislation aimed at controlling public houses. Lords, cities, princes,
parliaments and churches all issued floods of mandates, decrees and ordinances
to regulate numbers, licensing conditions, the duties of publicans and the moral
behaviour of patrons.[24] The high levels of income from marketing agricultural
produce, gathering licensing fees and raising excise taxes, on the other hand,
must have tempted many not to enforce restrictive legislation too harshly.[25] A
closer look at actual practice reinforces this suggestion. From a variety of
angles, scholarly concepts like 'social discipline' and 'confessionalization' can
be put to the test and often found wanting.[26]

---

[23] Most extensively discussed in Chartres.

[24] See in particular Frank and Hunter.

[25] Müller (noble incomes), Hunter (licensing fees and taxes), Snow and Tlusty (high excise
revenues).

[26] Insights into the debate on the ambitions and success of the early modern 'police state'
in J. Schlumbohm, 'Gesetze, die nicht durchgesetzt werden – ein Strukturmerkmal des
frühneuzeitlichen Staates?', in *Geschichte und Gesellschaft* 23 (1997), 647–63; K. Härter,
'Social control and enforcement of police-ordinances in early modern criminal procedure', in

Early modern communications – in the widest sense – provide a third leitmotiv. Chartres and Heiss emphasize the close interdependence between public houses and transportation networks, with travellers needing provisions and shelter on the one hand and boosting publicans' business on the other. As venues for feasts, games, dances and other entertainments, inns and taverns hosted much of local cultural life, as well as providing platforms for political and religious discussions. The latter at times evolved into subversive or openly rebellious activities (Brändle, Frank).

Fourth, public houses emerge as barometers of shifting consumer preferences, especially in terms of drinking tastes. The sources contain much detail on the types, quantity and quality of wine (Müller) and the rise of new beverages such as vodka in Russia (Snow), gin in England (Hunter), and hot drinks throughout Europe. These changes are not only a reflection of new fashions, but are also related to policies of taxation and other legislation.

A fifth issue appearing in several contributions is the tension that existed between 'private' and 'public' spheres. Public houses, by definition, accommodated hosts, servants and guests under one roof, with rooms permanently or temporarily assigned as 'public' or 'private'.[27] The semi-public space of taverns was the ideal location for meetings of all kinds, giving them a role in the development of the public sphere (Chartres). At the same time, activities occurring behind closed tavern doors could be viewed by authorities as 'secret' and therefore threatening to stability. The combination of private household with public rooms could also cause tension between guests and the publicans; as Tlusty emphasizes, particularly delicate problems arose in the context of quartering soldiers.

Moving to contrasts, there is naturally strong evidence for local peculiarities and regional differences. Both in terms of socio-political context and types of establishments, Snow's survey on Russian drinking houses is the most obvious case in point. Yet all contributions illustrate vastly heterogeneous constitutional, confessional and even climatic frameworks. Drinking cultures all varied accordingly. Variation existed, for example, with regard to drinks consumed (wine, beer or spirits); the degree of church interference with tavern life, as in the definition of legitimate entertainments; and the relationship of public houses to local problems, such as the disruptions caused by warfare. The status and appointment of publicans yields further distinctions: high-ranking members of local society, commanding offices and clout (Brändle) and wealthy innkeeper dynasties stretching over numerous generations (Pennington) contrast

---

H. Schilling (ed.), *Institutionen, Instrumente und Akteure sozialer Kontrolle und Disziplinierung im frühneuzeitlichen Europa* (Frankfurt, 1999), 39–63.

[27] See the examination of public houses in J. D. Melville, 'The use and organisation of domestic space in late seventeenth-century London' (Ph.D. Cambridge, 1999).

with poor temporary leaseholders, systems of rotation (Heiss) and even communal election (Snow). Patrons, finally, cannot be assigned a single social or gender profile. Tavern attendance reflected a great number of variables including location, type of establishment and specific occasion (Kümin).

Inevitably, not all facets of relevant work can be illustrated in a single collection. Additional recent tendencies have included closer interdisciplinary cooperation between history, sociology and anthropology, above all with regard to eating and drinking customs.[28] Another area of fruitful exchange promises to be literary studies, for instance through more thorough investigation of the social and historical context of references to public houses in epics and ballads, travel reports and other genres.[29] On the other hand, crucial aspects of the history of public houses remain obscure, certainly for the earlier periods: we know next to nothing about the armies of servants, cooks and waitresses who provided patrons with the desired services,[30] and – bar incidental evidence – comparatively little about regional gastronomic cultures and standards of accommodation.[31] 'Thick descriptions' of the world of individual publicans, exploiting all possibilities of record linkage and contextualizing their social and economic activities are also rather thin on the ground.[32]

---

[28] H. Spode, *Alkohol und Zivilisation: Berauschung, Ernüchterung und Tischsitten in Deutschland bis zum Beginn des 20. Jahrhunderts* (Berlin, 1991); S. Mennell, A. Murcott, and A. van Otterloo, *The Sociology of Food. Eating, Diet and Culture* (London, 1992); H. J. Teuteberg (ed.), *European Food History. A Research Review* (Leicester, 1992); see also the forthcoming proceedings of the 7th Symposium of the 'International Commission for Research into European Food History' ('Eating out in Europe'; 10–14 October 2001).

[29] J. F. Revel, *Un festin en paroles. Histoire littéraire de la sensibilité gastronomique de l'antiquité à nos jours* (Paris, 1995); B. Kaemena, *Studien zum Wirtshaus in der deutschen Literatur* (Frankfurt, 1999); S. Earnshaw, *The Pub in Literature: England's Altered State* (Manchester, 2000). The conference 'Drink and Conviviality in Early Modern England' (University of Reading, 10–11 July 2001) raised issues like political and religious stereotyping through specific forms of public drinking in literary texts.

[30] But cf. trial records involving a public house servant in R. Habermas and T. Hommen (eds), *Das Frankfurter Gretchen. Der Prozess gegen die Kindsmörderin Susanna Margaretha Brandt* (Munich, 1999).

[31] Travel literature is the single most promising, if very eclectic source. Some evidence on numbers of beds and shared accommodation in Chartres. For fascinating glimpses into confessional varieties in the standards of provision in early modern Switzerland cf. P. Hersche, 'Die protestantische Laus und der katholische Floh. Konfessionsspezifische Aspekte der Hygiene', in B. Bietenhard et al. (eds), *Ansichten von der rechten Ordnung* (Bern, 1991), 43–60.

[32] One example of microhistorical analysis involving the late seventeenth-century innkeeper Franz Stockhammer of Traunstein in Bavaria: N. Schindler, 'Skandal in der Kirche, oder: Die Strategien der kleinstädtischen Ehrbarkeit im ausgehenden 17. Jahrhundert', in *Salzburg Archiv* 26 (1999), 53–110.

Early modern public houses thus reveal a colourful world of social and popular customs, but much more beyond. As businesses and service institutions exposed to conflicting pressures from publicans, patrons and authorities, they mirror nearly all tensions of their time. For historians, thanks to the vast range of sources, they offer unique insights into patterns of consumption, communication and public life. These are prime objects for a 'new' cultural history indeed.

Satan's Servant or Authorities' Agent? Publicans in Eighteenth-Century Germany*

Michael Frank

'Wer nichts wird, wird Wirt' ('He who becomes nothing becomes a publican'). This proverb is familiar to most Germans and mirrors the low esteem attributed to the occupation of a publican in the past, at least by certain sections of the population. Even today the notion persists: those who have failed to learn an honest trade and have buried all hopes of securing a respectable livelihood can always, as a last resort, try their hand in the publican trade. The trade demands neither particular abilities nor specialist knowledge.

This negative assessment, which has remained firmly embedded in popular opinion throughout the centuries, was especially widespread among theologians of the early modern period. In 1679, Rothenburg's Superintendent John Ludwig Hartmann launched a damning attack on the publicans. From his pen, they emerge as godless and heinous individuals, willing to promote sin and sacrifice their customer's salvation for the sake of profit. They, he felt, were largely to blame for the omnipresence of the 'devil drink' in the German provinces.[1] Towards the end of the seventeenth century the celebrated Catholic preacher Abraham a Santa Clara voiced similar thoughts. He added the practice of cheating customers with bad drink and exorbitant prices to the list of transgressions.[2] The *Hausväterliteratur* (House Father Literature), a very popular adviser for ethical, medicinal, pedagogical and economical questions, contains similar sentiments – public houses, and of course with that the people who ran them, were labelled as irreligious and people were warned emphatically to avoid them.[3]

---

*   Translated from German by Eleanor Morrissey.

[1]   J. L. Hartmann, *Saufteufels Natur, Censur vnd Cur* (Rothenburg, 1679), 140, 145, 200.

[2]   M. Hübner and R. Hübner, *Der deutsche Durst: Illustrierte Kultur- und Sozialgeschichte* (Leipzig, 1994), 71.

[3]   See for example F. P. Florinus, *Oeconomus prudens et legalis: Oder Allgemeiner Klug- und Rechtsverständiger Haus-Vatter*, vol. 1 (Nuremberg, 1702), 82; J. J. Agricola, *Schauplatz des Allgemeinen Haußhaltens* (Nördlingen, 1676), 114. For an informative survey of the 'Hausväterliteratur' see J. Hoffmann, *Die 'Hausväterliteratur' und die 'Predigten über den christlichen Hausstand': Lehre von Haus und Bildung für das häusliche Leben im 16., 17. und 18. Jahrhun-*

Theologians were not alone in their condemnation of publicans. Members of the medical profession joined in the attack. According to the prominent doctor Johann Peter Frank, the wickedness of proprietors knew but few bounds. They made beer more potent by adding poppy or tobacco and made stale beer palatable with every kind of noxious trick, all with devastating effects on the health of the population at large.[4] This negative image of the cunning, the dishonest publican was known beyond the limits of learned society and also figured in seventeenth- and eighteenth-century popular farce and jokes.[5]

In the front lines of this impressive alliance of damnation we find the ruling orders. With the possible exception of the church, no other institution is mentioned more frequently in legislative texts than the tavern. According to an edict from Lippe (1691), which presents us with all the misgivings of the ruling bodies of the day in concentrated form, the sale of alcohol frequently led to crime and morally reprehensible behaviour such as swearing, cursing, defamation and fighting. This often resulted in bloodshed and threatened public peace and security. The tavern appears as a centre for illegal gambling, often initiated and promoted by the tavern keeper. There, contrary to church and state law, drinks were served during service time on Sundays and holidays.[6]

Looked at in this light, it seems quite logical that ruling bodies should have labelled the proprietors with such pejoratives as ruinous, godless, and suspicious.[7] In their opinion, tavern keepers encouraged idleness and idleness facilitated the greatest threat to the emerging state – public disorder. Seen

---

dert (Weinheim and Berlin, 1959).

[4]   J. P. Frank, *System einer vollständigen medicinischen Polizey*, vol. 3 (Mannheim, 1783), 451–2.

[5]   E. Moser-Rath, *'Lustige Gesellschaft': Schwank und Witz des 17. und 18. Jahrhunderts in kultur- und sozialgeschichtlichem Kontext* (Stuttgart, 1984), 216–18; idem (ed.), *Predigtmaerlein der Barockzeit: Exempel, Sage, Schwank und Fabel in geistlichen Quellen des oberdeutschen Raumes* (Berlin, 1964).

[6]   *Landesverordnungen der Grafschaft Lippe*, vol. 1 (Detmold, 1779), 'Verordnung wegen der Visitation der Wirtshäuser' from 3 January 1691, 705–6.

[7]   For 'ruinous' see article 8 of the contract with Peter Meerlenburg *et consortes*, parish of Stenderup (administrative district of Hadersleben) from 29 November 1783. According to this, the public house kept subjects from their work, which resulted in 'der Untertanen Verderb' – the subject's ruin. The term 'godless' can be found in Landesarchiv Schleswig Abt. 19 no. 65 II/I: Bericht zur Generalvisitation im Kirchspiel Hohenfelde 1775. For 'suspicious' see for example J. J. Scotti (ed.), *Sammlung der Gesetze und Verordnungen, welche in dem Königlich Preußischen Erbfürstenthume Münster ...,* vol. 2 (Münster, 1842) ('Öffentliche Sicherheit' from 20 January 1774), 215; *Hochfürstlich-Paderbörnische Landes-Verordnungen des Fürstbistums Paderborn*, vol. 2 (Paderborn, 1786), 'Kirchenordnung' of 1686, 266; *Landesverordnungen der Grafschaft Lippe*, vol. 1, 'Verordnung wegen Visitation der Wirthshäuser auf dem Lande', 13 April 1779, 663; 'Edikt wegen fremdem und unbekannten Volk', 2 January 1623, in F. D. C. von Cronhelm (ed.), *Corpus Statuorum Provincialium Holsatiae* (Altona, 1750), 145–8.

through the eyes of Sebastian Franck in 1531, they may not have created hell on earth but they had certainly created a godless place.[8]

The very dubious reputation of the tavern keeper was in part the product of projection. The negative image of taverns in contemporary opinion, especially among the ruling and educated orders, was superimposed on their proprietors. If the tavern was a source of sin, vice, crime and subversion, it followed that the people who ran them were to blame and must themselves be sinful, evil, criminal and subversive. For many contemporaries the verdict was clear: the tavern keeper was no less than Satan's servant. Christoph Weigel's effort to depart from official opinion presents an exception. In his *Ständebuch* (1698), with its description of the various trades and professions, he attempted, albeit very tentatively, a more positive characterization of the tavern keeper. Supporting his thoughts with Bible references, he argued that if in principle drinking was not dishonest, serving it was equally not dishonest. He stressed the positive aspects of alcohol and underlined its medicinal qualities. Given this, he questioned why persons who sold beer and wine should not be loved, tolerated, protected and supported.[9]

However, we must be wary when faced with seemingly conclusive evidence. Was the role of the publican defined within purely negative limits, i.e., was, as constantly claimed, their sole objective the promotion of crime and the fostering of vice and subversion? In the following pages we shall take a closer look at the role of the publicans primarily in the eighteenth century. We shall look in particular at the factors which set the framework for their actions; that is, the complex of dependencies and obligations created by the expectations and demands of the authorities on the one hand, and customers on the other. An analysis of the social and economic reality of the publicans, their income prospects and social standing in the local community, and of course a close look at the institution of the public house itself will help determine the publicans' scope of action within the bounds of this framework. In addition we shall examine to what extent they posed a threat to, or had a stabilizing effect on, public order, and assess claims of the public house as a breeding ground for agitation and rebellion. To allow us to answer these questions with authority, we will concentrate on evidence drawn from four regions in northern Germany – the Lutheran Duchy of Holstein, the reformed Earldom of Lippe and the two Catholic territories, Münster and Paderborn.

---

[8]   Sebastian Franck wrote that one forgot misery in the tavern; but those who forgot misery neither called nor shouted to God. S. Franck, *Von dem grewlichen Laster der Trunckenheit ...* (n. p., 1531).

[9]   C. Weigel, *Abbildung und Beschreibung der gemein-nützlichen Hauptstände* (Regensburg, 1698; rev. ed., Nördlingen, 1987), 547–50.

A simple characterization of the publican is impossible. Just as one will seek in vain a uniform type of public house, so too is the search for the typical publican doomed to failure. From the late Middle Ages, diverse forms of commercial hospitality developed.[10] The tavern (*Kneipe*), a fairly basic establishment, was licensed to sell beverages only. The inn (*Gasthaus*) provided both food and drink for its customers and could also provide accommodation for guests. The so-called *Strauchwirtschaft* opened its doors on a seasonal basis and, like the *Kneipe*, was restricted to selling drink. The list continues with the *Winkelkrug*, which operated illegally in the background, or the *Dorfkrug* and *Stadtkrug* which catered to the needs of its clientele in rural or urban areas respectively. *Zunft-*, *Gesellen-* and *Geschlechtertrinkstuben*, exclusive drinking places for guilds, journeymen and the members of the leading families of the city, complete the picture. Given this diversity of public houses and services, it is hardly surprising that even contemporaries found things confusing. This uncertainty was to no small degree the result of the bewildering range of graded privileges and concessions issued by the authorities. With their power to grant, extend or withdraw licences, they could bring pressure to bear on the publican and, in theory at least, regulate the location and incidence of drinking premises. Regulatory efforts were not always successful, however, as is well documented in the court records of the period, and many a publican used the general confusion regarding rights, obligations and services to their own advantage.[11] Moreover, in the general disarray a sub-system of illegal premises emerged, which was a thorn in the flesh of licence holders and authorities alike.

The possible range of public houses indicated above was of course not always mirrored in towns and villages. Understandably, major centres like the imperial free cities offered a greater selection of premises than did small towns like Detmold in Lippe or Wilster in Holstein. However, even here we find, in addition to the facilities reserved exclusively for journeymen or guild members, houses which served the needs of select local groups. In the later decades of the eighteenth century, Detmold's more respectable society met regularly for wine, beer and conversation at the so-called *Kestnersches Haus*.[12] In Wilster, a number of local prominents gathered twice weekly at one or the other of the town's two drinking houses, where they sat at their own table, conspicuously

---

[10]   H.C. Peyer, 'Gastfreundschaft und kommerzielle Gastlichkeit im Mittelalter', in *Historische Zeitschrift* 235 (1982), 265–88; 273.

[11]   This situation was the starting point for a report, which was presented from the archivist Clostermeier to the government on 13 March 1802. Staatsarchiv Detmold, L 92 N no. 17.

[12]   A fight which broke out in the *Kestnersches Haus* between Kriminalrat Heistermann, a higher civil servant, and Koch, the secretary of the local church adminstration (*Konsistorium*) demonstrates that 'polite' conversation was not always the order of the day. An affront to a person's dignity with a sharp-tongued remark could easily provoke a brawl of the kind usually associated with less elite establishments. Staatsarchiv Detmold, L 18 no. 82, fol. 254r.

segregated from the main body of customers.[13] In his biography, Friedrich Christian Laukhard (1757–1822) gives us insight into the day-to-day life and happenings in the special taverns for students (*Studentenkneipen*) in Gießen, Göttingen and Halle. He also tells of the company he kept in the many so-called 'peasant taverns' (*Bauernkneipe*) in the countryside around Halle. Aware that these connections beyond his station would damage his reputation and earn sharp criticism from the theologians, which proved to be true, he wrote: 'This behaviour weakened my standing with the clergy even more'.[14] Laukhard's uniform characterization of peasant taverns could lead us to believe that a differentiated system of public houses, which catered for particular groups of local society, was peculiar to the urban centres only. However, this was not so, as shown by reports from local officials in Krempermarsch and Wilstermarsch (1773). Based on their regular customers, we can distinguish roughly three categories for the public house in rural areas: those for day-labourers, farm-hands and travellers. It will be important to bear this wide variety in mind when, for example, we discuss the social profile and earning capacity of the publican further on.[15]

As different as the individual premises could be, one aspect was common to all. Their chief function lay in providing the general public with alcoholic beverages. If we take into account the immense importance of drink during the period in question, we come to appreciate the significant place of the public house in that society. At the time, alcohol was the only intoxicant available to the mass of the population in Europe and could offer escape from the sometimes oppressive reality of daily life or relief from everyday strains and anxieties. Beyond this, men drank for pleasure, but drinking also served to demonstrate masculinity. Drinking was bound up in fixed rituals which served to establish or reinforce a sense of community. Alcohol was also a critically important foodstuff in the early modern period. Especially beer, available as light beer with a low alcohol content, was used as a water substitute or to quench thirst. In addition, alcohol served as a valuable source of energy and helped secure the necessary calorie intake at a time when diets were generally poor. Whereas it was not uncommon for beer to be produced in private households, people generally bought their supplies of alcohol from their local public house.[16]

---

[13]   G. F. Schumacher, *Genrebilder aus dem Leben eines 70jährigen Schulmannes* (Schleswig, 1841), 262–4.

[14]   'Dieses Betragen schwächte meinen Kredit bei den Geistlichen noch mehr': F. C. Laukhard, *Leben und Schicksale*, vol. 1 (Halle, 1792; rev. edn. Frankfurt a.M., 1987), 343.

[15]   Landesarchiv Schleswig, Abt. 103 no. 175: 'Verzeichnis der Krugpächter aus dem Jahr 1773'.

[16]   In general for the history of alcohol see R. H. A. Blum, 'A History of Alcohol', in idem (ed.), *Society and Drugs*, vol. 1 (San Francisco, 1970), 25–42; H. D. Chalke, 'Alcohol and

However, the services of the public house were not only geared towards the needs of the local population. They were also expected to maintain the necessary infrastructure for the provision of travellers and the migrant population with the essentials of food, drink and shelter at night or in bad weather, a function usually fulfilled by those premises situated on the main highways. Beyond victualling and lodging, the public house often served as a staging point, thus making an important contribution to trade and commerce and enhancing the transport system. In the almost impassable terrain of the marshes in Holstein, this was one of the central functions of the public house, a fact which influenced the licensing policies of local authorities.[17]

As we have seen, the function of the public house went far beyond the provision of alcohol. We can gain further insight into the range of activities centred on the public house by consulting the corpus of leasing contracts made with the authorities. A lease from the parish of Stenderup in Holstein, made between parish officials and the local proprietors in 1783, is a typical example. For an annual rent of thirty Reichsthaler, payable each year at Michaelmas, they were granted a licence to run their individual premises, brew their own beer and distil brandy. In addition they were granted the exclusive right to supply parishioners with all the necessities for weddings, christenings and funerals – beer, brandy, pipes, tobacco and the like, and also granted the monopoly on the sale of minor wares. They alone were entitled to supply parishioners with country products (*Landwaren*): items such as bread, tar, train-oil, soap, shovels, spades, iron, and steel, to name but a few.[18]

It is only in recent times that research has paid closer attention to the public house as a centre where political and religious opinions were formed. Robert W. Scribner has shown how verbal communication in the public house greatly furthered the dissemination of Reformation ideas: the role of the Virgin Mary was a much favoured topic among guests. Themes such as the immaculate conception or the theory that Mary had born two children following the death of Jesus fired the imagination of contemporaries.[19] Such discussions sometimes became quite heated and it was not unusual for the parties involved to settle the

---

History', in *Journal of Alcoholism* 11 (1976), 128–49; P. Fouquet and M. de Borde, *Histoire de l'alcool* (Paris, 1990); H. Spode, *Die Macht der Trunkenheit. Kultur und Sozialgeschichte des Alkohols in Deutschland* (Opladen, 1993).

[17] Landesarchiv Schleswig, Abt. 103, no. 175: The registers of the local adminstration ('Kirchspielvögte') of the Kremper- and Wilstermarsch from July 1773.

[18] Landesarchiv Schleswig, Abt. 65.2 no. 814 III: Heuerkontrakt from 29 November 1783.

[19] R. W. Scribner, 'Flugblatt und Analphabetentum. Wie kam der gemeine Mann zu reformatorischen Ideen?', in H. J. Köhler (ed.), *Flugschriften als Massenmedium der Reformationszeit* (Tübingen, 1981), 65–76, esp. 68. For examples for such discussions in the public houses see P. Holenstein and N. Schindler, 'Geschwätzgeschichte(n). Ein kulturhistorisches Plädoyer für die Rehabilitierung der unkontrollierten Rede', in R. van Dülmen (ed.), *Dynamik der Tradition: Studien zur historischen Kulturforschung* (Frankfurt a.M., 1992), 41–108; esp. 62–3, 83.

outcome with their fists. The public house also served as a forum for open defiance of Catholic teaching, where guests demonstrated their disregard of the rules on fasting or derided sacramental rituals. In 1532, Wilhelm, Duke of Jülich-Berg, aware that popular religious discussion could easily sow the seeds of rebellion, banned all discussion of religious themes in public houses. He appears to have been more inclined towards the moderate path taken by Erasmus of Rotterdam and was obviously anxious not to aggravate the religious tensions in his territory during the sensitive stage of formation and demarcation of the confessions.[20]

Marion Kobelt-Groch has shown that it was not unusual for revolution and revolt to have had their origins in the public house. Her conclusions are based on source material from the German Peasants' war 1524–25, which shows that the public house was not only a place that bred discontent expressed in programmatic demands, but was also a centre where concrete plans of action were developed.[21] In our area, the sources frequently reveal the public house as a venue where criticism of the authorities was concentrated; a place not only for religious, but also for political opposition. Court records abound with such cases. Peter Scheel from Wilster was presented for directing 'dishonouring words' at the Magistrate on Whit Sunday in 1728.[22] In a similar incident from 1732, Christian Friedrich Petersen was charged with criticizing the work of council member (*Ratsmitglied*) Wieben, 'with very insensitive and strong expressions' while visiting his local tavern.[23] Johann Knickbein was prosecuted on a number of occasions in the 1750s for his verbal attacks on the local magistrate and the two mayors of the town.[24] Offences of this nature were not treated lightly. Ruling bodies apparently feared such expressions of discontent, which could spark off major incidents in the locality.

An incident from the district of Segeberg, Holstein, shows that their fears were not altogether unfounded. In 1795, the parish of Kaltenkirchen witnessed violence of such dimensions directed against local authorities that military intervention was necessary to restore order.[25] Participants were mainly drawn from the ranks of the socially displaced rural population; landless hirelings

---

[20] 'Kirchenordnung des Herzogs Johann' of 11 January 1532, in O. Redlich (ed.), *Jülich-Bergische Kirchenpolitik am Ausgang des Mittelalters und in der Reformationszeit*, vol. 1 (Düsseldorf, 1986), 251.

[21] M. Kobelt-Groch, 'Unter Zechern, Spielern und Häschern. Täufer im Wirtshaus', in N. Fischer and M. Kobelt-Groch (eds), *Außenseiter zwischen Mittelalter und Neuzeit* (Leiden et al., 1997), 111–26, esp. 125.

[22] Stadtarchiv Wilster, Man III b no. 398, 147.

[23] 'mit sehr empfindlichen und harten Redensarten': ibid., 398.

[24] Ibid., Man. III b no. 398a, 218, 221.

[25] 'Gedanken über den Zustand der Häuserinsten im Kirchspiel Kaltenkirchen, die Ursachen der von ihnen geäußerten Unzufriedenheit und die Mittel ihnen abzuhelfen', in *Schleswig-Holsteinische Provinzialberichte* 9 (1795), 63–92.

(*Insten*),[26] cottagers,[27] and also a number of retired farmers, who, having handed over their farms to the son and heir, were now struggling to subsist. The group of the landless poor predominated. Their numbers were rapidly expanding and their situation was marked by abject poverty and poor employment prospects.[28] Of particular interest to us, however, is that the incident originated in a number of local public houses. For the authorities, the case was clear. So-called liberty-criers had converged on the town and stirred up the discontented inhabitants. 'In these dangerous holes especially now so much false stuff of the two such fine words liberty and equality is spoken, and is more falsely understood, that it makes such stupid people the more easily dizzy, as their brandy courage already incites enough to outrageous insubordination'.[29] In Kaltenkirchen, the fears of the ruling classes had taken on substance, and the subversive energy of the public house had developed its full and dangerous potential. The considerable disruptive force of the incident was fired by rapidly worsening social conditions, by hopes kindled through the spirit of the French Revolution and, equally important, by discussions in the peculiarly male atmosphere of the public house. Alcohol did the rest.

Against this backdrop, can we argue that the public house lived up to its contemporary reputation as a centre for disorder? Both our sources and research publications suggest otherwise. Examples such as Kaltenkirchen, where rebellion originated in the public house, remain exceptions. We can thus agree with Peter Clark's assessment of drinking-houses playing, if any, but a very small role in the

---

[26] The *Insten* were characterized as follows: they 'rented a room from other people, lived sometimes in the one sometimes in the other village or parish, and had to try and earn their keep with their trade or daily wage' ('mieten sich bei andern Leuten eine Stube, wohnen bald in diesem oder jenem Dorfe oder Kirchspiel, und müssen durch ihr Handwerk oder Tagelohn ihren Unterhalt zu verdienen suchen.' Ibid., 65). Only three years previously the *Insten* had been described as a 'very useful class of person' ('sehr nützliche Klasse von Menschen'): 'They help the farmer with the field work in those times, when the hands which he has in readiness year in year out, are not sufficient and there they live with him' ('Den Bauern helfen sie bei dem Feldbau zu den Zeiten, wenn die Hände, die er Jahr ein Jahr aus bereit hat, nicht ausreichen und bei ihm bleiben sie wohnen.') See 'Ein Wort für Insten', in *Schleswig-Holsteinische Provinzialberichte* 6 (1792), 166–9, esp. 166. In Lippe the hirelings were referred to as *Einlieger*, in other north-German regions they were called *Heuerlinge* or *Heuerleute*.

[27] The cottagers, or *Kätner*, owned a small dwelling house, a so-called *Kate*, which rarely had a little land attached.

[28] *Schleswig-Holsteinische Provinzialberichte* 9 (1795), 65.

[29] 'In diesen gefährlichen Löchern wird besonders jetzt so viel verkehrtes Zeug über die beiden so schönen Worte Freiheit und Gleichheit gesprochen, und noch verkehrter verstanden, daß es so blöde Menschen umso leichter schwindlig macht, da ihr Branntweinmut sie ohnehin schon zu einer frevelhaften Widersetzlichkeit reizt.' 'Wahrscheinliche Ursache von den geäußerten Volksunruhen in dem Kirchspiel Kaltenkirchen und unvorgreiflicher Vorschlag, diese tiefliegende Ursache zu beheben', in *Schleswig-Holsteinische Provinzialberichte* 9 (1795), 279–90, esp. 283.

planning, organization or triggering of rebellion.[30] More importantly, we may argue that the public house actually helped stabilize the established political and social system. Like today's public house, the individual drinking houses of our period catered to their own select clientele. Side by side with those frequented largely by the lower orders we find establishments where the better ranks gathered. The retired schoolmaster Schumacher, looking back to Wilster of 1795, described how the petit bourgeois of Wilster had gathered twice weekly for a sociable evening in one or the other of Wilster's two more select taverns. 'We gathered in the evening, after dinner, i.e., at seven p.m. until at the very latest ten p.m. We drank beer for one or one and one-half shillings; the tavern keeper had to give tobacco free and this stood in two tins on the table. ... Conversation was not so very political, ... but much more dealt with events in the town'.[31] In other words, local gossip was the main topic of conversation, closing time was strictly observed, and they drank in moderation. This conservative picture hardly fits in with the subversive culture of the public house. Quite the contrary. With clientele of this nature, the public house guaranteed political and social stability.

We can, however, also view the less orderly gatherings, where criticism was voiced, in a more positive light. Expressions of discontent directed at the authorities had the character of cleansing rituals. By giving vent to their feelings, disgruntled citizens freed themselves of pent-up emotions, thus reducing the danger of individual situations getting out of hand and resulting in concerted disorder – somewhat on the principle of a pressure cooker, where the measured release of steam prevents an explosion. As court records reveal, protests were generally individual actions. Kept within certain bounds they were tolerated, and prosecutions followed only when the accepted limits were overstepped.

Thus far, our discussion has concentrated mainly on the licensed inns and taverns. As already mentioned, a sub-system of illegal premises also existed, the so-called *Winkelkrüge* or corner-houses. Our records contain frequent complaints of drink being sold from private dwellings, a source of unwelcome competition for the established publicans. Intervention on the part of the authorities is evidenced, for instance, by numerous entries in the administrative-district accounts in Holstein, such as the one mark fine paid by Katherine Tanterland from the parish of Meldorf, Dithmarschen, who had run a tavern (*Krug*) 'despite the existing prohibition'.[32] We often find these taverns strategically placed to attract

---

[30] P. Clark, *The English Alehouse: A Social History 1200–1830* (London, 1983), 66.

[31] 'Man kam zusammen Abends nach Tisch d.h. um 7 Uhr spätestens bis 10 Uhr. Man trank für 1 oder 1 ½ Schilling Bier; Tabak mußte der Wirt frei geben und dieser stand in 2 Dosen auf dem Tisch ... . Die Unterhaltung war nicht so sehr politisch, ... vielmehr handelte sie von Vorfällen in der Stadt.' Schumacher, *Genrebilder*, 262–3.

[32] 'Tanterlands Kathrine hat trotz des bestehenden Verbots einen Krug betrieben'. Quellenkartei Kiel; Landesarchiv Schleswig, AR 103 1569: Dithmarschen Süderdrittel, Kirchspiel Meldorf (The Quellenkartei Kiel is a collection of excerpts from the archives of Schleswig and

a maximum of trade. The beginning of the seventeenth century saw one of Detmold's gatekeepers exploit his advantageous location to the full by serving beer to persons travelling in and out of town.[33] While illicit sellers undoubtedly improved the supply of alcohol, it is difficult to quantify their contribution to the market. Understandably, they were anxious to evade detection and thus remain slightly obscure. Keith Wrightson has estimated that almost half of all alehouses in England were unlicensed, with keepers predominantly drawn from the ranks of the poor.[34] A survey of unlicensed sellers carried out in Lippe in 1791 does offer us a reasonable base for estimation. For the country areas, in which towns were excluded from the survey, a total of thirty-four illegal drinking-places were counted, representing almost one third (28.1 per cent) of all taverns.[35] These figures are likely only the tip of the iceberg, so that in all probability the incidence of illicit sellers was not less than fifty per cent. The main concentration of unlicensed premises is found, surprisingly enough, not on the periphery, but rather in the core district of the region, in the administrative district of Detmold, possibly an indication of demand structures and market chances.

Unfortunately, we have no sources which throw light on developments within the illegal market. Documents that allow a quantitative evaluation exist, when at all, only for the second half of the sixteenth century. However, our knowledge of the social groups that predominated in the trade does allow us to put forward some plausible arguments. From historical studies on general demographic and social developments we know how population expansion from early in the eighteenth century mainly affected the lower orders of society, whose earning prospects decreased rapidly in an ever narrowing market. We can thus safely assume an increase in the number of illegal sellers parallel with this expansion, given that this area offered one of the few means of subsistence. Competition in the tavern sector must have risen during the course of the eighteenth century.

Let us now shift our attention away from the institution of the public house and examine the social role of their proprietors. To begin with, we shall concentrate on the question of their social status and reputation within the community. A good point of departure is Heinrich Stiewe's assessment of the trade as having been in general 'a lucrative business'. Among the tavern keepers in Lippe, he found that while the majority were drawn from the ranks of the lesser small-

---

Holstein which is held at the Volkskundliche Seminar, University of Kiel).

[33] Staatsarchiv Detmold, L 18 no. 54: 'Schreiben des Braueramtes an den Magistrat der Stadt Detmold' of 9 July 1630, fol. 2r.

[34] K. Wrightson, 'Alehouses, Order and Reformation in Rural England, 1590–1660', in E. and S. Yeo (eds), *Popular Culture and Class Conflict 1590–1914* (Brighton, 1981), 1–27, esp. 3.

[35] This number has been determined from Staatsarchiv Detmold, L 92 N no. 6: 'Tabelle über die Brauereien, Brantweinsbrennereien und Krügereien, die im Lande ohne Cammercontracte exerciret werden.'

holders, a group normally destined to a life of poverty and deprivation, there were nonetheless clear indications of secure livelihoods and modest prosperity.[36]

We can test these findings for our region by examining the case of the Old Inn (*Alte Krug*) in the village of Heiden, Lippe. While the four hectares of land attached to the inn appear insignificant against the thirty-six hectares held on hereditary lease by the most substantial farmer of the village, it no doubt guaranteed the family's subsistence, at least in good harvest years.[37] However, harvest failure or slumps in demand, both not infrequent, would have endangered the family's survival had they not had recourse to the income from the inn. It is safe to say that it was the inn that formed the economic basis of the household. The Property Registry from 1770 shows that the keeper of the Old Inn (*Alte Krüger*) was authorized to brew beer, to sell the same on his premises and to take in paying guests. Households in Heiden and neighbouring communities were obliged to purchase their daily beer supplies and all alcoholic beverages for weddings and other festivities from the *Alte Krüger*.[38] The sources contain a number of indications that the proprietor was economically secure, indeed that he ranked amongst the wealthier of the villagers. One good indicator of wealth is the levy due to the Lord on the death of a villein, based on the financial resources of the deceased. When the *Alte Krüger* died in 1716 the staggering sum of thirty-five Reichsthaler fell due, an amount not equalled even by the wealthiest farmer of the village.[39] A further pointer towards wealth is the advantageous location of his premises. As the only public house within the village, it was also the central inn of the parish. Situated within view of the church, it had the added advantage of attracting the legions of churchgoers.

Later generations in the *Alte Krug* were subject to stiffer competition. The 1690s witnessed the establishment of an inn called The Alder (*Ellernkrug*) on the outskirts of the district, which soon attracted large numbers of customers. The *Ellernkrug* had a mere 0.12 hectare of farmland attached which was insufficient to secure a living.[40] The income from the inn was far more important

---

[36]   H. Stiewe, 'Zur baulichen Struktur und Nutzung von Krugwirtshäusern in Lippe', in J. Arndt and P. Nitschke (eds), *Kontinuität und Umbruch in Lippe. Sozialpolitische Verhältnisse zwischen Aufklärung und Restauration 1750–1820* (Detmold, 1994), 223–52, esp. 229, 240. Fritz Glauser reaches a similar conclusion in his study of a Swiss example. He established that the tavern keeper had quite considerable profit margins (20–27 per cent of the retail price) and generally had good earning opportunities: 'Wein, Wirt und Gewinn 1580. Wirteeinkommen am Beispiel der schweizerischen Kleinstadt Sursee', in H. C. Peyer (ed.), *Gastfreundschaft, Taverne und Gasthaus im Mittelalter* (Munich, 1983), 205–20, esp. 209–12.

[37]   Staatsarchiv Detmold, L 101 C I Amt Lage no. 5: 'Güterverzeichnis' of 1680.

[38]   M. Frank, *Dörfliche Gesellschaft und Kriminalität. Das Fallbeispiel Lippe 1650–1800* (Paderborn, 1995), 113.

[39]   Staatsarchiv Detmold, L 89 A I no. 116: Gogerichte, fol. 251v.

[40]   Staatsarchiv Detmold, L 101 C I Amt Lage no. 12: 'Kataster' of 1728.

here than was the case at the *Alte Krug*. If we take land ownership as a criterion for social classification, the tenants of the *Ellernkrug* clearly belonged to the lower orders of village society. The same applied to the owner of the New Tavern (*Neue Krug*) which opened its doors to the public in 1720.[41] Situated beside the churchyard and just a stone's throw away from the *Alte Krug*, the *Neue Krug* had no land attached and merely consisted of a small dwelling house, with one room reserved for serving guests. The family was completely dependent on the profits from the tavern so that in later years the keeper of the New Tavern (*Neue Krüger*) attempted to counteract this disadvantage by peddling linen and other wares not restricted by local monopolies. Again, these examples underline the considerable disparities that could exist within the trade.

A striking feature when we consider the trade as a whole is the relatively large number of livestock that the average publican called his own, which often enough outnumbered even those of prosperous farmers. No doubt this can be partly explained by the need to use the nutritional by-products of brewing and distilling. The two cows and four pigs listed for the *Alte Krug* in 1776 appear rather paltry compared to the three cows, three further horned cattle, two sheep and six pigs that the publican Adam Henrich Conrad Krüger kept on his holding in Bentrup at the same period. The tavern keeper in Hardissen, Johann Arnd Körner, had an amazing seven cows, three sheep, a goat and one pig.[42]

Roland Linde's profile of the keepers of inns and taverns in the Detmold region supports the observations made here: as a rule the publican held a small dwelling with very little land, yet was endowed with the economic features characteristic of substantial farmers. They had livestock in the stables and employed domestic servants, farm-hands and staff for the tavern.[43] Such symbols of economic success naturally increased their social prestige. Seventeenth-century sermons vividly illustrate the high regard enjoyed by individual proprietors in their community. One of many examples is the case of the journeyman who, believing he had been cheated by a tavern keeper, voiced an objection. He made no attempt to defend himself against the ensuing thrashing from his host, in whom he recognised the 'village king' (*Dorfkönig*). It would have been dangerous to offer resistance in such a case.[44]

---

[41] Ibid.

[42] Staatsarchiv Detmold, L 92 Z IV no. 31: 'Volkszählung' of 1776.

[43] R. Linde, 'Ländliche Krüge. Wirtshauskultur in der Grafschaft Lippe im 18. Jahrhundert', in S. Baumeier et al. (eds), *Beiträge zur Volkskunde und Hausforschung* 7 (1995), 7–50, esp. 42–3.

[44] For this seventeenth-century sermon see G. Lohmeier, *Bayerische Barockprediger. Ausgewählte Texte und Märlein bisher ziemlich unbekannter Skribenten des siebzehnten und achtzehnten Jahrhunderts* (Munich, 1961), 90.

To achieve success in the trade, the publican needed certain qualifications, which included literacy skills and a basic knowledge of mathematics. He stood at the centre of the local communication network, was often enough well-read and had a good knowledge of local events. These factors enhanced his standing in the community. Thus it is hardly surprising that, in conflicts with the authorities, the publican was often chosen to represent the interests of the community, as was the case in the Peasants' War.

However, it would be wrong to overstate the case of the publican as 'king of the village', just as it is an oversimplification to automatically equate wealth with prestige. Their reputation was determined by a variety of factors and much depended on the way they fulfilled their social role. Their reputation could suffer if, for instance, they were too fond of drink and became a disruptive factor in the community. In 1786 the publican of the *Ellernkrug* and his wife were presented at the lower court in Heiden following an anonymous charge of their being 'so very devoted to drink as to be close to destruction'.[45] Significantly, this devotion to drink was also the downfall of the couple who ran the other public house in the village, the *Alte Krug*. In 1788 charges were brought against them for repeated drunkenness. The judge threatened a spell of detention should they indulge in further excesses.[46] Proprietors could also gamble away their social assets by succumbing to the financial lures of the criminal world. To receive stolen goods or shelter prostitutes was guaranteed to meet with disapproval.

In addition, not every publican was wealthy and thus held in high regard. The sources show that many operated at subsistence level. An inspection of the economic situation of the tavern keepers in the Krempermarsch in Holstein has shown that for the year 1773, for instance, fourteen premises were so small as to be unlikely to survive.[47] The administrative-district accounts from Detmold list numerous newly established taverns between 1750 and 1820, not one of which survived.[48]

A prerequisite for success was the ability to make the most of market opportunities. The would-be licensee was well advised to secure a catchment area which offered a sufficient number of potential customers and it was vital that they obtained as wide a range of concessions and privileges as possible. Under such circumstances the alcohol trade could be quite a lucrative business.

But what was the fate of the unlicensed tavern keepers? By and large, our information tends to support the findings for England: they were predominantly poor and often unable to raise concession fees, and the profits from the drinking trade were an essential source of their income. A survey of the illicit sellers con-

---

[45] Staatsarchiv Detmold, L 89 A I no. 122: Gogerichte, fol. 69r.

[46] Staatsarchiv Detmold, L 89 A I no. 122: Gogerichte, fol. 126r.

[47] Landesarchiv Schleswig, Abt. 103 no. 175: 'Verzeichnisse der einzelnen Kirchspiele', July 1773.

[48] These figures are offered by Linde, 'Krüge', 27.

ducted in the administrative district of Steinburg, Holstein, in 1725 revealed, for the most part, a long-term involvement in the trade, between five to fifteen years. Because no prosecutions were made we can infer a certain acceptance of the unlicensed sellers both by the community and by local officials. Local attitudes were possibly influenced by the fact that, as small-scale traders, these drink-sellers were not perceived as a serious threat to the established drinking houses. In addition, this tolerance was motivated by an awareness that, without the extra income, these poverty-stricken people would have fallen on the parish for support.[49]

Considerably less tolerance was shown towards two hirelings from Heidenoldendorf, in Lippe, when they set up two barrels in their homes and served beer to paying guests. The two established village publicans, Christian Sievers and Johann Jost Obernkrüger, considered that the activities of the two men, who significantly enough are not mentioned in the records by name, would seriously affect their earnings. They argued that two drinking establishments were more than enough in Heidenoldendorf, more would not survive. Their stance was obviously adopted by the authorities who decreed that future illegal enterprises would be met with heavy sentences.[50] This example is also useful in that it demonstrates the minimal capital expenditure involved in such cases: a barrel or two of beer, a few adjustments in the living quarters, and business could begin.

A striking aspect of the unlicensed market is the high proportion of women involved in the trade. Of the five clandestine premises listed for the parish of Brockdorf, Holstein, three alone were run by women. Almost invariably, the women we meet in the illegal sector were widows.[51] The sources often make reference to their poverty just as they highlight them plying their trade at home, both indications that little capital expenditure was necessary to set them up in the business. One widow, Gretje Dreyers, admitted that she had illegally distilled brandy for twelve years past, but had sold little of this and had never had 'seated guests'. However, we should not give too much credence to her assurances. Under the circumstances it was in her own interest to play down her crime. It seems likely that widowed women first entered the trade following their husband's death. The loss of the main provider would have forced them to seek an alternative source of income. The drinking trade thus offered a subsistence

---

[49] This point is borne out by the comments of the parish administrator Knickbein. The interesting survey of the illegal tavern keepers, which dates from 8 October 1725, is to be found as an extract in Landesarchiv Schleswig, Abt. 103 no. 175.

[50] Staatsarchiv Detmold, L 92 N no. 297: 'Schreiben von Christian Sievers und Johann Jost Obernkrüger, Heidenoldendorf, an den Grafen' of 26 January 1711; 'Bescheid des Grafen' of 26 January 1711.

[51] Landesarchiv Schleswig, Abt. 103 no. 175: 'Extract des Schreibens des Kirchspiel Voigts Knickbeins zu Brockdorff an den Cantzeley Raht und Amts-Verwalter Hildebrandt', 8 October 1725.

niche. The very fact that such people worked illegally could indicate that their profit margins were too low to provide them with the means for the necessary licence fees. Gretje Dreyers bears this out with her plea to spare her from further demands which, as a 'poor widow', she could not pay.[52]

However, the difficulties of everyday life as a tavern keeper went well beyond the tensions caused by legal or illegal competition or the omnipresent authorities. Problems abounded. Court records show the tavern keeper at the centre of more conflicts than any other villager. Prosecutions in the lower courts outnumbered even those brought against the miller, a figure who always aroused a great deal of mistrust and animosity, with villagers constantly suspecting him of pocketing their valuable grain. An example from Heiden reveals that while the local innkeeper faced 125 charges between 1760 and 1795, the miller appeared on only seventy-nine occasions. Why was the publican more likely to be prosecuted than other members of the community? Correlating to the diverse social roles held by the publican in rural society in the early modern period, we can differentiate between various sources of conflict. For his role as a subject, we find conflicts arising from general offences such as infringements of the sumptuary laws. When the proprietor of the *Alte Krug* in Heiden invited more guests to his child's christening than the regulations allowed, he was fined the sum of two Reichsthaler. Heiden's miller and one Henrich Moritz met the same fate for this offence on a subsequent occasion.[53] As a farmer, the publican came into conflict with other farmers. Disputes arose over damage to crops, over the number of cattle pastured on common grazing lands, or over times for grazing.[54] When tempers were hot verbal exchanges sometimes ended in violence, as for example when negotiating the return of an escaped horse or cow. The records do not show a higher incidence of such offences for the publican. Other villagers faced the same or similar charges just as frequently. However, prosecutions which arose from his specific activity as publican are distinctive, both in quality and quantity. Customers presented them when drink was bad[55] or prices too dear.[56] Such a charge was brought against the publican in Heiden, who was accused of serving 'constantly bad beer' to his customers. As quite a few of his guests were severely indisposed as a result, the deputy-administrator was called upon to taste the offending brew. He declared the beer would 'better serve a pig than a human'.[57]

---

[52]   Ibid.

[53]   Staatsarchiv Detmold, L 89 A I no. 114: Gogerichte, fol. 83r.

[54]   For example, when the cows of the old innkeeper (*Alte Krüger*) broke into the field of a farmer from Trophagen and destroyed his crop of rye. Staatsarchiv Detmold, L 89 A I no. 113, fol. 71r.

[55]   Staatsarchiv Detmold, L 89 A I no. 113: Gogerichte, fol. 99v.

[56]   In 1692, the villagers of Heiden collectively complained of the overpriced drink served by the old innkeeper (*Alte Krüger*); L 89 A I no. 114, fol. 53v.

[57]   'allezeit schlechtes Bier'; 'daß es eher einem Schwein als einem Menschen dienlich'.

Prosecutions by the authorities also followed when publicans served beyond closing time or failed to report breaches of the law.[58] They were further involved in brawls and disputes of honour which could so easily break out in the drink-filled atmosphere of the tavern.[59]

Proprietors of inns and taverns also instigated prosecutions, namely when they saw their business in jeopardy: when, for instance, unlicensed sellers distilled or sold brandy or when customers failed to meet the bill for festivities.[60] All of this gives a clear indication of the potential risks associated with the trade. Publicans were in constant danger of being physically attacked or open to slurs on their honour. Over and above this, denunciations or official controls could leave them facing the full wrath of the authorities.

The publicans, open to pressure from two sides, were in a difficult position. When they adhered to the letter of the law, and, for example, refused to serve alcohol during worship time, they were likely to meet strong opposition from their customers. If they flouted the rules, they laid themselves open to the reactions of the authorities. Structurally, the problems involved here are similar to those faced by local administrators. They too operated on the boundary line between local society and the authorities, an area prone to conflict. Which way to turn when, on the one hand, attempting to safeguard one's own interests (e.g. to secure the sale of products) and, on the other, trying to avoid disputes with the legislators? The fact that this was not possible without conflict is evidenced by court records. In extreme cases, such conflicts could lead to licences being withdrawn or to customers boycotting the premises, as happened to the tavern keeper Starke in Kohlstädt, Lippe, in 1825.[61] In both instances, the publicans' economic existence was endangered. However, their position was not as weak as court records might suggest. They were an important force in their community, and their position was marked by a certain degree of economic power and social prestige. While publicans were at the centre of a web of interests, dependencies and obligations, they could, if they played the game right, free themselves to such a degree that both their economic existence and their reputation remained secure.

As source material indicates, the clientele of the public houses included people from every walk of life. For the rural area we can draw on Roland Linde's

---

This according to the details in Staatsarchiv Detmold L 89 A I no. 107, fol. 143r-v. The publican received a relatively minor fine of ½ Reichsthaler.

[58] No doubt as a result of their inclination to ignore regulations, publicans were forced from 1693 to swear an oath that they would observe the law; Staatsarchiv Detmold L 89 A I no. 114, fol. 81r.

[59] For example: Staatsarchiv Detmold, L 89 A I no. 114: Gogerichte, fol. 178r.

[60] Staatsarchiv Detmold, L 89 A I no. 114: Gogerichte, fol. 151v.

[61] Staatsarchiv Detmold, L 77 A no. 4905: 'Schreiben des Krugpächters Starke aus Kohlstädt an die Regierung in Detmold' of 25 August 1825, fol. 2r-v.

detailed analysis of the visitation records from Lippe: all groups of local society frequented the taverns, from the prosperous farmers down to the landless hireling.[62] Other regular customers included migrant workers, clergymen, farmhands, servants, travellers or members of marginal groups such as Jews and vagrants. A similar picture emerges for the town centres. In the Town Hall Cellar (*Ratskeller*) in Wilster we find not only the leading lights of the local establishment, but also ordinary inhabitants, journeymen and day-labourers. These findings reinforce the observations made by Erasmus von Rotterdam during his travels in the Empire; his *Colloquium* of 1520 records that without exception, all ranks are to be found in the German public house.[63]

While we encounter quite different social groups sharing the tavern, this is not to say the individual groups mixed. James S. Roberts has depicted nineteenth-century drinking houses as a type of social melting pot, where people of all occupations met and intermingled. The status divisions which dominated relations at the workplace were, according to his thesis, cancelled out in the more egalitarian atmosphere of the tavern.[64] Pre-industrial taverns, however, knew no such mingling of societal groups. The system of exclusive premises catering for particular social, professional or trade groups was mirrored in microcosm in the mixed tavern. Here the segregation manifested itself in the placement of tables, at which none but specific groups could be seated and served.[65] This is borne out by the visitation records from 1812 for the taverns in Lippe, which make frequent reference to the largely uniform groups of players.[66] By far the most impressive example of social segregation has been delivered by Regina Schulte for the Bavarian region. She claims the meticulous separation of the various groups was deemed necessary because of the very fact that people shared a room for drinking. Under the influence of alcohol, divisions could have become blurred and mixing 'would have meant anarchy'.[67] Accordingly, the tables were graded in descending order of social

---

[62]   Linde, 'Krüge', 35.

[63]   R. Schultze, *Geschichte des Weins und der Trinkgelage. Ein Beitrag zur allgemeinen Kultur- und Sittengeschichte nach den besten Quellen bearbeitet und populär dargestellt für das deutsche Volk* (Berlin 1867), 131.

[64]   J. S. Roberts, 'Wirtshaus und Politik in der deutschen Arbeiterbewegung,' in G. Huck (ed.), *Sozialgeschichte der Freizeit. Untersuchungen zum Wandel der Alltagskultur in Deutschland* (Wuppertal, 1980), 123–39; 125–6.

[65]   K. S. Kramer describes the situation for Schleswig-Holstein where closed groups sat together: guilds, patricians, farm-hands and servants, market suppliers. In idem, *Volksleben in Holstein (1550–1800). Eine Volkskunde aufgrund archivalischer Quellen* (2nd edn, Kiel, 1990), 143.

[66]   In a number of cases the inspectors noted both name and status of the players in their reports, such as farmer, servant, or hireling. See for example the report from the *Bauerrichter* Wissing; Staatsarchiv Detmold, L 77 A no. 5052, fol. 74r.

[67]   R. Schulte, 'Feuer im Dorf', in: H. Reif (ed.), *Räuber, Volk und Obrigkeit. Studien zur Geschichte der Kriminalität in Deutschland seit dem 18. Jahrhundert* (Frankfurt a.M., 1984),

standing. The first table, prominently marked, took up a place of honour and seated the prosperous farmers. This gradation continued down to the sixth table, reserved for tramping topers, gypsies, beggars, members of poorer trades and similar sorts. The seating plan of the individual tables was strictly determined along the lines of age, rank, office, wealth and reputation.[68] Thus, with its conspicuous demonstration of social difference, the tavern not only upheld but also reinforced the existing social hierarchy. Drinking was subject to strict social rules which prevented the overstepping of class boundaries. The tavern of the early modern period stabilized existing social structures by transferring the principle of social inequality to the interior.

Why did the average customer visit the tavern? One visitation inspector, reporting from Schieder in Lippe, summed up the motivation of the guests as follows: 'Some visit this place to hear what is new; others to find escape from boredom and others still drink a glass of beer and, with that, recover from the strains of the week gone by'.[69] While it seems fair to assume drinking itself was the main incentive for a visit to the tavern, it is significant that here the aspect of relaxation is highlighted. Drinking habits are described as moderate: 'a glass of beer'. What then of the stereotype charges of excessive drinking bouts normally attributed to the drinking houses that abound in legislative texts, sermons and moralist writings? The visitation records certainly contain examples of individual guests being 'under the influence', but this is the exception rather than the rule. A survey in Hohenhausen, Lippe, for instance, uncovered only one offender, the cottager (Straßenkötter) Güse, from the administrative district of Kirchheide.[70] A three-day inspection in Langenholzhausen listed 149 customers in the 10 local public houses, all of them sober. The inspectors judged that while on occasion a subject gets drunk and 'staggers home', generally they were not as addicted to drink as the authorities liked to suggest.[71] These 'on-site' reports are invaluable for our purpose because they help to counter-balance impressions gained from legal sources. There the tavern at times emerges as a forum for drinking excesses, excesses reflected in the records in the form of disorderly and violent conduct. Based on the moderate behaviour evidenced in the visitation sources, we may argue that cases involving excessive drinking appeared in court not least

---

100–152, esp. 124.

[68] J. Schlicht, *Bayerisch Land und bayerisch Volk* (1875), cited in Schulte, 'Feuer', 124.

[69] 'Manche besuchen das Wirtshaus, um etwas Neues zu erfahren; andere, um sich die Langeweile zu vertreiben, noch andere trinken ein Glas Bier, erholen sich dabei von der Anstrengung der verflossenen Woche und gehen wieder nach Hause.' Staatsarchiv Detmold, L 77 A no. 5052: 'Bericht des Amts Schieder' of 22 January 1812.

[70] Ibid., L 77 A no. 5052: 'Bericht der Vogtei Hohenhausen' of 29 January 1812, fol. 53r.

[71] Ibid., L 77 A no. 5052: 'Bericht der Vogtei Langenholzhausen' of 28 January 1812, fol. 51v–52v.

because disruptive behaviour was generally disapproved of, and customers were thus inclined to bring charges. At the same time, excessive drinking was expressly sanctioned at communal festivities such as weddings, christenings and other public diversions. Rules governing work or food and alcohol consumption were ignored and excess was allowed; indeed, it could be a social imperative on such occasions.[72]

However, as the inspector from Schieder noted, people not only drank at the tavern, they also exchanged the latest news. The tavern, at the hub of the local network of communication, was a place where one obtained information and formed opinions. Rumour, the most subtle form of local discourse, was equally at home there as were discussions on political, religious and economic questions. Moreover, and perhaps most importantly, contacts formed in public houses offered a specific and vital form of social support. Lars Magnusson has correctly pointed out how personal contacts, which had been made through communication in the tavern, could be activated and used as social capital when necessary, as in a time of individual crisis.[73]

The tavern also afforded customers an opportunity to relax from the stress and strain of day-to-day life. A drink with friends, pleasant conversation, games, song and dance: our material offers numerous examples of such diversions. Thus on Sunday, 17 October 1756, we see Hartig Schippmann and Jürgen Kröger singing 'outrageous songs' while visiting the tavern in Wilster.[74] Card and dice games were a favourite among all social ranks in town and country alike.[75] Bowling was particularly popular in Holstein, although it could pose a danger to life and limb if not given the players' undivided attention.[76] Entertainment was also offered in the form of raffles, run by the more enterprising publicans in an effort to attract more customers and increase profits.[77] Such recreational activities, enjoyed in the company of others, allowed guests

---

[72] Linde, 'Krüge', 37.

[73] L. Magnusson, 'Proto-industrialization, culture et tavernes en Suède (1800–1850)', in *Annales. Economies. Sociétés. Civilisations* 45 (1990), 21–36, esp. 32–3.

[74] 'Hartig Schippmann aus Mohrhusen und Jürgen Kröger aus Neuendorf haben am 17ten Sonntage post Trinitatis nach der Nachmittagspredigt in Claus Stegmanns Hause schändliche Lieder gesungen.' Stadtarchiv Wilster, Man III b, no. 398 a: Klageregister 1737–1822, 289.

[75] This is intimated in the frequently mentioned records of the tavern-visitations (e.g., the report of the district officer, the *Amtsbote* Wagner, Staatsarchiv Detmold L 77 A no. 5052, fol. 77 r/v) as well as in reports from the police commission, the *Polizeikommission* Detmold (e.g., the report of 8 July 1777; Staatsarchiv Detmold L 77 A no. 115, fol. 3v).

[76] Serious injury might result from bowling. In 1617, for instance, one Hans Vagell was fined a sum of 4 thaler for injuries caused when his bowling ball hit a spectator (Stadtarchiv Wilster Man II b no. 273, fol. 257v). In 1722 a fatality is registered for Heimsen near Minden. A child, injured by the bowler Reincke Kork, died three days later of wounds sustained in the accident. See Staatsarchiv Detmold, L 86 no. 1120 l, fol. 150r.

[77] Landesarchiv Schleswig, Abt. 19 no. 65 II 2: 'Generalvisitation im Kirchspiel Beyenfleth (Herzogtum Holstein) im Jahr 1769'.

to recharge and relax after a day's work. No doubt, the competitive element involved in games and drinking played its part in the regeneration process.

Source material leaves no doubt as to the expectations of the average guest. They sought a space where, free from official constraints, they could enjoy themselves and recover from their 'hard and heavy work'.[78] The publican provided just such a space. If he failed to fulfil their needs, customers withdrew to other establishments where, regardless of official closing time, they could sing and dance into the early hours 'free from all supervision'.[79] With customer demands often diametrically opposed to official requirements, conflicts with the authorities were inevitable.

As people tended to visit the public house on weekends and church holidays, rather than on weekdays (when attendance was usually quite sparse),[80] it seems appropriate to view the tavern culture of this period primarily as a leisure culture.[81] With the week's work completed, the free hours of the weekend were devoted to worship and tavern, preferably in this order. While it was fairly common for men to retire to the 'local' after services, some, less concerned with spiritual needs than with worldly appetites, bypassed the church and chose the direct path to the tavern. Hence the frequently voiced charges of Sabbath-breaking directed at Catholics and Protestants alike. Feast days such as Christmas saw the inns and taverns full to capacity. Sometimes they were the venue for family festivities. However, we can distinguish class preferences here, with the poorer orders more likely to celebrate in a public house. The 'better sort', or those who considered themselves such, tended to celebrate such occasions as weddings or christenings in their homes. By this means they demonstrated that both space and domestic comfort were such that they could adequately cater to the needs of a large crowd.[82]

---

[78] 'sauren und schweren Arbeit': Staatsarchiv Detmold, L 77 A no. 5052: 'Bericht der Vogtei Langenholzhausen' of 28 January 1812, fol. 52v.

[79] 'ohne alle Aufsicht': Staatsarchiv Detmold, L 77 A no. 164: 'Supplik der Vorsteher des Braueramtes der Stadt Detmold' of 8 January 1771, fol. 29v.

[80] In this context, the tavern-visitations from Lippe, 1812, which offer surveys for different weekdays, are an invaluable source. They list the highest attendance rates for Sunday night.

[81] For a positive answer to the question of whether it is appropriate to speak of 'leisure' with regard to the early modern era see P. Münch, *Lebensformen in der Frühen Neuzeit 1500 bis 1800* (Frankfurt a.M., 1996), 415.

[82] Felix Platter, a highly respected citizen of Basel, thus writes of his wedding in 1577 that 150 (!) guests were invited to the feast that took place at his father's home. See F. Platter, *Tagebuch (Lebensbeschreibung) 1536–1567*, ed. V. Lötscher (Basle, 1976), 324–5. Court records also support the thesis that poorer people tended to celebrate in the public house, wealthier citizens in their homes. No doubt, the more prosperous members of urban society rented the town's ballroom for such occasions.

While the publicans and their trade represented a lucrative source of revenue for the authorities, official interest extended well beyond their fiscal function. Ruling bodies recognized the sphere of the public house as a critical centre for public influence and control and attempted to exploit this for their own purposes. It is hardly surprising then that they endeavoured to use the public house as a publicity forum for the contents of ordinances.[83] Publicans in Münster were even obliged to keep a record of edicts (the so-called *Edikten-Buch*). This was to contain all ordinances, in systematic order, and to be so displayed as to ensure free access by the customers.[84] This measure, it was hoped, would make the dissemination of the contents of ordinances more efficient. Ordinary inhabitants were only too inclined to forget the details of rulings from above and this could occasion legal uncertainty.[85]

The authorities had other expectations of the publicans. In the course of time, numerous ordinances intended to suppress the worst problems in the trade were directed at keepers of inns and taverns. Four broad areas of concern may be distinguished: the need to establish quality standards and to set down maximum prices; the wish to exercise official control over travellers; the desire to influence the number of public houses; and the need to exert direct control on alcohol consumption. Each of these will now be examined in turn.

Keepers of taverns and inns were repeatedly accused of serving adulterated or even stale drink and were no less notorious for the exorbitant prices they charged. The authorities of the time were deeply concerned with the adverse effects of stale or adulterated drink on public health and safety. As far back as 1587, members of the legislative assembly of Wilster in Holstein addressed themselves to the issue of quality when they ordered the publicans of the town to serve 'fresh' beer.[86] National legislation, while remarkably reserved on the issue of curbing alcohol consumption, was less reticent on the question of price control. The National Police Regulations of 1530 required that all local authorities should set down prices for 'wine, beer, bread and meat' sold by the publican, 'according to the given conditions of time and region'.[87]

---

[83]   Stadtarchiv Wilster, Acta IV G 1 no. 1532: 'Schreiben der Stadt Wilster an den König' of 2 October 1732.

[84]   See Scotti, *Sammlung*, vol. 2 ('Jagdordnung' of 10 February 1792), 356.

[85]   Klaus Scholz has shown this in his convincing discussion of legislation in Lippe in the early modern period. He cites the characteristic assessment of the estates' legal advisor: 'After one year scarcely anyone knows the contents [of ordinances] any more. The printed copies are quickly snapped up. And thus the subject, even the young lawyer, runs risk, to involuntarily act unlawfully and to commit a criminal offence'. Cited in Scholz, 'Edikte, Landesverordnungen und Amtsblätter als Quellen der der Geschichtlichen Landeskunde Westfalens bis 1800', in *Archivpflege in Westfalen und Lippe* 24 (1986), 10–14, here 13.

[86]   F. D. C. von Cronhelm (ed.), *Corpus Constitutionum Regio Holsaticarum*, vol. 3 (Altona, 1753), 396.

[87]   J. J. Schmauss and H. C. von. Senckenberg, (eds), *Neue und vollständigere Sammlung der*

Beyond the provision of services for local inhabitants, inns offered a guarantee that strangers could find food, drink and safe lodgings on their journeys. But along with the more respectable traveller availing of these services while on private or commercial business, the inn drew members of the less reputable marginal groups, the migrant poor. Characterized as they were by a high degree of mobility, these tramping beggars, gypsies, beggar Jews, mercenaries, minstrels, and criminals frequently evaded official control. The early modern state, increasingly concerned with the need to exercise control over its subjects, could only be suspicious of groups whose high mobility enabled them to evade supervisory efforts. The ideal subject was the virtuous, disciplined citizen, whose integration in a rural or urban community facilitated the state's growing demand for control.[88] Initial regulative attempts were mirrored in a series of ordinances which obliged the innkeeper to register and submit the names of strangers lodging on their premises. They were further forbidden to shelter beggars, gypsies and other members of the marginal groups. Unannounced inspections, the so-called *Visitationen,* served to guarantee adherence to the rules. As early as 1572 the authorities in Münster responded to a petition from the estates by forbidding the innkeepers under threat of 'severe punishment' to give support or lodging to 'these stray itinerant idlers and other suspicious rogues'. This was also intended to prevent the innkeeper from dealing in or accepting goods 'extorted' from unsuspecting inhabitants.[89] The innkeepers in Lippe risked banishment, according to the local Police Regulations from 1620, if found harbouring 'evil dishonest society'. 'Considerable penalties' were threatened on innkeepers who failed to report foreigners availing of their hospitality for a period of three days. On receipt of such information, local officials were obliged to summon the registered guest, establish the reasons for their visit, and either decide the case themselves or file a report to central government.[90]

Reichs-Abschiede, Welche von den Zeiten Kayser Conrads des II. bis jetzo, auf den Teutschen Reichs-Tägen abgefasset worden ..., vol. 2 (Frankfurt, 1747; rev. ed. Osnabrück, 1967), 340.

[88] To date, one of the most important, and both theoretically and conceptionally stimulating discussions on marginal groups is the article by F. Graus, 'Randgruppen der städtischen Gesellschaft im Spätmittelalter' in *Zeitschrift für historische Forschung* 8 (1981), 385–437. Robert Jütte offers a research review in 'Mythos Außenseiter. Neuerscheinungen zur Geschichte der sozialen Randgruppen im vorindustriellen Europa', in *Ius Commune 21* (1994), 241–66. See also R. Scribner, 'Wie wird man Außenseiter? Ein- und Ausgrenzung im frühneuzeitlichen Deutschland', in N. Fischer and M. Kobelt-Groch (eds), *Außenseiter zwischen Mittelalter und Neuzeit* (Leiden etc., 1997), 21–46.

[89] 'bei schwerer Strafe ... diesen herrenlos herumziehenden Müßiggängern und anderen verdächtigen Buben': Scotti, *Sammlung*, vol. 1, 'Verordnung' of 5 December 1572, 167. See also ibid., vol. 2, 'Oeffentliche Sicherheit' of 20 January 1774, 213, 215.

[90] 'böse unehrliche Gesellschaft': *Landesverordnungen der Grafschaft Lippe*, vol. 1, 370–71; for one example of many for the eighteenth century: ibid., vol. 2, 'Verordnung wegen der Häuslinge und Einlieger' of 12 November 1749, 22.

With their power to grant or withdraw licences, the authorities had an instrument at their disposal with which to regulate the number of drinking houses. This regulatory tool allowed them to intervene in the market as demand or political considerations dictated. They could close illegal premises at will, a power no doubt envied by licensed publicans, who were interested in keeping illegal competition at a minimum. A further factor in favour of controlling the market was voiced by the *Policey-Wissenschaftler*[91] Joseph von Sonnenfels in 1787 when he demanded that the number of existing houses be reduced in order to control the incidence of drunkenness.[92] In practice, however, licensing policy was frequently determined by economic interests. The ruling orders, with an eye to their finances, were not averse to increasing revenue by issuing new licences. Here we have a clear demonstration of the conflicting aims of official drug policies, which can be witnessed down to the present day: commercial interests conflict with issues of health and public order.[93]

Noteworthy against this background is the situation in Holstein, where, from the early eighteenth century, some efforts were made to reduce the number of public houses. In a letter to the government in 1733, the head of the Church Council in Münsterdorf referred to complaints from preachers that the population would no longer obey police regulations. A survey had revealed tippling, gaming and brawling as the most serious disorders. The church notable proposed a concrete remedy for the problem: 'But since it is public and evident that tippling originates in the many taverns, and through tippling the most disorder arises, thus I hold it above all necessary that such seductive taverns be limited'.[94] This was the beginning of a campaign against drunkenness which the authorities hoped to win by reducing the opportunities for alcohol consumption. While some progress was made, it was not until 1790 that the provincial government in Holstein made a more concerted effort by introducing measures for rural areas that sought to reduce the number of

---

[91] Of professorial rank, the *Policey-Wissenschaftler* was involved in the research and development of matters pertaining to public order.

[92] J. von Sonnenfels, *Grundsaetze der Polizei, Handlung und Finanz: zu dem Leitfaden des politischen Studiums* (Vienna, 1787), 148.

[93] One topical issue is, for instance, the position of governments on alcohol and tobacco. While on the one hand they profit through taxes by the greatest possible consumption, on the other side, they instigate information campaigns to increase awareness of the health risks involved with both substances. An early modern example of this conflict is explored in B. A. Tlusty, 'Water of Life, Water of Death: The Controversy over Brandy and Gin in Early Modern Augsburg', in *Central European History* 31 (Fall 1998), 1–30.

[94] 'Weil aber kund und offenbar ist, daß von den vielen Schenken das Saufen herrührt, und durch das Saufen die meiste Unordnung entsteht, so halte ich es vor allem für notwendig, daß solchen verführerischen Schenken ein Maß gesetzt ... würde'. Landesarchiv Schleswig, Abt. 65.2 no. 881 II: 'Schreiben des Probstes Kirchhoff' of 5 November 1733.

taverns to no more than one in every village.[95] Only eight years later the first positive effects could be reported. The general guidelines were then specified to the effect that only establishments situated on main or public roads were to be tolerated. With this, the government wished to reduce numbers to the minimum necessary for the provision of services for travellers.[96]

While measures implemented to curb alcohol consumption varied regionally, both in intensity and enforcement, all territories adopted the basic principle of fixing strict hours for the sale of drink, a principle fully endorsed by prominent *Policey-Wissenschaftler* such as Justi and Sonnenfels.[97] It was thus strictly prohibited for all but travellers and the sick to drink during service time while 'seated' in a public house. The confessions were largely in agreement as to where such behaviour would lead: church attendance would suffer; drunken behaviour would disrupt religious services; and drunkenness, disorder and foul language would profane the Sabbath.[98] This would be offensive to both God and the community at large. Beyond this it was felt that offenders thoughtlessly put their salvation at risk by denying themselves access to 'God's holy words'.[99] While the stiff fines dealt out for such offences were imposed on publicans and tippling customers alike, proprietors could find themselves confronted with substantially higher fines than those demanded from offending guests.[100] The perception of the inn- or tavern keeper as the person responsible for the guests' actions seemed to justify this, and direct pressure on them would ensure observance of the newly established norm. In sixteenth-century Wilster, publicans were even bound by oath to refuse drink to

---

[95] This was alluded to in a communication from Kiel dated 12 November 1790. Here again we see the ambivalent position of the authorities; one of the arguments brought against reducing the number of drinking places was that this measure would cause a loss of revenue in the domaines.

[96] Landesarchiv Schleswig, Abt. 65.2 no. 804 II: 'Circulare' of 28 April 1798.

[97] J. H. G. Justi, *Die Grundfeste der Macht und Glückseligkeit der Staaten; oder ausführliche Vorstellung der gesamten Polyzei-Wissenschaft II* (Königsberg, 1760; rev. ed. Aalen, 1965), 175; Sonnenfels, *Grundsaetze*, 148.

[98] See for example *Hochfürstlich-Paderbörnische Landes-Verordnungen*, vol. 1, 'Polizeiordnung' from 1655, 8; ibid., vol. 1, 'Kirchenordnung' from 1686, 249; on Münster: Scotti, *Sammlung*, vol. 1, 'Kirchen- und Schulordnung' from 1693, 314; on Lippe: *Landesverordnungen der Grafschaft Lippe*, vol. 1, 'Kirchenordnung' from 1571, 39; ibid., 'Polizeiordnung' from 1620, 371; on Holstein: Cronhelm, *Corpus Constitutionum*, vol. 3, 'Buersprake der Stadt Wilster 1587', 394; ibid., vol. 1, 'Gemeinschaftliche Polizeiordnung von 1636', 296.

[99] For example: Cronhelm, *Corpus Constitutionum*, vol. 1, 'Verordnung wegen gebührender Heiligung der Sonn- und Feyer-Tage' of 16 April 1736, 301–9; 304.

[100] Thus, for example, we see in Münster a tavern keeper fined six gold gulden but the customer only two when they infringed the Church and School Regulations of 1693. Scotti, *Sammlung*, vol. 1, 314. An ordinance from 1710 in Lippe laid down a fine of only one gold gulden for the offending guest but ten for the tavern keeper: *Landesverordnungen der Grafschaft Lippe*, vol. 1, 738.

their customers during service time.[101] Both Lippe and Holstein extended these regulations. 1710 saw Lippe generally prohibit the sale of brandy,[102] while premises in Holstein were forbidden to open between nine p.m. on the eve and five p.m. on the Sunday or church feast, with the stipulation that drinking should then be moderate and overindulgence avoided.[103]

Compared to their Catholic neighbours, Protestant territories tended to be both more consistent and harsher in their legislative efforts to curb drinking on the Sabbath and feastdays. While the Catholics remained true to the principle of prohibiting drinking during service time only, restrictions were harsher in the Protestant areas. Calvinist Lippe went so far as to generally forbid 'women-folk' drinking in the tavern.[104] The relatively permissive Catholic attitude is exemplified in the Police Regulations for Paderborn from 1655: the sale and consumption of alcohol during worship time were prohibited, thereafter inhabitants might visit the tavern and 'take delight in drink', but overindulgence would not be condoned.[105]

A further step in the campaign against alcohol was the introduction of fixed closing times, a measure adopted in all regions. Times were adapted to suit the natural rhythm of the seasons, eight p.m. in wintertime and nine p.m. during the brighter months (in Holstein an hour later respectively). A bell reminded both publicans and those inclined to tarry that time was up. A timely departure, it was felt, would ensure that customers headed for home in a sober and orderly fashion.[106]

The battle against the demon drink was also fought on a second front: drinking on credit was perceived as one of the root causes of inebriety. Both Lippe and Paderborn launched a massive campaign to suppress this outrage. In

---

[101] This according to instructions contained in the file 'Punkte und Artikel worauf die Krüger in den Städten und Marschen vereidigt werden' of 20 December 1591; Stadtarchiv Wilster Acta IV G 2 no. 1548. In her dissertation, Ruth Mohrmann correctly states that no evidence of this oath is to be found in commonplace practice for seventeenth- or eighteenth-century Wilster: R. Mohrmann, 'Volksleben in Wilster im 16. und 17. Jahrhundert' (Ph.D. University of Kiel, 1975), 313 n. 177.

[102] Landesverordnungen der Grafschaft Lippe, vol. 1, 'Verordnung wegen der Brantwein- und Bier-Gelage' of 27 March 1710, 738.

[103] Cronhelm, Corpus Constitutionum, vol. 1, 'Wiederholte und extendirte Verordnung, wegen gebührender Heiligung der Sonn- und Feyer-Tage' of 16 April 1736, 304–5.

[104] Landesverordnungen der Grafschaft Lippe, vol. 1, 'Polizeiordnung von 1620', 371. This ordinance was valid until 18 July 1843; B. Ebert, 'Kurzer Abriß einer lippischen Rechtsgeschichte für die Zeit seit Simon VI.', in Mitteilungen aus der lippischen Geschichte und Landeskunde 25 (1956), 12–60; here 21, 41.

[105] Hochfürstlich-Paderbörnische Landes-Verordnungen, vol. 1, 8. An eighteenth-century example can be found in ibid., vol. 3, 'Verordnung wegen der auf gewisse Art erlaubter Einfuhr fremden Brantweins, und dessen Verzapfung' of 17 December 1740, 60.

[106] Ibid., vol. 1, 9; Landesverordnungen der Grafschaft Lippe, vol. 1, 372; Cronhelm, Corpus Constitutionum, vol. 1, 296.

a report to the government in 1789, we see the chief administrator Hoffmann from Lippe cautioning that every opportunity be taken to undermine the 'tendency to drink', an inclination fostered by the publicans' willingness to extend credit, which animated subjects to keep on drinking. Hoffmann suggested that credit limits be set, scaled according to the income of the customer, from the substantial farmer down to the poor cottager, hireling and day-labourer.[107] Hoffman's perception was endorsed by voices from other regions. In Brake, for instance, the all too 'accommodating' credit of 'greedy inn- and tavern keepers' was seen to facilitate the tendency to drink to total inebriation.[108] However, there were some who questioned the efficacy of such a step, aware firstly that determined drinkers would avail of credit facilities in a number of premises,[109] but also conscious of the difficulties involved in supervising such a complicated system of credit limits.[110] A government ordinance of 16 March 1790 mirrored Hoffmann's fundamental ideas but went a step further by totally prohibiting credit facilities in the taverns, a measure which had been introduced in Paderborn fifty years previously.[111]

An overview of government efforts to exert control over the publican reveals that measures to effect observance of the Sabbath and the efficient surveillance of travellers predominate in Catholic and Protestant territories alike. There was also a large degree of correspondence between the individual regions in both the issues they addressed (e.g. price and quality standards, numbers of drinking premises, limitation of sale) and the penalties imposed (clear dominance of low to moderately severe fines). Over time, a clear trend can be distinguished: while efforts to restrict drinking in the first half of the seventeenth century concentrated on the introduction of strict time limits for the sale of alcohol, towards the end of the seventeenth century and during the first half of the eighteenth, direct influence was exerted on the publican and

---

[107] Hoffmann's report of 25 July 1789 is contained in Staatsarchiv Detmold, L 37 Tit. XXV no. 2. He suggested the following scales for credit: substantial farmers were to be limited to 24 *Mariengroschen*; less substantial farmers could be granted credit up to 18 *Mariengroschen*; substantial, middling and small cottagers no more than 12; and all other groups a maximum of 9 *Mariengroschen*.

[108] Staatsarchiv Detmold, L 37 Tit. XXV no. 2: 'Bericht des Amtes Brake' of 12 September 1789.

[109] This was the central argument in the report from the administrative district of Horn of 21 October 1789; Staatsarchiv Detmold, L 37 Tit. XXV no. 2.

[110] See the report from Detmold from 27 August 1789: Staatsarchiv Detmold, L 37 Tit. XXV no. 2. Guided by a very pessimistic view of the situation in their area, it suggests a far more radical solution: the prohibition of all brandy drinking bouts. As an ordinance to this effect already existed (from 1710, see *Landesverordnungen der Grafschaft Lippe* vol. 1, 738), it is to be doubted that this measure would have been very effective.

[111] *Landesverordnungen der Grafschaft Lippe*, vol. 4, 8; *Hochfürstlich-Paderbörnische Landes-Verordnungen*, vol. 3, 'Verordnung wegen der auf gewisse Art erlaubter Einfuhr fremden Brantweins, und dessen Verzapfung' of 17 December 1740, 60.

customers, for instance, by prohibiting the tavern keeper from granting credit. Finally, in the second half of the eighteenth century, it was deemed necessary to directly combat the proliferation of public houses and reduce numbers to the necessary minimum. A further trend also deserves attention: throughout the early modern period, but in particular during the course of the eighteenth century, there was a steady increase in regulatory legislation by governments, with the main initiative falling in the final third of the period. With this, the early modern state demonstrated its claim to control, at least on paper.[112]

In furtherance of their objectives, ecclesiastic and state bodies were only too aware of the potential offered by the exploitation of publicans, with their myriad contacts and intimate knowledge of local events. Accordingly, a non-stop barrage of ordinances was directly aimed at the publican. It was incumbent on them to refuse requests for drink during service times, to ensure official closing times were observed, to report law infringements, to keep the authorities informed on travellers or strangers attempting to recruit soldiers, to forbid proscribed games, to mediate in disputes, and much more besides.[113] Publicans, if effectively exploited for the government's regulatory concept, would have served as ideal agents for bringing social disciplining policies on to the level of the ordinary inhabitants. An effective integration of the publican in the system of social control would have brought the government significantly closer to success.

That publicans failed to live up to these expectations, we know, and the reasons are apparent. The demands made of them were at variance with their own and their customers' interests. Their main concern was, of course, to secure a reasonable profit, and the sale of alcohol was their chief source of income. Customers expected to enjoy their drink in a pleasant atmosphere, uninhibited by official controls. The potential for conflict was given. If proprietors catered to official demands, profits suffered; if they disregarded regulations, they faced severe sanctions, and even stood to lose their licence (and, with that, their means of subsistence). The inevitable result of this conflict of interests is mirrored in the records.

---

[112] A development also to be observed in other areas, as in efforts to exert control of marginal groups. See M. Frank, 'Daß hochdero Lande und Unterthanen davon rein und unbeschwert bleiben sollen. Lippische Obrigkeit und Sinti in der Frühen Neuzeit', in K. Bott-Bodenhausen (ed.), *Sinti in der Grafschaft Lippe. Studien zur Geschichte der 'Zigeuner' im 18. Jahrhundert* (Munich, 1988), 43–65.

[113] The obligations of the publican are detailed in an ordinance from 1606; Landesarchiv Schleswig, Abt. 103 no. 175. On the duty to keep the authorities informed on travellers or strangers attempting to recruit soldiers, see for example *Landesverordnungen der Grafschaft Lippe*, vol. 1, 'Verordnung wegen der fremden Werber und Kriegsdienste' from 29 September 1688, 698.

In 1591 an official from Steinburg in Holstein complained that drinking premises were full during Sunday worship time. Publicans, he claimed, ignored regulations and failed to report offenders and were generally too lax in enforcing regulations.[114] The publicans had little choice but to ignore the rules. When Henning Ahrend from Wilster refused beer to Claus Ratie during worship time, Ratie solved the problem by drawing his own beer from the barrel.[115] Records from the district courts are full of Sabbath-breaking offences. In Wilster, from the seventeenth century onwards, such crimes, involving either just one of the offenders or both publican and customer, predominate. In 1623, Hinrich Berendts drank brandy 'on a day of prayer in service time', for which he paid a fine of one thaler.[116] The innkeeper Hans Santzer, who had 'drawn beer during service time' paid a markedly higher fine of five thaler in 1638.[117] Sentences for non-observance of the strict times for serving drink could be quite severe and damaging for the parties concerned, as is evidenced by two cases from Wilster and Detmold. While the tavern keeper Marten Arent in Wilster was incarcerated in the town jail for a period, the innkeeper Schild from Detmold was fined the enormous sum of fifty gold gulden, which sum he had to borrow from the court Jew Moses Jacob.[118] Despite the severe sentences that could be imposed on proprietors for infringements of this nature, in the long term, it is doubtful that they were persuaded to observe the rules. Fines were generally low or moderate, direct pressure from their clientele was strong and, as we shall see, the supervisory efforts of the authorities were not as effective as court records might suggest. Indeed, rather than being a sign of efficiency, the relatively numerous indictments could indicate that it was commonplace practice to disregard regulations.[119]

---

[114] Stadtarchiv Wilster, Acta III G 1 no. 1121: 'Bericht des Amtmanns Benedikt v. Ahlefeldt' of 6 November 1591. For an eighteenth-century example see the report in Landesarchiv Schleswig, Abt. 19 no. 65 II/1: 'Pro memoria' of the Generalvisitation of 1775 in Hohenfelde, Holstein.

[115] Stadtarchiv Wilster, Man III b no. 398: 'Klageregister der Stadt Wilster' of 12 January 1716, fol. 325r.

[116] Ibid., Man. II b, no. 273, fol. 293r. For the eighteenth century see the case of Ernst Schliemann, Paul Bobbert and Hans Meyfart, who drank in a tavern during the sermon on Sunday 12 February 1743: ibid., Man. III b, no. 398a, 131.

[117] Ibid., Man. II b, no. 273, fol. 354v. The tavern keeper Jochim Ehlers was sentenced on 6 October 1739; ibid., Man. III b, no. 398a, 68.

[118] Staatsarchiv Detmold, L 18 no. 73: Actum Detmold of 15 May 1714, fol. 3r-v. For the case of Marten Arent see Stadtarchiv Wilster, Man IIb, no. 273: Brücheregister 1601, fol. 151v.

[119] These findings apply not only to Sabbatarian offences; publicans were often indicted for other reasons, such as for granting credit. See for example the case of the alcoholic Hermann Henrich Faßemeyer: in 1787, publicans in the parishes of Hohenhausen and Talle in Lippe were explicitly forbidden, under threat of severe punishment, to serve him alcohol on credit. However, Faßemeyer repeatedly found keepers willing to give him credit.

Well aware that successful enforcement of their standards required stronger measures, the authorities in all the examined territories introduced a system of regular visitations intended to supervise the publican. Holstein led the way in 1636. According to the Police Regulations of Schleswig and Holstein, 'diligent investigations' were to be carried out, in the urban centres by summoners, with the rural areas covered by persons designated by local officials. As an incentive, inspectors were promised twenty per cent of the collected fines.[120] The remaining regions followed this lead in the eighteenth century but stipulated more frequent inspections, which ranged from the unannounced monthly visits in Münster[121] to the minimum of two per month demanded in Lippe.[122] The highest rate of control has been found for urban areas, where we see priority given to Sabbath-breaking offences.[123] In general, the supervision of travellers and the strict observance of closing times were also high-priority issues. As in Holstein, the other regions attempted to motivate inspectors by offering them a share of any fines imposed: 1792 saw Lippe increase this share to an astounding third of the takings.[124]

While inspectors tended to be drawn from the lower ranks of public servants, some private citizens were recruited to carry out the task.[125] Not surprisingly, this task proved to be quite unpleasant at times. Trouble often lurked at the entrance to the tavern. Thus we see Anna Jacob Foppens indicted in 1662 for refusing entry to an inspector wishing to check 'if someone tippled there within' during worship time.[126] The same offence brought Matthias Knickbein to court in 1697. The records show he had good reasons for obstructing the inspector: he indeed had 'seated guests'.[127] Once inspectors had gained entry, they were obliged to control guests for possible alcohol consumption and to question them on dancing and games. Understandably, such measures often caused hefty reactions. Both publicans and customers offered resistance, which in the drink-filled atmosphere of the tavern could be dangerous. Seen in this

---

[120] Cronhelm, *Corpus Constitutionum*, vol. 1, 'Gemeinschaftliche Polizeiordnung aus dem Jahr 1636', 296.

[121] Scotti, *Sammlung,* vol. 2, 'Verordnung aus dem Jahr 1774', 215.

[122] *Landesverordnungen der Grafschaft Lippe*, vol. 2, 'Verordnung wegen Visitation der Wirthshäuser auf dem Lande' of 13 April 1779, 663.

[123] Stadtarchiv Wilster, Acta III G1 no. 1121.

[124] *Landesverordnungen der Grafschaft Lippe*, vol. 4, 64.

[125] For seventeenth-century Holstein, I have found a number of private citizens acting as inspectors. In Steinburg, a district in the marches of Holstein, they were referred to as *Eidgeschworne* which can be loosely translated as 'those who have sworn an oath'. In the remaining districts of the Duchy they were called *Krugsucher* which is roughly equivalent to tavern-searcher.

[126] Anna Jacob Foppens was fined one Reichsthaler for her offence. See Landesarchiv Schleswig, Abt. 163: Amtsrechnungen Eiderstedt (Historische Quellenkartei Kiel).

[127] Landesarchiv Schleswig, Abt. 163: Amtsrechnungen Eiderstedt.

light, the case of Michael Böge from Wilster, who grabbed, shook and beat the inspector Carsten Eckhoff, was no doubt only one of many such incidents.[128] In view of the unpleasantness and dangers involved and, in the long term, the possible social consequences that could follow for all-too-diligent inspectors, one can understand the lack of motivation mirrored in the records. Least motivated were the private citizens recruited for the purpose. Some failed to report offences,[129] others failed to report for duty, and others still hired replacements, who, in turn, failed to turn up.[130] There are indeed clear indications that inspectors joined forces with the publicans and their customers. An example from Lage shows one inspector answering charges of giving advance notice of his visits.[131] The probable logic behind cooperation of this type is easy to appreciate: when official directives were formally complied with, none of the parties involved suffered a disadvantage, thus none could take offence.[132] Publicans themselves developed a variety of survival strategies. A number of proprietors in Lippe secretly converted back rooms into drinking parlours, where guests adjourned after official closing time to drink and gamble into the early hours.[133] Tavern keepers, and in some cases the guests themselves, employed men to keep watch for approaching inspectors.[134] As we can see, intelligent strategies for evading official constraints are not an invention of the American Prohibition era. Against this background, the efficiency of official controls could only be very limited. The original plan, whereby control of the public house and publicans would equally control drinking, was thus doomed to failure.

---

[128] Stadtarchiv Wilster, Man. III b, no. 398a, 332.

[129] Two tavern visitators, Laurentz Bahnß and Paul Eddens, were each fined a hefty 10 Reichsthaler in 1665 'as they had stated in court that nothing had happened, but that from the pastor's letter the opposite was to be seen'; Landesarchiv Schleswig, Abt. 163: Amtsrechnungen Eiderstedt (Historische Quellenkartei Kiel).

[130] This extreme case is documented in the report of the general visitation from 1769 in the diocese of Münsterdorf, Holstein. It notes that whereas the official visitators in the parish of Hohenfelde should have visited the local drinking houses during worship time, 'however they do not execute the their post, but hire to that end others for money, who however neglect the duties incumbent on them'. Landesarchiv Slesvig, Abt. 19 no. 65 II 2.

[131] See the magistrate's report to the government of 4 December 1811 from Lage; Staatsarchiv Detmold, L 77 A no. 5052: 'Bericht des Magistrats der Stadt Lage an die Regierung', fol. 2r. The magistrate, in view of the integrity hitherto demonstrated by the defendant, considered the accusations to be unfounded. No closer investigation was carried out.

[132] This, of course, was only applicable as long as the unholy alliance held.

[133] Staatsarchiv Detmold, L 77 A No. 5052: 'Pro memoria des Oberamtmannes Hoffmann' of 6 January 1812, fol. 12v.

[134] Ibid., 'Bericht des Amtes Detmold an die Regierung' of 20 December 1811, fol. 6v; ibid., 'Pro memoria des Oberamtmanns Hoffmanns' of 6 January 1812, fol. 12v.

On Easter Sunday of 1741 the village church in Heiden was the scene of an incident of some significance. Two members of the congregation, Johann Jost Wend and Jost Heinrich Meinert, were so engrossed in conversation that the words of the sermon were apparently lost on them. One Johann Hermann Gröne, none too pleased with this behaviour, demanded they should 'kindly hold their tongues'. To his question of whether they believed themselves in a tavern, they laconically replied 'there is no difference'. Understandably, contemporaries saw their remark as an ungodly provocation and the offending parties were subsequently fined.[135] However, recent research, in particular the work of French historians, underpins their perception of the situation, namely that the church and the tavern shared the same central functions. Robert Muchembled and Jean Delumeau have shown how both institutions were critical centres for community and, as such, served as the 'cornerstones of social relationships' (Muchembled).[136] In both, specific identities were shaped and community was manifestly formed.

Church and tavern have long since lost their position as the cornerstones of society. Other institutions dominate today and push forward the process of secularization and modernization. The past 200 years have seen the tavern undergo changes which have undermined its role as a social institution. While it regained some of its previously held importance during the nineteenth century as a meeting place for the German working-class movement,[137] an ongoing process of depoliticization, particularly in the post-war era, has significantly reduced its relevance in society. No less important is the fundamental change in patterns of sociability during the same period, which involved a shift away from public towards private activities. Whereas during the early modern period drinking centred mainly on the tavern, today people generally drink in the comfort of their homes. This process of transformation naturally had consequences for the publican. They are now only one of many offering their services on the recreation market. Open to strong competition from servers catering to the 'event-culture', they are faced with new demands, which require different talents from those required of their predecessors.

Nonetheless, pressure has been removed in one area. If, against the backdrop of regulatory legislation, with the tavern keeper exploited in an effort to effect social discipline, relationships between publicans and guests were often

---

[135] Staatsarchiv Detmold, L 89 A I no. 119: Gogerichte, fol. 26r.

[136] R. Muchembled, *Die Erfindung des modernen Menschen. Gefühlsdifferenzierung und kollektive Verhaltensweisen im Zeitalter des Absolutismus* (Reinbek bei Hamburg, 1990), 188–9; J. Delumeau, *Angst im Abendland. Die Geschichte kollektiver Ängste im Europa des 14. bis 18. Jahrhunderts*, vol. 1 (Reinbek bei Hamburg, 1985), 258.

[137] J. S. Roberts, 'Der Alkoholkonsum deutscher Arbeiter im 19. Jahrhundert', in *Geschichte und Gesellschaft* 6 (1980), 220–42, esp. 238; U. Wyrwa, *Branntewein und 'echtes' Bier. Die Trinkkultur der Hamburger Arbeiter im 19. Jahrhundert* (Hamburg, 1990).

strained in the early modern era, they relaxed over time, parallel to the diminishing significance of the tavern as a social institution. Efforts to exploit the publicans as a means of securing social discipline became less and less. But one shadow from the past remains: both publican and public house have retained their rather dubious reputation. The occupation of the publican is often seen as the final chance for those who have failed to secure a respectable livelihood. However, today's tavern proprietors may find some consolation in the fact that, freed from the burden of past obligations, they are no longer in danger of being seen either as Satan's servant or the authorities' agent.

Public Houses and their Patrons in Early Modern Europe

Beat Kümin

The study of popular activities remains a difficult task for early modern historians. Official guidelines emerge sharply from laws and regulations, but it is less certain what impact they had.[1] Confessional doctrine appears lucid in theological tracts, yet more ambiguous in grass-roots behaviour. Town halls and parish churches highlight communal concerns, but who actually attended political and religious assemblies? Similar problems beset research into public houses, another ubiquitous local institution. We know much about norms and individual offences, but less about daily routine. On 2 May 1782, for instance, Pope Pius VI attracted large crowds when his party changed horses at the Bavarian inn of Schwabhausen, while the appearance of a magician worried the neighbours of a seventeenth-century Swiss tavern.[2] These, presumably, were extraordinary cases, but what kind of people can we expect among more regular patrons?

This essay investigates attendance patterns at early modern public houses. After a brief introduction to the range of primary and secondary sources, I will examine the issue of clientele from different perspectives, with particular emphasis on the number, social profile and gender of patrons. The focus thus lies on customer profiles rather than individual behaviour. While most examples are drawn from German-speaking areas, the geographical perspective extends over wider parts of the Continent.[3] It will be argued that there was no 'typical' early modern tippler, but that the composition of patrons depended on a number of dynamic variables. There are some indications of general trends over

---

[1]   J. Schlumbohm, 'Gesetze, die nicht durchgesetzt werden – ein Strukturmerkmal des frühneuzeitlichen Staates?', in *Geschichte und Gesellschaft* 23 (1997), 647–63. For legal frameworks affecting public houses see for example *Sammlung Schweizerischer Rechtsquellen. Section II: Die Rechtsquellen des Kantons Bern*, pt 1, vol. 8.1 (Aarau, 1966).

[2]   J. Bogner, 'Postgasthaus und Postanwesen in Schwabhausen, Landkreis Dachau', in *Amperland* 8 (1972), 306–13, esp. 310; Staatsarchiv Bern (hereafter StABE), B V 142, 51 (concerns about magical activities at the tavern of Etoy in the Bernese district of Vaud).

[3]   This essay draws on a broader study of early modern public houses in the Reformed city republic of Bern and the Catholic duchy / electorate of Bavaria: Beat Kümin, 'Das Wirtshaus im alten Europa: Kommunikation und Konsum in der kommunalen Gesellschaft' (Habilitationsschrift, University of Bern, in progress).

time, but these were far from uniform and less unequivocal than is often suggested.

Historiographical treatment of the topic has been somewhat impressionist. Early 'cultural' surveys of the hospitality trade focused on colourful anecdotes rather than critical evaluation of context or sources.[4] The rise of social history then prompted attempts to define patrons more closely; most famously, perhaps, when Peter Clark endorsed contemporary claims that English alehouses around 1600 were 'run by the poor for the poor'. Similarly pronounced views emerged among protagonists of the 'acculturation' thesis, which saw popular culture in the periphery successfully challenged by concepts radiating out from early modern elites. For Robert Muchembled the world of the tavern was a 'mass school' for crime and a powerful competitor of the church, championing a fundamentally different set of values. Such an environment, it was felt, alienated women and social superiors, who increasingly stayed away. By the seventeenth century, according to Richard van Dülmen, patrons were almost exclusively men from the lower orders. The overall trend in gender relations has been conceptualized as a gradual 'masculinization' of the atmosphere, paralleled by an 'erotic functionalization' of female waiting staff, reaching its climax in the neatly separated gender spheres of bourgeois society. The early modern period appears as a crucial transition phase, even though precious little evidence is offered to bolster the thesis.[5] Public houses also attracted much interest as battlegrounds in epic struggles such as the civilizing process, social polarization and the campaign for greater moral discipline.[6] After all this emphasis on 'grand theory', however, the time may have come to re-examine the evidence.

Recent work provides a number of stimulating approaches. Historical anthropologists include extensive tavern information in their surveys of popular lifestyles,[7] interdisciplinary projects investigate early modern food and alcohol

---

[4] A typical representative of this genre is O. D. Potthoff and G. Kossenhaschen, *Kulturgeschichte der deutschen Gaststätte* (Berlin, 1933; reprint Hildesheim, 1996).

[5] P. Clark, 'The Alehouse and Alternative Society', in D. Pennington and K. Thomas (eds), *Puritans and Revolutionaries* (Oxford, 1978), 47–72, esp. 53; R. Muchembled, *Popular Culture and Elite Culture in France, 1400–1750* (Baton Rouge, 1985), 119; R. van Dülmen, *Entstehung des frühneuzeitlichen Europa 1550–1648* (Frankfurt, 1982), 208; B. Beneder, *Männerort Gasthaus? Öffentlichkeit als sexualisierter Raum* (Frankfurt, 1997), 151 and passim.

[6] H. Spode, *Alkohol und Zivilisation* (Berlin, 1991); K. Wrightson, 'Alehouses, Order and Reformation in Rural England 1590–1660', in S. and E. Yeo (eds), *Popular Culture and Class Conflict 1590–1914* (Brighton, 1981), 1–27.

[7] See the collection of excerpts ('Archivalische Quellenforschungen') initiated by K.-S. Kramer and now deposited at the 'Bayerisches Institut für Volkskunde' in Munich.

consumption,[8] and there is growing interest in the 'theatre' of public houses among students of crime, communication, sociability and popular culture.[9] A number of case studies, furthermore, offer comprehensive discussions of the hospitality trade in heterogeneous contexts: among them, a principality in north-western Germany, a Swiss rural district and one of the foremost imperial free cities.[10]

As for primary sources, the picture is not as bleak as might be expected. Detailed information from various angles for any one establishment is rare, of course, and quantitative evidence is notoriously hard to uncover, but a surprising number of records throw light on the composition of patrons. The spectrum includes guest books kept by individual publicans, lists of menus and diners at top-level establishments, official surveys of strangers or tavern visitations, administrative records such as innkeepers' petitions and government registers, court cases involving tavern offenders, lists of debtors, diaries, travel reports, sermons and moral literature.[11] Visual and material evidence – discussed elsewhere in this volume – provides further clues about the size of establishments and the likely spectrum of patrons.

---

[8] G. Hirschfelder, 'Bemerkungen zu Stand und Aufgaben volkskundlich-historischer Alkoholforschung der Neuzeit', in *Rheinisch-westfälische Zeitschrift für Volkskunde* 39 (1994), 87–127; B. A. Tlusty, 'Crossing Gender Boundaries. Women as Drunkards in Early Modern Augsburg', in S. Backmann et al. (eds), *Ehrkonzepte in der frühen Neuzeit* (Berlin, 1998), 185–98; K. Hürlimann, 'Öffentlicher Konsum in Wirtshäusern. Soziale Funktion des Konsums in den Zürcher Landvogteien Greifensee und Kyburg im 15./16. Jahrhundert', in J. Tanner et al. (eds), *Geschichte der Konsumgesellschaft* (Zurich, 1998), 147–63; the 7th Symposium of the 'International Commission for Research into European Food History' in 2001 discussed the topic 'Eating out in Europe'.

[9] B. Müller-Wirthmann, 'Raufhändel. Gewalt und Ehre im Dorf', in R. van Dülmen (ed.), *Kultur der einfachen Leute* (Munich, 1983), 79–111; M. Hohkamp, 'Vom Wirtshaus zum Amtshaus', in *Werkstatt Geschichte* 16 (1997), 8–18; H. T. Gräf and R. Pröve, *Wege ins Ungewisse. Reisen in der frühen Neuzeit 1500–1800* (Frankfurt, 1997); S. Teuscher, *Bekannte – Klienten – Verwandte. Soziabilität in der Stadt Bern um 1500* (Cologne, 1998), esp. ch. 6; T. Brennan, *Public Drinking and Popular Culture in Eighteenth-Century Paris* (Princeton, 1988), esp. 16–19.

[10] R. Linde, 'Ländliche Krüge. Wirtshauskultur in der Grafschaft Lippe im 18. Jahrhundert', in S. Baumeier and J. Carstensen (eds), *Beiträge zur Volkskunde und Hausforschung* 7 (Detmold, 1995), 7–50; F. Brändle, 'Toggenburger Wirtshäuser und Wirte im 17. und 18. Jahrhundert', in *Toggenburgerblätter für Heimatkunde* 41 (1999), 7–51; B. A. Tlusty, *Bacchus and Civic Order: The Culture of Drink in Early Modern Germany* (Charlottesville, VA, 2001), esp. chaps 6–9 (with particular emphasis on Augsburg).

[11] Many examples are used below, but see also L. Vöchting-Oeri, 'Der Gasthof zum Wilden Mann in Basel als Herberge vornehmer Reisender zu Beginn des 30-jährigen Krieges', in *Basler Zeitschrift für Geschichte und Altertumskunde* (1944), 91–118 (guest book with coat of arms and signatures of noble patrons); B. Roth-Lochner, 'Les repas du graveur Fournier à l'auberge de Grange-Canal (1778–83)', in *Revue du Vieux-Genève* (1991), 42–51 (list of debtors).

A first question, then, concerns attendance levels. The apparent variety provides a first indication of core variables such as location, type of establishment and specific situation. On a number of Sunday evenings in 1812, officials carried out unannounced visitations of public houses in different districts of the German principality of Lippe. In forty per cent of all cases – that is, on twenty-four occasions – they found no guests at all; on ten visits, between one and five patrons; on fourteen, six to ten; on eight, eleven to fifteen; and on four, over sixteen (with a maximum of eighteen).[12] No comparable surveys have yet come to light for earlier periods, but individual pieces of information add up to an equally heterogeneous picture. Tax records, for instance, reveal vastly differing levels of alcohol sales and consumer demand: in the Bavarian district of Dachau, where beer dominated, a turnover of over 22,000 litres at the public house of Schweinbach in the year 1788–89 contrasted with a mere sixty-eight litres at Mariabrunn. Some distance away, in the isolated village of Unterfinning, the publican sold a daily average of no more than twelve litres in the 1720s, while the Ox in rural Münsingen, located on a busy transit route in the wine-growing region of Bern, reached a more impressive seventy-seven litres during the 1680s. Estimating that a typical customer drank perhaps a litre per visit towards the end of the early modern period, the daily number of guests would have varied from 0.2 at Mariabrunn to 77 at Münsingen.[13] A character in Erasmus's tongue-in-cheek colloquy on early sixteenth-century inns, to add a literary voice, claimed that 'often eighty or ninety met together in the same stove room', and a similarly large group of fifty to seventy diners appears in a travel report from the Swiss town of Thun in 1788. Eighteenth-century London inns, judging from period surveys, may have had an average of forty to fifty beds; those in smaller English towns, however, only about four, and rural establishments fewer than three.[14]

The timing, frequency and length of visits varied just as widely. Occasionally, people actually lived at an inn, but what gave the trade a bad name was the steady trickle of individuals who spent nearly all their time

---

[12] Linde, 'Krüge', 36.

[13] Bayerisches Hauptstaatsarchiv, Munich (hereafter BayHStA), GR 1551/2, Heft 1788–89; R. Beck, *Unterfinning. Ländliche Welt vor Anbruch der Moderne* (Munich, 1993), 255–6; StABE, B VIII 499, 1687–8. Per-capita estimates for premodern alcohol consumption vary between ½–1½ litres a day, with a falling tendency after the sixteenth century: R. Sandgruber, *Die Anfänge der Konsumgesellschaft* (Munich, 1982), 186–9; in the 1790s, a half-measure (0.84 l.) of wine seems to have been a typical serving in Bern: J. Ebel, *Anleitung, auf die nützlichste und genussvollste Art in der Schweitz zu reisen* (Zurich, 1793), pt 1, 22.

[14] D. Erasmus, 'Diversoria', in C. R. Thompson (ed.), *The Collected Works of Erasmus*, vol. 39: Colloquies (Toronto, 1997), 368–80, esp. 371; C. Meiners, *Briefe über die Schweiz* (4 pts, 2nd edn, Berlin, 1788–90), pt 3, 339 (*Neuenhof* inn at Thun); for numbers of beds in English inns cf. Chartres in this volume.

drinking. Contemporaries, and especially wives, took a grave view of people who jeopardized their household economy by spending a fortune on beer and wine. Chronic offenders could be formally banned from attending public houses by a court order, a measure aimed at protecting relatives and shaming the drunkard.[15] Such people, however, should not be taken as representative of patrons as a whole. For most townspeople and peasants, alcohol was something of a luxury. A measure of wine bought at the pub could easily absorb over a third of a day-labourer's wages.[16] Although a great deal was spent on special occasions, average consumption was less spectacular. At Unterfinning, water was the everyday fare and only about two dozen major feasts brought substantial numbers of customers to the local inn. Per household, the publican's beer sales amounted to a very modest 0.23 litres a day. The peasants of this village clearly did not spend all their time drinking. Urban establishments – benefiting from denser population, regular markets and specialized services – were normally busier, not least because commercial deals had to be sealed with a drink at the tavern (*Weinkauf*).[17]

It was not unusual to see people frequenting public houses in the middle of the day. Around 1720, the Bavarian cobbler Simon Hölzl from Hirschhausen stopped for a drink at Wangen before visiting customers at Gauting, while ten years earlier, according to another piece of incidental information, two tipplers sat in a beerhouse in the district of Starnberg between eight and nine o'clock on a Monday morning. Given work commitments, however, people were most likely to visit public houses in the evening, when attending a market or kermis, on family occasions such as weddings and above all on Sundays and feast days.[18] The existence of markets invariably boosted turnovers: the Sun at

---

[15] In 1786, the Lippe hunting official Jürges apparently lived at an inn (Linde, 'Krüge', 21); a constant frequenter of taverns, causing serious 'damage to his household', was Uli Freiburghaus in the Bernese parish of Neuenegg: Gemeindearchiv Neuenegg, Chorgerichts-Manuale (from 1650, hereafter GANC), e.g. 13 August and 27 September 1671; for tavern bans and the implications on personal honour, see Tlusty, *Bacchus*, 118–24.

[16] A measure (1.67 l.) of wine cost 3–5 *Batzen* at the Weiermannshaus tavern near Bern in 1786 (StABE, B VIII 517, 4), at a time when building workers earned between 5–10 *Batzen* a day: H. Ebener, 'Staatsbauten auf der Berner Landschaft im 18. Jahrhundert' (Ph.D. University of Bern, 1997), 221–31.

[17] Beck, *Unterfinning*, 255–6; on *Weinkauf* cf. Hürlimann, 'Konsum', 156, and *Handwörterbuch zur deutschen Rechtsgeschichte* (5 vols, Berlin, 1964–98), s.v. Weinkauf.

[18] Examples for drinking during the day: Wirthmann, 'Raufhändel', 103, 95. For the predominance of evening attendance see J. Heinzmann, *Beschreibung der Stadt und Republik Bern* (2 pts, Bern, 1794–96), pt 1, 63; G. Hanke, 'Anweisungen des Dachauer Rates für den Tafernbesuch', in *Amperland* 22 (1986), 271–2; on Sunday visits: J. C. Füssli reported in 1766 that the inhabitants of Catholic Engelberg in Central Switzerland took to the wine 'on Sundays and feast days, but only in small measures': G. Dufner, *Spielendes, Tanzendes Alt-Engelberg* (Engelberg, n.d.), 23; 'cabarets, auberges, tavernes, cafés et guinguettes représentent la plus

Herzogenbuchsee (Bern), a large village with three annual fairs, sold the staggering amount of 38,744 litres (106 litres per day) of wine during the fiscal year 1787–88, and additionally benefited from an agreement with local butchers, allowing publicans to slaughter cattle themselves if they catered for over seventy people on the day of a fair.[19] Great crowds of revellers are shown outside inns on the sixteenth-century kermis images by the Beham brothers and large numbers of guests gathered for wedding celebrations at public houses. At Dachau near Munich, the wedding party of coppersmith Erasmus Mayr occupied three tables at a wheat beerhouse in 1638, while that of the prosperous brewer Georg Hueber took up no less than twelve tables at Heigl's inn in 1662.[20] Sunday visits, meanwhile, caused great concern among clergymen of all confessions. Johann Jacob Hürsch, Zwinglian minister of Neuenegg, a Swiss rural community on the Bern-Fribourg border, preached against 'those people who preferred to be in the house of gluttony rather than that of the Lord', while his Catholic counterpart Father Jordan of Wasserburg warned Bavarian flocks that the merry feeling after Sunday drinking amounted to a most treacherous deception.[21]

As for business hours, innkeepers had to open their premises year in and year out, but last orders came early. Disregarding small regional variations, locals were expected to leave at eight o'clock in the winter and nine o'clock in the summer, with overnight guests only allowed to linger thereafter. These regulations, as well as attempts to restrict weekday attendance – Monday afternoons only (reflecting the 'Blue Monday' of artisan tradition) in Bavaria in 1616 – or maximum drinking times – one to two hours according to sixteenth-century Bernese consistory ordinances – proved notoriously difficult to enforce.[22]

---

importante occasion de convivialité marquant le dimanche aussi bien dans les sociétés urbaines que rurales': R. Beck, *Histoire du Dimanche. De 1700 à nos jours* (Paris, 1997), 79.

[19] A closer examination of the relationship between markets and the hospitality trade in B. Kümin and A. Radeff, 'Markt-Wirtschaft. Handelsinfrastruktur und Gastgewerbe im alten Bern', in *Schweizerische Zeitschrift für Geschichte* 50 (2000), 1–19, esp. 16 (*Sonne/* Sun Inn).

[20] For Sebald and Barthel Beham cf. Stewart in this volume; A. Kübler, *Strassen, Bürger und Häuser in Alt-Dachau* (reprint Dachau, 1996), 61, 97.

[21] GANC, 9 January 1659; E. Moser-Rath, *Dem Kirchenvolk die Leviten gelesen ... . Alltag im Spiegel süddeutscher Barockpredigten* (Stuttgart, 1991), 302 (early eighteenth century).

[22] On year-round hospitality see for example *Rechtsquellen des Kantons Bern*, pt 2, vol. 1 (Aarau, 1914), 67 (District of Niedersimmental 1504); on closing times, e.g. Linde, 'Krüge', 41 (Lippe), and StABE, B V 147, 1263 (Bernese district of Morges); on rules re drinking days / time: *Landt Recht [und] Landts= vnd Policeÿ Ordnung der Fürstenthumben Obern vnd Nidern Bayrn* (1616), Book 3, Title 3, art. 13 (Bavaria); StABE, A I 479, fol. 235r (Bern); plentiful violations of closing times e.g. in GANC, 10 April 1659, 17 February 1667 and elsewhere.

Aggregating different types of evidence, the 'world of the tavern' looks remarkably comprehensive. An early sixteenth-century inn, reverting to Erasmus's witness, accommodated 'travellers on foot, horsemen, traders, sailors, carriers, farmers, youths, women, the sick and the whole'.[23] There is little ground to dismiss this as purely fictional, for public houses were legally bound to offer general access. Countless laws and licences charged innkeepers with the duty to admit all members of the public, apart from a narrow range of marginal or dangerous individuals.[24] Early travel reports from before 1500 reveal prelates, diplomatic envoys and high-ranking pilgrims among the innkeepers' clientele, without implying that this was somehow unusual: Hans von Waldheim, patrician and mayor of Halle in Germany, stayed at the Bell in Bern and at the Blue Tower in Fribourg on 8–9 April 1474, and a party including the Venetian nobles Giorgio Contarini and Paolo Pisani used numerous inns like the Lamb at Brixen or the Golden Crown at Ulm on a cross-Alpine journey in the summer of 1492.[25] The majority of customers, however, were of middling status, judging from records of tavern offenders. Equipped with some spare cash, respectable householders clearly considered attendance at this site of social exchange an important part of civic life.[26] Yet humbler people were far from excluded. A Bavarian mandate of 1627 ordered that 'worthy' poor be catered for in inns at communal expense, while a tavern concession issued by the Bernese council in 1756 explicitly mentioned the 'local' poor as likely beneficiaries.[27] Old and sick people enjoyed similar legal protection. Moderate drinking of alcohol was considered a source of strength in illness and old age. In case of an emergency, normal opening hours could be waived and the provision of wine to needy neighbours was a powerful argument in applications for a government licence.[28] Less welcome, no doubt, were more marginal elements

---

[23]   Erasmus, 'Diversoria', 371.

[24]   U. Heise, *Der Gastwirt* (Leipzig, 1993), 68–70. Examples include the lease of the *Löwen* at Idstein in the German county of Nassau-Idstein in 1692 (printed in Potthoff and Kossenhaschen, *Kulturgeschichte*, 486–7), the oath of Neuchâtel innkeepers in 1694 (to accept 'tous estrangers passans et autres allans venans et séjournans tant à pied qu'à cheval': Arthur Piaget, 'Octrois de "schild"', in *Musée neuchâtelois* (1901), esp. 97–8) or the common law principle known as the 'innkeepers' rule'.

[25]   F. Welti (ed.), 'Hans von Waldheims Reisen durch die Schweiz im Jahre 1474', in *Archiv des Historischen Vereins des Kantons Bern* 25 (1920), 89–154, esp. 93–4; H. Simonsfeld (ed.), 'Ein venetianischer Reisebericht über Süddeutschland, die Ostschweiz und Oberitalien aus dem Jahre 1492', in *Zeitschrift für Kulturgeschichte* 2 (1894), 241–83, esp. 246, 261.

[26]   Tlusty, *Bacchus*, 132–3, 149–52.

[27]   BayHStA, Mandatensammlung, 1627/XI/19, Art. 25; StABE, B V 144, 134 (Heimenschwand).

[28]   At Worb (Bern) in 1556, sick people could be served outside normal opening hours (StABE, B V 147, 776); at about the same time, customary law in the manor of Niederaichbach (Bavaria) charged the local publican with house deliveries of wine for needy neighbours ('soll

like the twenty-four strange beggars and peddlers who called on the publican of Küter's Jug near Heesten in Lippe over a mere three-week period in 1786–87. Around 1800, according to an official register compiled by Bavarian authorities, the isolated public house at Kolmstein catered 'mainly for scoundrels', while the beerhouse of Johann Hamberger at Blumberg had to be closed as a 'haunt of evil people', which threatened public order.[29]

Small wonder, therefore, that public houses set the stage for some interesting encounters. Well-documented combinations include meetings between locals and strangers (from neighbouring villages as well as more distant lands); young and old people; townsfolk and peasants; Christians and Jews; and soldiers and civilians, not to mention men and women.[30] In a tavern at Lio Maggiore on the Venetian coast in 1314, locals enjoyed a game of cards with complete strangers who had just disembarked from a visiting galley. In his memoirs, Thomas Platter remembered the mixed welcome he received from publicans and local patrons as an itinerant scholar in the 1520s. In a court case involving a public house near Munich in 1721, witnesses appeared not only from local Neuried, but also the neighbouring villages of Planegg, Steinkirchen, Gräfelfing and Forstenried. On a better *table d'hôte* in late eighteenth-century Geneva, diners enjoyed the cosmopolitan company of Swiss, German, French, Italian and English travellers and parties including academics and clergymen as well as noble ladies.[31] The Bear at Neuenegg accommodated both young 'boys' and elderly members of the consistory, while the typical patron of a Lippe *Krug* (inn) around 1800 appears to have been middle-aged. In the villages outside Augsburg around 1700, Jews and Christians met in public houses in a variety of contexts, among them the conclusion of business deals and purely social occasions. Country people, finally, flooded the countless wine cellars of early modern Bern whenever a market was held in the city.[32]

---

vilgedachter Würth abermalen schuldig sein, den alten, schwachen, krankhen Mann- oder Weibspersohnen ... bei Tag oder Nachts das Getrankh, es sey Wein oder Pier, gerecht, gueth und unverfelscht gegen Bezalung zu uberschickhen'): W. Hartinger (ed.), *Dorf-, Hofmarks-, Ehehaft- und andere Ordnungen in Ostbayern* (Passau, 1998), vol. 1, 266.

[29]   Linde, 'Krüge', 20–1; BayHStA, GR 878/186, 209, 515.

[30]   Swiss bathing resorts and their inns offered a unique 'melting of peoples and estates' ('Jneinanderschmelzen der Völker und Stände'): Heinzmann, *Beschreibung*,   pt 1, 251; historians of premodern sociability draw similar conclusions: Teuscher, *Soziabilität*, 197.

[31]   G. Ortalli, 'Il giudice e la taverna. Momenti ludici in una piccola communità lagunare', in idem (ed.), *Gioco e giustizia nell' Italia di Commune* (Treviso, 1993), 43–70, esp. 68; T. Platter, *Lebensbeschreibung*, ed. A. Hartmann (2nd edn, Basel, 1999), 39; Wirthmann, 'Raufhändel', 102; Meiners, pt 2, 335–6.

[32]   GANC, e.g. February 1686; Linde, 'Krüge', 35; S. Ullmann, 'Kontakte und Konflikte zwischen Landjuden und Christen in Schwaben während des 17. und zu Anfang des 18.

Even so, it would be wrong to envisage informal mingling of patrons on every occasion. Several factors prompted social separation and thus more homogeneous groups. One important aspect was the acute awareness of status among authorities, customers and publicans alike. In its section on public houses, the Bavarian police ordinance of 1616 specified a set menu for regular customers, but allowed optional extras for 'higher' or foreign patrons, as long as they ate at a separate table. Servants, in turn, had to be seated and catered for in accordance with their master's instructions. Spatial separation of social groups by tables or even rooms, a feature much emphasized for the period after 1800, was thus a possibility in early modern Europe, but not universal practice. Fynes Moryson, an Englishman travelling on the Continent around 1600, saw servants sharing their masters' tables in German public houses. When a seventeenth-century moral reformer called for the introduction of socially exclusive establishments, he envisaged something clearly not customary at his time.[33]

Informal barriers may have been much more effective. Ulrich Bräker, once a mercenary in the Prussian army and in 1789 a small trader in cotton based in the Swiss valley of Toggenburg, encountered many distinguished gentlemen on his travels. In one of his diary entries, he remembered that they 'rapidly raised their eyebrows ... when such a mean, insignificant little man' dared to interrupt their table conversations. Then as now, furthermore, publicans were reluctant to admit certain guests. Albrecht Moser, landlord at the Toddler in Zurich in 1474, 'does not accommodate everybody', while 'river people' found Vilshofen in Bavaria very inhospitable some three hundred years later. There were no fewer than fourteen different inns vying for custom, but 'even the most honest among [the river people] are accepted almost nowhere and drag themselves laboriously from house to house in order to find lodging for the night'. Public health considerations, as well as social preference, could play a part. Horace-Bénédict de Saussure, a scholar and usually welcome guest, was given short shrift at Obergesteln (Valais) in 1783 because the landlord feared that his bad cold would frighten away other customers.[34]

Jahrhunderts', in Backmann et al. (eds), *Ehrkonzepte*, 288–315, esp. 306–7; Heinzmann, *Beschreibung*, pt 1, 63.

[33] *Policeÿ Ordnung*, Book 3, Title 3, Art. 1–2 (1616); M. Krauss, *Herrschaftspraxis in Bayern und Preussen im 19. Jahrhundert. Ein historischer Vergleich* (Frankfurt, 1997), 366–70 (hierarchy of tables in nineteenth-century Bavaria); F. Moryson, *An itinerary ... containing His Ten Yeeres Travell [1617]* (Facsimile, Amsterdam, 1971), pt 3, book 2, ch. 3, 85; H. Guarinonius, *Die Grewel der Verwüstung Menschlichen Geschlechts* [1610], ed. E. Locher (Bozen, 1993), 846. By 1778, however, the hospice on the Gotthard pass provided regular and 'better' travellers with accommodation in two distinct houses: Gräf and Pröve, *Wege*, 152–3.

[34] U. Bräker, *Tagebücher*, ed. A. Messerli and A. Bürgi (3 vols, Munich, 1998), vol. 3, 262 (1789; 'die angesehenen männer speeren gar geschweind maul und augen auf – wann so ein gemeines, nichtsbedeütetes männchen ... etwas drein reden will'); Welti, 'Waldheims Reisen', 125 (the *Kindli*/ Toddler 'herbergit nicht allerleye luthe'); BayHStA, GR 878/186, 667

Topographical location and type of establishment further affected the social profile of patrons. Public houses in isolated villages primarily catered for locals,[35] those on transit routes additionally for a wide spectrum of strangers, and the multiplicity of establishments in larger cities offered scope for specialization. An inn, by definition, was the logical choice for travellers in need of overnight accommodation, a tavern for a quick drink among craftsmen, a cheap beerhouse for customers of limited financial means, while distinguished visitors always looked out for the local VIP-establishment. After a personal visit in 1773, the German scholar Philipp Gercken happily reported that the Sword in Zurich had lived up to its reputation as Switzerland's foremost inn and, a little later, Professor Christoph Meiners of Göttingen stayed at the Geneva Arms in Geneva on the basis of recommendations by friends, although he had heard that the service at the Scales had also dramatically improved in previous years.[36] Every larger town knew such a hierarchy in its hospitality trade. At Landau in Bavaria around 1800, Mathias Wolfers owned the 'premier' inn, where 'guests of distinction ... almost exclusively' took quarter. Official registers of strangers' lodgings kept at the city gates of Bern in the 1790s show similar gradations in clientele: foreign elites went to the Falcon, humbler craftsmen and servants stayed at the Small Convent, while several 'middling' choices were available as well.[37] Top hotels like the Falcon also catered for state banquets. Among many similar functions, the Bernese council wined and dined 'son exelence Mons. de Beville', governor of the King of Prussia in the nearby Duchy of Neuchâtel, on 26 December 1779, and 'Deputes de Frybourg', envoys of the neighbouring Swiss city republic, on 16 June 1783.[38]

For a variety of reasons, including topography and activities of the publicans, certain establishments developed a specific professional or ideological profile. A number of examples from around 1800 may illustrate this point. Thanks to its riverside location, boatmen were conspicuous among patrons of the Little Horse at Wangen on the Aare in Bern, and the beerhouse at

---

(1806; 'Waßßerleute, auch die honetesten, werden fast nirgends eingenohmen, und schleppen sich mühesam von Hauß zu Hauß um in Vilshofen eine Nachtherberge ... zufinden'); R. Arnold, 'Gasthof- und Wirtshauswesen im Wallis des 18. Jahrhunderts', in *Blätter aus der Walliser Geschichte* 18 (1985), 489–500, esp. 499 (de Saussure).

[35] H. Heidrich, *Wohnen auf dem Lande* (Munich, 1984), 106, 110.

[36] P. W. Gercken, *Reisen durch Schwaben, Baiern, angränzende Schweiz ...* (4 pts, Stendal 1783–88), pt 2, 236; Meiners, pt 4, 92. Christoph Meiners' letters about Switzerland became one of the most widely used travel guides of the late eighteenth century.

[37] Wolfers' inn was deemed necessary 'indem dieses hier das erste Gasthaus ist wo die Gäste von Distinktion beinahe ausschlüßig ihr Absteigquartir nehmen' (BayHStA, GR 878/186, 29); guests at the *Klösterli/* Small Convent in Bern included Elisabeth Singeri, a 'maid' (StABE, B II 692, 15 February 1795).

[38] Extracts from catering records edited in M. Rageth-Fritz, *Der Goldene Falken* (Bern, 1987), 212–16, esp. 212–4.

Herzogsägmühle near Schongau proved convenient for rafters on the Lech in Bavaria. Some distance away, the inn at Neuhausen was approved by the authorities 'because of the presence of royal huntsmen', while the forester of Hartröhren in Lippe catered especially for people who worked in the woods.[39] Carriers, wagoners and coachmen formed the natural customer base for inns along highways. In Bavaria, timber transports boosted sales at the beerhouse of Ramersdorf; the inn at Otterfing was 'indispensable' for carriers travelling to Holzkirchen; and that at Grünwald catered for military personnel with business at the local powder depot. Early industrial sites such as mines promised similar spin-offs for the hospitality trade. When plans were made for a bigger inn at Roche in the French-speaking part of Bern, the initiators appealed for government support as it 'would undoubtedly be a convenient and useful establishment, especially for the salt works at Roche, but also for the Lord Salt Director'. The latter, it was argued, could then accommodate all riders, servants, traders, coachmen and other visitors at the public house rather than in his official residence.[40] Students and academics, unsurprisingly, had regular haunts in university towns and there were houses with a distinct confessional or ideological profile: in the 1520s, the White Hart at Cambridge played host to some of the most prominent early English religious reformers, openly Jewish taverns flourished in eighteenth-century Swabia, and even Anabaptists, usually vociferous in attacking feasting and drinking, appreciated public houses as recruitment bases and for practical services. Political parties, finally, used public houses right from the start: as early as the 1680s, Northampton's Whigs went to the Swan, whilst the Goat Inn attracted the Tories.[41]

But what about changes over time? A crude, but valid method to test the hypothesis of a linear decrease in the presence of social elites is to look for inconsistencies and contradictions. The first point to note is a marked difference in timing: while polarization is seen as complete by the seventeenth century in some accounts cited in the introduction, a French study observes a withdrawal of 'bourgeois' circles from *cabarets* and *ginguettes* only after 1750. Elsewhere, there is plenty of evidence that public houses still attracted the 'better' sort around 1800: most unambiguously in Lippe, where the visitation of 1812 revealed that no level of the village hierarchy was significantly under- or

---

[39] Bräker, vol. 3, 525; BayHStA, GR 878/186, 549, 527; Linde, 'Krüge', 24.

[40] BayHStA, GR 878/186, 524, 691, 523; StABE, A V 1167, 83.

[41] BayHStA, GR 878/186, 706 (beerhouses catering for 'academics' at Ingolstadt); Ullmann, 'Landjuden', 307; C. Marsh, *Popular Religion in Sixteenth-Century England* (New York, 1998), 169 (White Hart); M. Kobelt-Groch, 'Unter Zechern, Spielern und Häschern. Täufer im Wirtshaus', in N. Fischer et al. (eds), *Aussenseiter zwischen Mittelalter und Neuzeit* (Leiden, 1997), 111–26; A. Everitt, 'The English Urban Inn 1560–1760', in idem, *Perspectives in English Urban History* (London, 1973), 111 (Northampton).

over-represented among patrons.[42] Early Appenzell industrialists practised a lively tavern culture, founding numerous associations and developing a rudimentary 'public sphere' in the process. Personifying the *crème de la crème* of eighteenth-century society, Emperor Joseph II of Austria happily used public houses, while a Russian grand duke and duchess descended at the Golden Lion in Lausanne (Bernese Vaud) in September 1783.[43] At much the same time, travel reports still document contacts between guests of unequal standing: Christoph Meiners, German champion of enlightened ideas, recalls a dinner at an inn near Delémont (Swiss Jura) in September 1788, where his party ate with 'coachmen, carriers, and various pedestrians in the same lounge'. Ulrich Bräker, our small businessman, spent the night of 18 September 1794 at the Eagle in Lucerne, where he dined in a room 'full of gentlemen and ladies', ministers and other 'distinguished' guests. He felt embarrassed, as nobody actually talked to him, but he listened carefully to the conversation.[44]

Apart from acknowledging regional, typological and situational differences, a more balanced view of chronological trends should distinguish between *individual* establishments and the trade as a whole. A decline in top-level customers was often the consequence of changes in management or decreasing standards at a particular institution. The landlady of the Key at Wiedlisbach (Bern), for instance, proudly reported that the Black Horse had been the better inn at the beginning of the eighteenth century, but that her father's diligence and industry had convinced the travelling elites to prefer the Key instead.[45]

Sketching an adequate gender profile is an equally difficult undertaking. With regard to male patrons, the tavern has been described as a 'theatre', in which men were meant to perform, reasserting their masculinity through generous (but not debilitating) consumption and spirited defence of personal honour. Fuelled by alcohol, provocations and insults were readily forthcoming, and local court records are packed solid with ensuing confrontations. While these were often violent, they followed almost ritualized forms and normally stopped short of serious injury.[46] Women, in turn, faced different social constraints and expectations. Perceiving alcoholism as a grave threat to their household economies, they found support in local courts willing to discipline irresponsible

---

[42] Beck, *Dimanche*, 81; Linde, 'Krüge', 35.

[43] A. Tanner, *Spulen - Weben - Sticken. Die Industrialisierung in Appenzell Ausserrhoden* (Zurich, 1982), 301; W. May, 'Reisen "al incognito". Zur Reisetätigkeit Kaiser Josephs II', in *Mitteilungen des Instituts für österreichische Geschichtsforschung* 93 (1985), 59–91; Meiners, pt 2, 345.

[44] Meiners, pt 4, 267; Bräker, vol. 3, 519–20.

[45] Testimony to the Bernese bailiff in 1790, cited in K. H. Flatt, 'Gaststätten zu Wangen und im Bipperamt', in *Jahrbuch des Oberaargaus* 7 (1964), 147–59, esp. 158.

[46] Detailed evidence in Tlusty, *Bacchus*, 126–33; and Müller-Wirthmann, 'Raufhändel'.

husbands, while knowing that the same judges – like society as a whole – looked yet more disapprovingly at excessive tavern consumption of their own.[47]

As signalled above, historians usually draw a marked contrast between the Middle Ages, when female attendance appears perfectly common, and later periods, when women allegedly disappeared from public houses. It has been stated that early modern Württemberg patrons were drawn 'almost exclusively' from among the male inhabitants and that women did not go to English ale-houses without a very good reason.[48] And yet, there is plenty of contrasting evidence. For a start, norms and practice diverged: where authorities formally banned female attendance, as in late eighteenth-century Madrid, people evidently disapproved.[49] On another level, we may again face regional and situational differences. On the basis of her pioneering work on Augsburg, Ann Tlusty suggests three basic contexts in which women formed a regular part of early modern tavern society: first, as landladies or servants; second, as 'respectable' guests (wives accompanying husbands or on 'business'); and third, appearing most often in court records, as singles or women unaccompanied by their husbands, who were almost invariably suspected of sexual licence if not prostitution.[50]

From a comparative perspective, women certainly played a most conspicuous role in the running of the hospitality trade, from medieval alewives right through to present-day hoteliers.[51] Over five per cent of individuals currently identifiable as publicans in early modern Bern were female, a considerable proportion given the fact that women appeared much less frequently in official sources. There is also plenty of evidence for married couples attending public

---

[47] H. R. Schmidt, 'Ehezucht in Berner Sittengerichten 1580–1800', in R. Po-chia Hsia and R. Scribner (eds), *Problems in the Historical Anthropology of Early Modern Europe* (Wiesbaden, 1997), 287–321, esp. 296, 304; Tlusty, 'Women as Drunkards'.

[48] Medieval evidence: In 1474, pilgrim Waldheim encountered 'many beautiful women' at inns in the Swiss spa of Baden (Welti, 'Waldheims Reisen', 131); see also B. Hanawalt, 'The Host, the Law, and the Ambiguous Space of Medieval London Taverns', in idem, *Of Good and Ill Repute. Gender and Social Control in Medieval England* (Oxford, 1998), 104–23, esp. 109, and Hürlimann, 'Konsum', 150; A. Landwehr, *Policey im Alltag. Die Implementation frühneuzeitlicher Policeyordnungen in Leonberg* (Frankfurt, 2000), 245 (Württemberg); Clark, *English Alehouse*, 130–1.

[49] 'En dépit des ordonnances interdisant l'entrée des femmes dans les tavernes, le cabaret ne semble donc pas avoir été à Madrid le cadre d'une sociabilité exclusivement masculine': J. Soubeyroux, *Pauperisme et rapports sociaux à Madrid au XVIIIème siècle* (Lille, 1978), vol. 1, 197.

[50] Tlusty, *Bacchus*, 138–45.

[51] See for example J. M. Bennett, *Ale, Beer and Brewsters in England. Women's Work in a Changing World 1300–1600* (Oxford, 1996); M. E. Wiesner, *Women and Gender in Early Modern Europe* (Cambridge, 1993), 96; H. Heiss, 'Selbständigkeit auf Widerruf? Zur Rolle von Gastwirtinnen bis 1914', in I. Bandhauer-Schöffmann and R. Bendl (eds), *Unternehmerinnen* (Frankfurt, 2000), 49–88.

houses together. On 11 January 1678, Margareth Kilcher joined her husband Bendicht Krattinger at the rural inn of Biberen (Bern), where they had 'a jolly time and ... were friendly with each other' and the presence of wives was still apparent during the Lippe visitations of 1812. Female peddlers or 'business' women offering some commercial service like mending or washing were not uncommon, either.[52]

Festive and ceremonial life, however, provided additional contexts for 're-spectable' female attendance. Urban society may have had specialized venues for different kinds of public entertainment (theatres, guild and dance halls, coffee houses), but rural inhabitants knew little else than public houses. Among the most prominent occasions were weddings and dances. Countless women – wives as well as maidens, individuals as well as larger groups – frequented public houses in early modern Neuenegg and there is little indication that popular opinion objected. In Bern's Reformed territory, dancing was officially banned almost throughout the early modern period, but people carried on regardless. At Neuenegg, for example, 'Barbli Marschall has been presented for dancing at the inn, which she admits and is fined x s[hillings]', 'Elsi Herren has danced at the inn, [she] confesses and is fined like others x s.', 'Leni Tschirren last summer also danced at the inn, and as she always evades appearing before the consistory, she is earnestly reprimanded and fined x s.'. In a series of proceedings from late 1671, maid servant Madleni, nine other women and eleven men incurred penalties for dancing at the innkeeper's wedding.[53] The official ban was particularly vulnerable in a community located only a short walk from the nearest Catholic public house, the Customs House at Sensebrücke in Fribourg. Large numbers of Neueneggers flocked to this inn on religious or agricultural feasts, apparently unimpressed by the strong likelihood of a court summons back home. Among scores of individual names, we find no less than forty-five women accused of dancing during kermis in 1752. Barbara Freiburghaus, meanwhile, committed a series of offences in 1671: after yet another Sunday spent dancing at the Customs House, she preferred to pay the large sum of five pounds to spending two days in prison. Her husband's response is not recorded and it is unclear whether she actually committed her

---

[52] B. Kümin, 'Useful to Have, but Difficult to Govern: Inns and Taverns in Early Modern Bern and Vaud', in *Journal of Early Modern History* 3 (1999), 153–75, esp. 159 (per centage); StABE, A V 1111, 673 (Kilcher; 'sich lustig gemacht habind, hiemit fründtlich mit einandren ... gsin seÿind'); Linde, 'Krüge', 34 (wives), 17 (peddlers).

[53] GANC, 16 January and 13 February 1681 (Marschall, Herren, Tschirren); 26 November, 3 and 17 December 1671, 14 and 28 January and 10 February 1672 (innkeeper's wedding). Explicit references to 'wives', 'daughters' and 'maidens' (e.g. GANC, 29 July 1666) make it clear that both married and unmarried women danced at inns. Similar church court evidence in H. R. Schmidt, *Dorf und Religion. Reformierte Sittenzucht in Berner Landgemeinden der frühen Neuzeit* (Stuttgart, 1995), 133; Willy Pfister, *Das Chorgericht des bernischen Aargaus im 17. Jahrhundert* (Aarau, 1939), 66–7.

infringements without him. Elsi Flühmann was an equally hopeless case in the eyes of her minister, who felt scandalized by her repeated visits to Sensebrücke, where – as he put it in the court book – 'unpunished papist dancing and other wantonness suited a loose whore like herself'. In the end, she opted to find work (and a husband) in the neighbouring Catholic canton.[54]

The search for a marriage partner provided a further motive for participation in tavern society. Church courts in sixteenth-century Zurich heard of vows being exchanged on the premises, while young Appenzell peasants and textile workers (but apparently not women from the industrial elite) frequented public houses with similar intentions two hundred years later.[55] Markets and fairs encouraged mixed gender groups as well. Late eighteenth-century visitors to Switzerland observed how young peasant males brought local girls into public houses and how many couples shared a drink during markets.[56] Along the main transit routes, men and women met regularly throughout our period. Publicans were urged to take particular care of single female travellers by a seventeenth-century moral writer, and in the early tourist age, inns accommodated entire families. 'We slept at Chamonix, where there was only one inn. The table d'hôte supper charmed me: the company was a mixed one of men and women from every country in Europe'.[57] Future mothers – to round off with an intriguing, but often overlooked aspect – commanded special privileges at public houses. Many establishments were legally bound to supply high-quality wine during childbirth.[58]

But women did not always need a peculiar context or excuse to visit public houses. Court evidence suggests that many simply enjoyed a sociable drink, behaving just as merrily and at times reprehensibly as male patrons. Of twenty individuals appearing before the Neuenegg consistory for tavern-related offences in 1650–54, four were female (two landladies and two patrons). The latter did not get in trouble merely for attending, but for overindulgence or suspected moral and sexual offences. Because of frequent drinking after hours with her husband, for instance, Hans Flühmann's wife was called to account in March 1650. A little later, Madleni Mader, also a married woman, was asked why she kept two *other* men company at the inn until late on a Sunday in 1657,

---

[54] GANC, 15 October 1752 (kermis), 4 March 1671 (Freiburghaus) and 21 June 1673 (Flühmann; because 'das Papistische Vngestrafft tantzen vnd anderer mu[o]htwill [ihr] als einer leichtfertigen hu[o]ren so wol beliebet'). In areas under the old religion, dancing at inns was also regulated, but usually not banned altogether. At Engelberg, for example, an 'honest boy' was allowed to bring an 'honest daughter' to an inn for officially approved dances (mandate of 1730; Dufner, *Alt-Engelberg*, 15).

[55] Hürlimann, 'Konsum', 150 (Zurich); Tanner, *Spulen*, 300–301.

[56] Meiners, pt 1, 315; J. Reinach, *Kleine Schweizerreise von 1788* (Heidelberg, 1790), 63.

[57] Guarinonius, *Grewel*, 841 (1610); quote by François de Frénilly (1787) cited in G. R. de Beer, *Travellers in Switzerland* (Oxford, 1949), 79; Meiners observed in 1783 that Englishmen in particular took their wives, daughters (and mistresses) along to the *table d'hôte* (pt 2, 336); for early Alpine tourism see C. Pfister, *Im Strom der Modernisierung* (Bern, 1995), ch. 5.1.3.

[58] One example in StABE, B V 143, 8 (tavern in Buchholterberg near Thun).

while Verena Freiburghaus admitted vomiting after drinking heavily at the Bear on 'Palm day' in 1671. Cathrina Ferren was heard swearing there in 1670 and – after some beating round the bush – two local wives confessed to encouraging a male patron to 'uncover himself and ... publicly show his privy parts' in the summer of 1663. Sowing 'discord' in the public house on a Sunday brought two further female defendants before the consistory in 1661 and many other cases could be added. The allegedly wanton behaviour of peasant girls in public

Figure 1:   Sigmund Freudenberger, Scene outside a cellar tavern in the city of Bern [*Kellerschryssete in Bern*] (perhaps under today's City and University Library on Münstergasse?). Ink drawing, late eighteenth century (Kunstmuseum Bern. Photo: Peter Lauri. Used by permission).

houses is still commented on in a late eighteenth-century description of the
republic of Bern.[59] Far from being a unique case, much similar evidence appears in court records elsewhere. In London, to select a dramatically different
location, a widow Pollard visited one of the capital's alehouses 1630 'on business', two female patrons were overheard arguing in St John Street tavern in
1611 and three women, who had shared 'a pott of beere or two' at Kingsland in
Hackney, appear as witnesses in 1590.[60]

To emphasize the presence of a wide range of 'respectable' women is not to
deny obvious links between social drinking and sexual licence. Public houses
played host to everything from innocent innuendo to outright prostitution, and
the borderlines were often blurred. Figure 1, showing a scene outside a late
eighteenth-century cellar tavern in the city of Bern, is suggestive. A young man,
probably a member of the urban patriciate, urges a hesitant woman, perhaps a
servant or visitor from the countryside, to accompany him to the public house,
which is clearly marked with the sign of a bush.[61] In the doorway, an elegant
lady of somewhat ambiguous status raises her glass in an inviting gesture, representing the merry world awaiting patrons inside. Was she the landlady?
Contemporaries were well aware of a correlation between sexual allurement
and increased alcohol consumption. In the seventeenth century, the Neuenegg
consistory censured the local landlady for dancing with her patrons, while in
England, innkeeper Elizabeth Barwicke of Wapping provoked slanderous accusations whenever her sailor-husband was absent.[62] Waitresses and tavern
servants fuelled the imagination of patrons and moralists as well. Shrewd publicans, according to Hippolytus Guarinonius, who deplored the moral decline of
his fellow Tyroleans, deliberately employed beautiful women to exploit male
weaknesses, and Christoph Meiners related the 'chastity' of tavern patrons directly to the age of their waitresses![63] In February 1787, Ulrich Bräker fancied
an attractive maid servant from Kempten, but feared that this 'vain woman –
serving at an inn, where she faces daily advances from lewd fellows ... will in
time become a genuine whore'. That was not the only calamity, as many a fellow servant incurred unwanted pregnancies, some even charges of infanticide.

---

[59]   GANC, 31 March 1650, 23 August 1657, 7 May 1671, 26 June 1670, 29 July – 2
August 1663 ('das er sich entblößt vnd ... sein Scham gezeigt'), 15 September 1661;
Heinzmann, *Beschreibung*, pt 2, 234–41.

[60]   L. Gowing, *Domestic Dangers: Women, Words, and Sex in Early Modern London*
(Oxford, 1998), 15, 92, 241.

[61]   Contemporaries could interpret acceptance of such an invitation as legitimizing a sexual
approach: U. Rublack, 'Metze und Magd. Krieg und die Bildfunktion des Weiblichen in
deutschen Städten der Frühen Neuzeit', in Backmann et al. (eds), *Ehrkonzepte*, 199–222, esp.
214, 216.

[62]   GANC, 17 February 1675; Gowing, *Dangers*, 134.

[63]   Guarinonius, *Grewel*, 824 (1610); Meiners, pt 4, 180 (1788); medieval female staff
encountered comparable prejudices: Hanawalt, 'London taverns', 105, 108.

Working in the hospitality trade, to add to their predicament, was not something that predisposed judges and juries in their favour.[64]

When Bräker met a friendly, well-mannered girl on the road to Zurich and agreed to join her for a drink that evening at the Hart in town, he agonized later whether she could be a whore. However unjustified his fears were on this occasion (as about female patrons in general), prostitutes clearly frequented public houses. Inns on medieval highways have been described as precursors of specialized brothels (*Frauenhäuser*), and an oath administered to Bernese innkeepers in 1617 urged particular vigilance against 'whores' and people infected with the French disease.[65] References to the sale of sexual favours in taverns are legion, both in literary and legal or administrative sources. In 1646, a German woman was evicted from Bern for leading a 'scandalous life' at the bathing inn of Gutenburg near Burgdorf. She admitted being a 'whore', but vigorously denied any other 'misdeeds or thefts'. The Neuenegg consistory supplies a steady trickle of cases, as for example in 1650, when publican Daniel Feller was cited for accommodating notorious prostitutes; in 1665, when the village constable received instructions to evict a whore from the inn; or in 1664 and 1673, when several female patrons were (rightly or wrongly) suspected of indecent behaviour.[66] Over one hundred years earlier, two whores from the *Frauenhaus* at Basle joined Hans Heitzen for a drink at the nearby Hare, while a Genevan official complained in 1791 that 'there were undoubtedly many prostitutes at Carouge; and it is also true that some publicans stage dances and attract such girls' deliberately, in order to boost the number of guests.[67]

---

[64]   Bräker, vol. 2, 537 ('ein eitels weibsbild – dient auf einem gasthoff, wo sie täglich von geilen böken angefahlen wirdt ... jch steh vor sie in sorgen, sie werde mit der zeit ein ordentlich bordelmensch'; 11 February 1787); for a moving infanticide case, leading to the execution of a female servant of the *Einhorn* public house at Frankfurt in 1772, see R. Habermas and T. Hommen (eds), *Das Frankfurter Gretchen: Der Prozess gegen die Kindsmörderin Susanna Margaretha Brandt* (Munich, 1999). Brandt was convicted of killing an infant conceived after a drinking bout with a patron. 'Inn servants in France were the one group of women denied the right to sue their seducer if they became pregnant': Wiesner, *Women*, 96.

[65]   Bräker, vol. 3, 202–3 (22 July 1789); A. Lömker-Schlögell, 'Prostituierte', in B. U. Hergemöller (ed.), *Randgruppen der spätmittelalterlichen Gesellschaft* (Warendorf, 1994), 56–88, esp. 59; *Rechtsquellen des Kantons Bern*, pt 1, vol. 8.1, 205–7.

[66]   F. Junker, *Gutenburg und seine Geschichte* (Gutenburg, n.d.), 93; GANC, 31 March and 28 April 1650, 30 April 1665, 30 June 1664 and 20 August 1673. See also the presence of whores in carnival plays like H. R. Manuel, *Das Weinspiel (1548)*, ed. T. Odinga (Halle, 1892), 238–9, 352–3, and the survey in A. L. Martin, *Alcohol, Sex and Gender in Late Medieval and Early Modern Europe* (Basingstoke, 2001), 58–78.

[67]   G. Schwerhoff, 'Starke Worte. Blasphemie als theatralische Inszenierung von Männlichkeit an der Wende vom Mittelalter', in M. Dinges (ed.), *Hausväter, Priester, Kastraten* (Göttingen, 1998), 237–63, esp. 238 (Basle 1520); G. Maistre, 'La lutte du clergé contre les cabarets du XVIIe au XIX siècle', in *Vie religieuse en Savoie* (Annecy, 1988), 307–31, esp. 308 ('il n'es pas douteux qu'il y ait un très grand nombre de filles de joie à Carouge; il est encore vrai que quelques cabaretiers font danser chez eux et y attirent de ces filles').

Early modern public houses were not always full and far from homogeneous. There is no 'one' guest profile to match all functions and activities. Sophisticated *table d'hôte* conversations are documented alongside violent conflict, and nobles attended as well as the poor. Social barriers could be overcome, at least temporarily and in particular contexts. Alleged chronological trends, particularly a decreasing proportion of women and social elites, are not always borne out by the sources.

A large number of variables affected the composition of patrons. Official norms, established gender roles and moral attitudes certainly mattered, but so did regional custom, location, type of establishment and seasonal or festive situation. From a social perspective, market-days and busy highways yielded a mixed clientele, while isolated village taverns or VIP-houses had more homogeneous patrons. With a view to gender, 'respectable' women were naturally rare in male environments such as foresters' lodges or soldiers' taverns, but very conspicuous at dances or weddings in local inns, the latter throughout our period and often in spite of restrictive legislation. Ladies of high social standing may have shunned public houses at home, but could not avoid them when travelling. Underlying causes for regional differences remain to be determined, but was there, for instance, more comprehensive social exchange in a relatively 'free' environment like the Swiss Confederation? Did early Alpine tourism foster a particularly diversified culture in Bern's public houses? Tavern attendance, in any case, seems as varied as early modern experience as a whole.

PART TWO

Thematic Approaches

English Inns, Taverns, Alehouses and Brandy Shops: The Legislative Framework, 1495–1797[*]

Judith Hunter

To the writer of glossy tourist literature, an inn is simply an old public house; to many a novelist, historian, or even translators of the Bible, use of the word 'inn' implies that at the house in question a traveller might expect to obtain food and a bed for the night. Both concepts are widely accepted and cause no great confusion, but the word is also used as an alternative to tavern, alehouse or public house, to give variety to a piece of writing. Yet, as it will be argued in this essay, in the past the various establishments from which our present public houses and hotels have evolved were essentially different types of retail outlets, with different histories and, to a varying extent, subject to different laws. Their role in the community also frequently differed.

The first act that required retailers of ale and beer in England to be licensed was passed in 1552. It was not, however, the first act to be concerned with selling ale and the earliest, dated 1266, was still in force in the 1550s.[1] The 1266 act had introduced the assize of ale, a form of government price control based on the local price of corn. Local ordinances and other laws dealing with the sale of victuals quickly extended the conditions of the assize to cover the use of true measures for retailing ale – the gallon, pottle and quart – and the price and quality of differing strengths. The enforcement of these regulations was the business of the hundred, manor and borough courts, a task that was extensively exercised almost everywhere in England. The number of presentments to the courts would seem to suggest that some form of local control, an embryonic licensing system, may often have been in operation. But there was no national statute that regulated the way in which ale sellers (of whatever

---

[*]   The essay is based on: J. Hunter, 'Legislation, Royal Proclamations and Other National Directives affecting Inns, Taverns, Alehouses, Brandy Shops and Punch Houses, 1552 to 1757' (Ph.D. University of Reading, 1994).
[1]   1552, 5/6 Edward VI c25; 1266, 51 Henry III c6.

kind: alehouse keepers, tippling house keepers, brewers, victuallers or innkeepers) ran their houses.

This situation did not begin to change until the Tudor period. In 1495, an Act of Parliament, which was primarily concerned with the problem of vagabonds and rogues, gave authority to the justices of the peace to 'reject and put away common ale-sellers ... wherever they (thought) convenient', and to take surety from them for their 'good behaviour'. The justices could also 'punish alehouse keepers for allowing dicing in their houses'. The suppression of 'unlawful' games was not a Tudor invention, but this act of Henry VII's was the first specifically prohibiting such games in alehouses. It was also the first statute to give authority over ale-selling and alehouses to the justices of the peace.[2]

Although no other statutes regulating the trade were passed for another fifty years, various royal proclamations sought to enforce laws already on the statute books, specifically relating them to alehouses and inns although the original laws did not. In many cases the relevant clauses were only a small part of the subject matter of the proclamations. But the fact that alehouses are mentioned at all is indicative of the general growth of concern about their role in society. Rather different was a proclamation of 1551 reminding people that it was forbidden to eat meat during Lent or on 'fish days' (Fridays and Saturdays). The law prohibiting this had been passed in 1548, but now victuallers were also forbidden to serve meat dishes at the prohibited times.[3]

The following year, 1552, the government passed the first Licensing Act, the opening words of which set the tone not only for this statute but for most of the legislation and proclamations for the next hundred years:

> For as much as intolerable hurts and troubles to the Commonwealth of this
> Realm doth daily grow and increase through such abuses and disorders as
> are had and used in common alehouses and tippling houses.

There was a widespread opinion that alehouses were a threat to orderly society and that the poorer sort of people who frequented them had become a new and

---

[2]   1495, 11 Henry VII c2.

[3]   P. L. Hughes and J. F. Larkin, *Tudor Royal Proclamations*, vol. 1, 1485–1553 (1966). In this example, the term 'victualler' includes various traders selling food and drink, but the use of the word is complicated. However, it is frequently used to mean alehouse keepers, or alehouse keepers and innkeepers. Significantly, the registers of licensees kept by the clerks of the Quarter Session Courts in the eighteenth and early nineteenth centuries were either called Alehouse Registers or Victuallers Registers. See J Gibson and J. Hunter, *Victuallers' Licences: Records for Family and Local Historians* (Bury, 1994). Today publicans are often referred to as licensed victuallers.

increasingly dangerous force. Thus, the aim of this first Licensing Act was to bring the keepers of alehouses – the establishments that catered for the lower strata of the population – under the jurisdiction of the justices of the peace. The 1495 act had been permissive, but it now became mandatory for the justices to act. Furthermore, from 1552 keeping an alehouse became a 'privileged' occupation, open only to those who were licensed.

Licences could only be issued at the quarter sessions or by two magistrates acting together out of sessions. Justices, however, were ordered to license only as many alehouses as they thought necessary and convenient for the area. To ensure proper conduct in the houses, each prospective licensee was to be bound by recognizance, with two sureties, that they would maintain orderly houses and not allow unlawful games to be played therein.

No further acts making any direct reference to the ale trade were passed during the Tudor period, but this first Licensing Act was soon amended, expanded and refined by several other means. These included royal proclamations, orders of the Privy Council, and the conditions laid down by the recognizances drawn up by the county benches and the town councils. The conditions required by the various authorities varied considerably, but those laid down by a proclamation of 1621 were the most detailed imposed by central government. They included prohibitions against serving meat on 'fish days' and during Lent, playing unlawful games, drinking during times of church service, tippling, buying stolen and pawned goods, selling tobacco, and harbouring rogues, beggars or masterless men. The licensees had to sell beer and ale at the correct prices and only from pots that had been inspected and marked with the proper seal; provide at least one lodging for travellers; and report any strangers who stayed more than one night. The justices were ordered to hold special licensing sessions annually and to grant licences only to men of 'trust', honest conversation and suitability for keeping an alehouse.[4]

Most of these clauses can be traced to an Act of Parliament or royal proclamation, but the reasoning behind a particular clause is not always obvious. For example, the prohibition of eating meat during Lent and on fish days (Wednesdays, Fridays and Saturdays from 1562) had little to with religion and a lot to do with ensuring a good fishing industry which would be a source of ships and sailors should they be needed in time of war. From 1600 licensees were intermittently ordered to enter into special Lenten recognizances with the monarch, rather than the magistrates.[5]

---

[4] P. L. Hughes and J. F. Larkin, *Stuart Royal Proclamations: Royal Proclamations of King James I*, Vol. 1 1603–1625 (Oxford, 1973).
[5] 1562, 5 Elizabeth I c5; London, Public Record Office (PRO), E 180: Victuallers' recognizances; F. Youngs, *Proclamations of the Tudor Queens* (Cambridge, 1976), xii, 124.

The proliferation of alehouses was almost unanimously recognized by central government, church leaders, assize and county justices, and the landed gentry in general as one of the great social evils of the Tudor and early Stuart periods, and part and parcel of the greater problems of poverty, unemployment and homelessness. Parish and borough officers did not want 'strangers' to become a burden on the poor rates, and both central and local government saw the unsupervised lodging of travellers as a threat to the security of the community. Because the government was concerned about the possible break-down of law and order, innkeepers and alehouse keepers were required to report the presence of any strangers – travellers staying more than one night – to the local magistrate or other suitable officer. However, should a stranger need accommodation the constable could demand that he be accommodated at the alehouse, or inn if there was one, where he could be kept under observation. Thus alehouse keepers could, and sometimes were, presented at the quarter sessions for refusing to accept travellers brought to their house by a parish officer.[6]

Ale and beer, however, were essential to the well-being of the population, and as vital as bread to the diet of the working population. In times of bad harvest and severe shortages of grain, the government needed to act to ensure that the poor did not starve for want of bread or small ale. Although they sought to reduce the number of alehouses, they also needed to ensure that cheap ale was available. To this end a *Book of Orders* was issued in 1586, and re-issued or revised in 1597, 1608, 1622 and 1630.[7]

In spite of all the efforts of the Privy Council during the latter years of the sixteenth century, the proliferation of alehouses continued unabated, and soon after James I took the throne statutory restrictions against inns and alehouses took on a new dimension. Four acts were passed in the first decade of the seventeenth century for the better suppression of alehouses, and for 'restraining the inordinate haunting and tippling' and the 'odious and loathsome sin of drunkenness'.[8] Whereas the 1552 act had only ordered the punishment of alehouse keepers, these new acts ordered the punishment of brewers who delivered to unlicensed alehouses, parish officers (usually constables) who failed to uphold the law, and local customers for tippling or being drunk.

However, the laws were frequently not upheld and in the 1620s three new acts were passed dealing with the same problems.[9] Punishments were increased

---

[6]   F. G. Emmison, *Elizabethan Essex: Disorders* (Chelmsford, 1976) 209; J. Pound, *Tudor and Stuart Norwich* (1988), 110–11; D. L. Powell (ed.), *Surrey Quarter Session Records: Order Books and Sessional Rolls, 1666–1668* (1951), 72; M. Dalton, *The Countrey Justice* (1630 edn.).

[7]   P. Slack, 'Books of Orders: the Making of the English Social Policy, 1577–1631', in *Transactions of the Royal Historical Society,* 5th series 30 (1980), 1–21.

[8]   1603, 1 James I c9; 1606, 4 James I c4; 1606, 4 James I c5; 1609, 7 James I c10.

[9]   1623, 21 James I c7; 1625, 1 Charles I c4; 1627, 3 Charles I c4.

and the fines from some offenders were given to the parish as an encouragement to the officers to act. Tippling was prohibited in inns and wine taverns to travellers as well as local customers. The reasons given for the continued proliferation of unlicensed alehouses are significant: fines were seldom levied, many offenders were too poor to pay or to bear 'their own charges of conveying them to gaol', and if they were imprisoned the parish would be obliged to maintain their wives and children. It might also be added that the justices themselves did not always administer the law as it was intended. As landowners and landlords they sometimes found it to their own advantage to favour one prospective licensee against another, or to turn a blind eye to offenders.

The Tudor period saw the development of a national system of government that stretched from Parliament and the illustrious members of the Privy Council, through the assize judges and justices of the peace, to the borough officers, the high constables, and the humblest parish officer. All of these were involved in the regulation of alehouses, but it was the justices of the peace in the counties and their equivalents in the boroughs who were the main instruments through which legislation and royal proclamations were administered. By Elizabeth I's reign the duties of the magistrates had become so numerous and important that a new literature of manuals had come into being to instruct the justices of their duties and authority.[10] The abstracts from the various statutes, along with accompanying advice, are given under alphabetically arranged subject headings, with 'Alehouses' the first or second subject. It was one of the longest sections; but to cover all the laws relating to the alehouse trade, the justices also needed to consult additional sections entitled 'Drunkenness', 'Fish Days', 'Games (unlawful)', 'Sabbath Day', and 'Weights and Measures'. Administrative and judicial responsibilities for alehouses were clearly amongst the more onerous tasks laid upon the justices of the peace.

The situation did not change much in the century following the Civil War. The same laws remained in force, and for much of the second half of the seventeenth century, it would seem that the county benches continued to act against surplus alehouses and the same types of disorderly behaviour. The picture, however, varies from county to county, and by the early eighteenth century there was a general absence of strict control or even concern for the increased number and character of the various retail outlets for the sale of liquor. Only a few of the clauses listed in Tudor recognizances are to be found in those for Georgian licensees.[11]

---

[10] Dalton, *Countrey Justice*.
[11] Aylesbury, Buckinghamshire Record Office, Q/RLv/10: Alehouse recognizance of Joseph Hill.

The sale of beer attracted little new licensing legislation – just two acts, both of which came about through the campaign for licensing spirit retailers. In 1729 it became mandatory for justices to hold annual licensing sessions in September and to act only for the petty session division in which they lived. Furthermore, alehouse keepers could only apply for licences in their own local division where, it might be reasoned, their character and standing, and the location of their alehouse, would be known. No longer could a prospective licensee apply to a magistrate anywhere in the county, and if refused, try his luck elsewhere. However, holding brewster sessions did not necessarily mean that the magistrates were vigilant in controlling the trade. In some places the justices took no part in the proceedings; they merely handed a pile of blank forms to the clerk of the peace.[12]

The second act, passed in 1753, effectively repealed all previous Licensing Acts, but confirmed their tenets and made it much easier for the law to be enforced. Licences were not to be issued to prospective licensees without a certificate of good character, and justices could summon unlicensed alehouse keepers before them, together with the local excise officer, and examine both of them under oath. Recognizances still had to be taken, but now a record of these had to be sent to the next quarter sessions and a register duly kept.

In the sixteenth century wine was as important as ale and beer, and the term 'tavern' referred to a house specializing in the sale of wine, or a drinking room within an inn. The 1553 act for licensing retailers of wine stands apart from the mainstream of legislation concerned with the history of public houses for several reasons.[13] It was not concerned with alehouses, which at this date rarely sold wine. The establishments addressed in 1553 were the inns and taverns, the latter being the specialist retail outlets for wine. Almost all the other Tudor and early Stuart legislation regulating public houses was directed at alehouses, and by extension to inns, but only occasionally to taverns. The terms under which the wine retailer was licensed also differed considerably from those binding ale and beer retailers. Moreover, much of the act would appear to have been overridden by the Crown almost as soon as it had received the royal assent.

According to the 1553 act, wine was to be sold at the low prices mentioned therein; prices which did not take into account fluctuations of the cost of wine to the vintners. Not surprisingly, disputes occurred when vintners were forced to buy at high prices and to sell at low. Wine was to be retailed in towns, not villages, the licensees being appointed by the towns' chief officers; and only the twenty-two towns named in the act were to be allowed more than two

---

[12]   1729. 2 George II c17; 1753, 26 George II c31; T. Skyrme, *History of the Justices of Peace*, vol. 2 (Chichester, 1991), 113, 136.
[13]   1553, 7 Edward VI c5.

retailers. London, for example, was allowed forty, although there were already more than 300 taverns in operation there, so that obeying the law would have meant the closure of most of those already in existence. No guidance was given as to how the forty were to be selected.

Over the next half century, several town councils did attempt to implement the law, but in 1554 Queen Mary began issuing wine licences to individual wine retailers by letters patent, setting at naught most of the clauses in the act.[14] There was considerable confusion and several licensees found it wise to pay for licences from both the Crown and the local council. Stephen Thwatye, vintner of London and taverner of the Red Bull in Thames Street, obtained two licences, even though as a member of the Vintners' Company he was exempt from needing an individual licence.[15]

At least 300 licences were granted by Queen Mary under the royal prerogative, and another dozen by Queen Elizabeth. By the mid 1560s a central wine office had been established in London. In 1570, however, Queen Elizabeth granted to Sir Edward Horsey, one of her favourites at Court, the privileges of issuing wine licences, fixing the price of wine, and fining offenders.[16] He was the first of a long line of Receivers of Wine Rents.

In 1583 Horsey was replaced by Sir Walter Raleigh, and when he fell out of favour, by the Earl of Nottingham and his son, Lord Effingham.[17] By James I's reign the profits of the 'wine licence business' had risen substantially, and in 1604 it was farmed to three Londoners for £6,000. The new receivers had considerable difficulties in persuading retailers to pay the fees and there were many 'bad and desperate debts'. A few councils continued to appoint licensees and occasionally the king also licensed retailers.[18]

In spite of all the difficulties, wine licensing was clearly a profitable business. An act passed in 1623 in the wake of an enquiry into the abuses of monopolies, however, made it illegal for the privilege of licensing wine retailers to be granted to anyone for private gain, except the king.[19] The Receiver of Wine Rents had become an employee of the Crown.

---

[14] W. H. Stevenson and Rev. Canon J. Rainer (eds), *Records of the Borough of Nottingham*, vol. 4, 1547–1625 (1889), 113; J. A. Twemlow, *Liverpool Town Books*, vol. 1, 1550–71 (Liverpool, 1918), 334–5; Norfolk Record Office, Norwich Mayors' Court Book no. 7, fol. 532; PRO (ed.), *Calendar of Patent Rolls, Philip and Mary*, vols 1–4 (1936–9).

[15] K. Rogers, *Mermaid and Mitre Taverns in Old London* (1928), 16–17; PRO, *Calendar of Patent Rolls, Philip and Mary*, vol. 1.

[16] PRO, *Calendar of Patent Rolls, Elizabeth*, vol. 5, 72–3.

[17] A summary of Raleigh's wine patent is given in: PRO, index to wine licences, C 380; PRO, *Calendar of State Papers Domestic*, 1603–1610, 10.

[18] PRO, *Calendar of State Papers Domestic*, 1603–10.

[19] 1623, 21 James I c28.

Whatever the original intention of the 1553 act, wine licensing was now seen primarily as a useful source of income for the Crown. Many alehouses now sold wine and taverns were to be found in villages in all the counties surrounding London, if not all over the country.[20] Legally, like alehouses and inns, taverns were forbidden to sell meat at prohibited times, or to allow tippling, but as regards licensing and orderly conduct taverns remained largely outside the responsibility of the justices.

The situation did not change much after the Civil War, except that the importance of the wine licence as a source of income for the Crown was increased. The Wine Act of 1660 confirmed the authority of His Majesty's agents to grant licences at a yearly rent payable to the Exchequer.[21] This income, together with excise and custom duties, formed the basis of the king's hereditary income. Unlike other licensing acts, this statute had no concern for the character of the licensee or the orderly running of the tavern and no provision was made for closing disorderly houses. Such a situation was open to abuse and during the mid and late eighteenth century, when it was not possible to obtain a spirit licence unless one already had an alehouse or wine licence, anyone who had been refused an alehouse licence from the magistrates could purchase a wine and spirit licence from the Wine Licence Office with no questions asked.[22] John Fielding, the chief magistrate at Westminster, campaigned against this unrestricted issuing of licences, alleging that they enabled disorderly coffee houses, bawdy houses and gaming houses, as well as irregular taverns, to sell alcohol as they pleased.[23] It was not until almost the end of the century that the situation was remedied and wine licensing became the responsibility of the justices of the peace.

Unlike alehouse keepers and taverners, who could conduct their business of selling liquor only if they were properly licensed, innkeepers, except for a very short period in the early seventeenth century, did not need a licence to run an inn – that is, to provide accommodation and refreshment to travellers. The requirement for inn licences came about not because of any new statute, but through the machinations of Sir Giles Mompesson, who persuaded James I to grant him the authority to license inns, old and new, throughout England.[24] After some three and a half years, Mompesson and his agents had licensed some twelve hundred inns, a mere fraction of those in existence in 1617 when

---

[20]   J. Taylor, *Taverns in the Ten Shires round London* (1636).

[21]   1660, 12 Charles II c25.

[22]   1736, 9 George II c23; 1753, 24 George II c40.

[23]   J. Fielding, *Penal Laws relating to the Metropolis* (1768), 414.

[24]   W. Notestein, F. Relf and H. Simpson (eds), *Commons Debates,* vol. 7, Appendix B (1935), 379–86.

he had been commissioned.[25] On the other hand, many of those that had been licensed by Mompesson were new inns and unwelcome competitors. He also licensed alehouses which had been closed by the magistrates for disorderly behaviour. There were many other complaints as to the way in which Mompesson had executed his commission, and by 1621 the grievances against his authority had become an outcry – not only by the innkeepers caught up in the system, but also by justices of the peace, the assizes, and travellers who were finding that the cost of using the inns was soaring.[26] An enquiry by Parliament found abundant evidence of Mompesson's abuse of his patent, and in March that year the House of Lords gave judgement against him.[27] A few days later the patent was repealed. Innkeeping no longer required a licence and new inns could be opened without any permission from the justice. However, if they sold ale, beer or wine, the requisite licences were still required – a practice which had long been accepted in many counties.[28]

Spirits had been drunk in England since the sixteenth century, but mainly for medicinal purposes, and socially only in very small quantities. By the 1640s, however, home produced spirits were being distilled in sufficient quantities to attract the attention of a Parliament that desperately needed to raise revenue to fight a civil war. In 1643 excise duties, an innovative tax, were imposed on a variety of home produced commodities, including beer, ale, cider, perry, and strong waters (spirits).[29]

The manufacture of spirits on the Continent and in Britain, however, was in its infancy and as yet so little was imported that spirits were not listed in the *Book of Rates* until 1649. During the mid seventeenth century, several new types of beverage began to be imported into England – tea, coffee, chocolate, and spirits, variously referred to as strong waters, hot water, spirits from cider or wine, brandy, or burnt wine. They rapidly became very popular, and new retail houses opened specializing in the sale of these drinks – coffee houses, chocolate houses and brandy shops. During the Nine Year War (1688-97), however, French brandy, along with other French goods, was prohibited, and under the influence of William III, gin became the fashionable drink, its

---

[25] Aylesbury, Buckinghamshire Record Office, D/X 648: Sir Giles Mompesson's Account Book. This is a copy of the original held in private hands.

[26] Notestein et al., *Common Debates*, vol. 7, 364; vol. 4, 85–6.

[27] J. R. Tanner (ed.), *Constitutional Documents of the Reign of James I, 1603–1625* (Cambridge, 1961), 322–4.

[28] Dalton, *The Countrey Justice* (1636 edn.), 31.

[29] C. H. Firth (ed.), *Acts and Ordinances of the Interregnum, 1642–1660* (1919).

distillation encouraged by the low duties set on spirits made from English corn by the Distillation Act of 1690.[30]

No licence, apprenticeship, or permission of any kind was required to set up as a distiller. No licence was required to sell the spirits, and low duties meant low prices. Not surprisingly the production and consumption of gin increased year by year, and by the 1720s it was being sold from a multitude of different outlets: victuallers of all kinds, including inns and alehouses; specialized shops variously called dram shops, brandy shops, or geneva shops; street sellers; and all kinds of other tradesmen. According to the returns made in 1725 by London parish constables, excluding the City and Southwark, there were over six thousand houses and shops selling spirits.[31]

The keepers of many of these establishments were also 'compound' distillers (the term used in the excise accounts), who flavoured and redistilled the raw alcohol they bought from large-scale distillers and then sold it to the public. Most of these spirit retailers sold some form of gin, but there was also a wider choice of British and imported spirits on sale in inns, taverns, up-market alehouses, coffee houses and punch houses, where customers could afford higher prices.

For some thirty years, the government fostered the growth of the British distillation industry, believing it to be essential for the support of the landed interests. The amount of gin drunk increased at a phenomenal rate, especially in London, to the detriment of the working population. In 1729, the Middlesex justices sent a petition to Parliament, blaming gin for a rise in the death rate in London, as well as a worsening crime problem.[32] The government was at last persuaded to take action.

Two acts were passed, the first of the so-called Gin Acts.[33] Justices were to have the same powers over spirit retailers as they had over alehouse keepers. Their licences were to be renewed annually, but at twenty pounds each the cost of a spirit licence was very high. A new and prohibitively high duty of five shillings a gallon was also laid on all spirits ready for sale; it was to be paid by the compound distillers.[34] The excise commissioners were made responsible for the collection of the money and the local excise officers were ordered to keep a register of stills. Street selling was prohibited. The acts were not a success and it took twenty-two years and eight Acts of Parliament before the retail of

---

[30] 1688, 1 William and Mary, Session I c24 and later acts; 1690, 2 William and Mary, Session II c9.

[31] D. George, *London Life in the XVIIIth Century* (London, 1966), 45.

[32] W. Maitland, *The History of London from its Foundations to the Present Time*, vol. I (London, 1756 edn.), 544.

[33] 1729, 2 George II c17; 1729, 2 George II c28.

[34] In today's currency, twenty-five pence.

spirits, like that of beer and ale, was effectively brought under the control of the justices of the peace in 1751.[35]

Spirit licences could only be obtained by those already granted an alehouse or wine licence, and who were the ratepayers of the property they occupied. Distillers were no longer allowed to sell by retail, and conversely taverners, innkeepers, and alehouse keepers were not allowed to distil. This separation of the retailing and distilling trades concentrated the latter into a smaller number of larger scale enterprises, making it much easier to ensure that the correct duties were paid and that the spirits sold were of good quality. The act also strengthened the authority of both excise officers and magistrates in other ways, and thus, wherever the law was enforced, the old type of gin shops disappeared from the scene.

Little evidence has been found to show the pattern of consumption and the effects of the acts outside London. However, in 1737, distillers in Cambridge sent a petition to Parliament explaining that the recent Gin Act had forced them to reduce their business and, in order to make provision for themselves and their families, they had set themselves up as vintners, obtaining the necessary licences from the London Wine Office. This was despite their lack of an apprenticeship in the wine trade, a factor that had been anticipated by the Gin Act. Conflict had occurred because Cambridge University had a charter granting the Chancellor the right to issue wine licences in Cambridge. Fortunately for the former distillers, their petition was successful and a clause in a new act relating to the University confirmed the rights of the distillers to act as vintners and to retail under the aegis of a wine licence.[36]

The prices, quality, quantity and availability of liquors on sale in public houses were the subject – or result of – numerous statutes, the majority of which were concerned with excise and custom duties. Altogether more than fifty Customs Acts and some 130 Excise Acts affected the liquor trade to a lesser or greater degree between 1552 and 1757.[37] At the Restoration of the monarchy in 1660, custom and excise duties, together with the rents from wine licences, became the basis of the king's regular income.[38] Excise duties had become a permanent and vital part of the national economy. During the ensuing century additional customs and excise duties were not only used for raising money for a variety of other causes, but to foster particular home industries and to encourage or discourage trade with other countries.

---

[35] 1733, 6 George II c17; 1736, 9 George II c23; 1737, 10 George II c17; 1743, 16 George II c8; 1747, 20 George II c39; 1751, 24 George II c40.

[36] *Journal of the House of Commons*, vol. 13 (London, 1803), 768, 820.

[37] A full list of all the acts, 1552–1757, is given in Hunter, 'Legislation', 382–95.

[38] 1660, 12 Charles II c23; 1660, 12 Charles II c24.

The price at which a barrel of beer should be sold to the victuallers was set by the Excise Act of 1660. The excise duties, payable by the brewer, could also be passed onto the licensees, but according to the law retail prices in the inns and alehouses were still controlled by two earlier acts that had not been repealed. The earliest of these was the Assize of Ale Act of 1266, and as late as the mid eighteenth century, alehouse recognizances still included a clause to the effect that licensees would keep the assize.[39] With no regard to this, however, the 1603 Licensing Act had set the maximum price for best, or strong, beer at one penny a quart, and halfpenny for small beer.[40] Not until 1671 could retailers legally raise their prices to take into account inflation and the additional excise costs.[41] What prices were actually charged is not known.

In 1689 and 1690, Excise Acts substantially increased the taxes on ale and beer, at the very time when differential duties gave the advantage to producers and retailers of gin.[42] The following year, in order to improve the collection of duties, victuallers were forbidden to brew their own beer if there was a common brewer in the town. The number of brewing victuallers was already in decline and this measure helped to further reduce the numbers; nearly nine thousand ceased to brew between 1689 and 1695.[43] Whereas the story of the production and sale of gin in the late seventeenth and early eighteenth centuries was one of increase, for the beer trade it was one of contraction. By the 1690s, excise duties on beer and ale had become oppressive, acting against the smaller establishments and the poorer members of the community. The price of beer had almost doubled so that a 'twopenny pot, which had formerly held a full ale quart', was said to hold a half of this amount. Many alehouse keepers went bankrupt leaving brewers with big debts. From 1703 onwards, annual acts maintained additional taxes on malt, cider, perry and mum (a type of strong beer). According to a report to the Treasury by the Excise Office itself, the main blame for the decline in the ale trade lay with the high taxes. Not until spirit licensing came under the control of the magistrates did the situation begin to change, and by then porter, a new type of beer, was beginning to challenge the popularity of gin.

The 1690 Distillation Act had been primarily a protective measure, a means of using up the surplus corn produced during a period of excellent harvests. The new duty set on the raw spirits made from British grain was only a quarter of that which had been set by the previous act, and only half that paid on strong

---

[39] Aylesbury, Buckinghamshire Record Office, Q/RLv/9–19: Victuallers' recognizances, 1763–91.

[40] 1603, 1 James I c9. One penny is approximately ½ pence.

[41] 1671, 22/23 Charles II c5.

[42] 1689, 2 William and Mary, Session I c3; 1690, 2 William and Mary Session II c3.

[43] P. Clark, *The English Alehouse: A Social History 1200–1830* (London, 1983), 208; London, PRO, CUST 48/6: Excise Board, Entry Book of Correspondence, fol. 19–22.

beer. Even good gin was cheap, perhaps as little as a penny a pint, but much of what was made in dram shops, alehouses, and by other small time operators, scarcely deserved the name of gin. There could be little control of the quality of spirits on sale until the problems of excessive production and licensing had been solved.

Most other drinks were also highly taxed and expensive, including home-produced spirits such as British brandy and those distilled from cider and perry. There was also quite a range of imported beverages – brandy, geneva, rum, spruce beer, and arrack to name but five of the thirteen listed in the 1724 *Book of Rates*; the most highly taxed was a cordial known as citron water that commanded an astonishing tax of one pound per gallon.[44]

Wine, still the country's most important individual import, was mostly dealt with under the Customs Acts. High duties kept all wines relatively expensive, but there was a considerable variation in custom charges according to the country of origin of the wines, and the port into which they were brought. London was usually more expensive than other ports. The dictates of mercantile and foreign policies also meant that custom duties were used at various time to make wines from some countries relatively scarce, very expensive or comparatively cheap. The retail price of wine was also a concern of the government since the 1660 Wine Act had given authority to the Chancellor of the Exchequer to proclaim the wine prices each year.

During the First Dutch War, 1652–54, Parliament's prohibition of Dutch ships in British Waters brought about a virtual dearth of wine in England. Preferential treatment halved the price of sack and mullagoes from Spain during the Second Dutch War.[45] French wine was made relatively scarce in 1670 when additional duties were imposed on French goods in an attempt to improve an unfavourable balance of trade between Britain and France. During the Nine Year War, French wines were either subjected to prohibitively high duties or actual prohibition; both circumstances led to a drastic shortage of French wines and brandy on sale in English inns and taverns. In 1706 wine was in such short supply that Sir William Congreve, one of the wine commissioners, was driven to complain, 'If I have the spleen, it is because the town of London affords not one drop of wine outside a private house'.[46] Although French wines were again allowed into England in 1711, they remained scarce and expensive, their pride of place taken by wines from Spain and Portugal. Spanish wines had long been enjoyed in England, but although Portuguese wine had been available since the 1670s, in general they were of inferior quality. However, the Methuen Treaty of 1703 gave them preferential treatment and the seal of patriotic approval.

---

44 1724, 11 George I c7.
45 A. D. Francis, *The Wine Trade* (London, 1972), 92.
46 Francis, *The Wine Trade*, 125.

According to Cesar de Saussure, who visited England in the early eighteenth century, a bottle of the cheapest Portuguese wine cost only two shillings (ten pence in today's currency), a mere trifle in contrast to a bottle of French claret at five shillings (twenty-five pence).

According to the Inspector General of Customs the interference in the wine trade through custom duties led vintners to adulterate their wine, using gin, sweets and 'viler liquors to strengthen the common draft'. In 1727 de Saussure commented that most wine merchants, especially tavern proprietors, possessed the art of doubling or even trebling the quantity of their wine. Adulteration of beer was also widespread, the blame for which can also be laid upon the high taxes that made it difficult for brewers and victuallers to make a living.[47]

The legislation so far discussed has been almost entirely concerned, one way or another, with the sale of liquor; but from time immemorial, inns – and to a lesser extent the other establishments – had been involved with a wide range of other services. Inns, taverns, alehouses and punch houses all provided meals and, under the Statute of Victuals, they should have been regulated by the clerk of the market whose responsibility it was to ensure that victuals for men and horses were sold at reasonable prices.[48] In 1623 this obligation was re-enforced by a new Act of Parliament, which also dealt with the provision of bedding for horses belonging to guests at the inn.[49] For this no fee should be taken. No statute regulated the quality and cost of accommodation, but occasionally the maximum prices that should be charged in a particular town were set by a royal proclamation, such as that proclaimed in Windsor in 1563.[50] Amongst the prices announced were:

A featherbed for one man one night and so depart: 1d
A featherbed with necessary apparel thereunto for one
     man alone by the week: 6 d

Inns and alehouses have long been venues where social and public events could take place, from simple meetings and celebrations with family, friends and acquaintances, to official meetings of parish vestries, manor courts, petty sessions, assize courts and the feasting enjoyed by members of town councils. Such activities, however, were not directly the concern of statutes, except in so far as the behaviour of the participants contravened the conditions laid down by

---

[47]   Ibid., 103, 129; Madam Van Muyden (ed.), *England in the Reigns of George I and George II* (London, 1902).
[48]   1318, 23 Edward III c6.
[49]   1623, 21 James I c23.
[50]   Hughes and Larkin, *Tudor Proclamations,* vol. 2, 1553–1603 (London, 1969), no. 701.

the licensees' recognizances or in any other way that could be said to be 'disorderly'.

Closing the alehouse to customers during the time of divine services was a condition of every recognizance, but in the mid seventeenth century Puritan ideals on the matter of Sunday observances brought about increased restrictions of all sorts of activities. Most of these were not specifically aimed at public houses, but the prohibition of travel (except to church) and all sorts of leisure and work activities, inevitably affected the business of the inns and other establishments.[51] In 1695 swearing and cursing were also prohibited.[52] Such vices were not confined to alehouses and dram shops, but drink has always loosened tongues and in public places it is easy for informers to find victims. Under an act of 1746 parish constables could apprehend anyone heard to curse or swear profanely.

There was little concern for disorderly behaviour or excessive eating and drinking at the clubs and other establishments frequented by the upper and middle classes. But, just as the multiplication of alehouses during the Tudor period had been seen as a threat to the good order of the country, so the excessive number of places of entertainment used by the lower ranks of society also began to be regarded as a dangerous development. In 1710 justices were given authority to examine and bind over for twelve months, or commit to prison, the 'divers lewd and dissolute persons' who were suspected of living by gaming. A clause in the 1729 Gin Act confirmed the prohibition of unlawful games, authorizing the justices to commit to prison without bail anyone playing them, in particular tradesmen, artisans, apprentices and labourers. In 1745 the penalties for those convicted of gaming were increased and magistrates were empowered to convict both keepers and frequenters of gaming houses. An act of 1757 was specifically directed against working men who misspent their time gambling and were thus reduced to poverty. Licensees of public houses and other establishments who allowed games to be played in their houses could also be convicted and fined.[53]

During the Tudor period many a play was performed in an inn yard, with privileged spectators watching from the inn galleries. Under the Vagrancy Act of 1572, however, itinerant actors and other entertainers were classified as rogues and vagabonds, unless they were licensed; few were. In 1713 and 1737 new legislation confirmed that common players were still to be regarded as rogues and vagabonds and no person could legally perform any interlude, play,

---

[51] W. P. Baker, 'The Observance of Sunday' in R. Lennard (ed.), *English Men at Rest and Play* (London, 1931), 105, 116–18.

[52] 1695, 6/7 William III c11; G. H. Jennings (ed.), *The Diary of a Georgian Shopkeeper* (Oxford, 1979), 36–7.

[53] 1710, 9 Anne c14; 1745, 18 George II c34; 1757, 30 George II c24.

farce, or any other entertainment without a licence from the Lord Chamberlain. The 1737 act made it clear that inns and public houses were not exempt from this legislation, and from December 1752 every room, garden, or other place in the Cities of London and Westminster and within a radius of twenty miles thereof, which was kept for public dancing, music and entertainment had to be licensed. Landlords of inns and alehouses who continued to offer entertainment without a licence could be fined, and as keepers of a disorderly house their alehouse recognizance could also be revoked. Those that were licensed could not open for entertainment on Sundays, Christmas Day, Ash Wednesday, or other days of fast and humiliation. Nor were they allowed to open before five o'clock of the afternoon or stay open at unreasonable hours. This act also allowed justices to examine any person apprehended during any search by constables, and to charge them for being a rogue or vagabond, an idle or disorderly person.[54] It was a short-sighted policy that restricted the use of inns and alehouses on Sundays to drinking; there were few other amusements or places of recreation for working people and their families.[55]

Inns and alehouses were also a vital element in England's transport and communication network, but of the numerous laws concerned with roads and traffic that were passed during the period under study, very few applied, even indirectly, to public houses. In the sixteenth and seventeenth centuries many postmasters were also innkeepers, and in the towns where they were established they had a virtual monopoly on providing post horses for travellers. Under the 1710 Post Office Act, however, this privilege became an obligation and burden. Postmasters were duty bound to keep a sufficient number of horses and post-boys in readiness, but as the coaching trade expanded the number of people travelling by horse declined. Other innkeepers provided post horses and post-chaise in competition with the postmasters, but unlike the postmasters, they could give up keeping post horses for hire when business was slack. The discontent of the postmasters increased in 1747 when a tax of four pounds was imposed on all four-wheeled coaches, and two pounds on all two-wheeled vehicles. As owners of stage coaches and postchaise many innkeepers were liable for this tax. The matter came to a head in 1779 when postmasters and innkeepers who let post horses for hire had to be licensed.[56]

Soldiers were a special group of travellers whose accommodation requirements became a vexatious issue in the seventeenth and eighteenth centuries, and an unfair burden on the publicans. There was much opposition to compulsorily billeting soldiers in private houses, but by the mid seventeenth

---

[54]   1713, 12, Anne c23; 1737, 10 George II c28; 1752, 25 George II c36; 1757, 30 George II c24.

[55]   F. Place, *Improvement of the Working People* (London, 1834), 19–20.

[56]   1710, 9 Anne c10; 1710, 9 Anne c23; 1747, 20 George II c10.

century it had become accepted that they could, and should, be billeted in public houses.[57] The notion that the rights of alehouse keepers and innkeepers might also be violated does not seem to have been considered. In 1689 a new Mutiny Act gave compulsory billeting legal status. All types of establishment were included, except taverns which only sold wine. The act was for one year only, but from 1701, it was renewed annually with only a few changes.[58] The army may have solved its problem, but for the innkeepers and other retailers, billeting was to be a problem for another hundred years.

However convenient it was for the government to place the burden of quartering soldiers on public houses, it frequently led to a financial loss for the licensees and even to bankruptcy. Payment for the soldiers' accommodation and food, and hay and straw for horses, was usually at minimum rates and in arrears, or not paid at all, and no provision was made for such necessities as fire and candles. Local villagers and townsfolk were discouraged from visiting the alehouses when soldiers were in residence and there might be no room for the ordinary traveller to stay. Wagons and stage coaches might have to be turned away with all the consequent loss of business. Numerous petitions tell the story of hardship, bankruptcy and closure, but if the licensees revolted and 'pulled down their signs' to avoid quartering, they were likely to lose their licence at the next brewster session.[59]

By the end of the eighteenth century, as a result of some two hundred and fifty years of legislation, the licensed victualling trade was firmly established as an essential feature of the financial, military and economic life of the country. Some acts had been on the statute books for a long time and, while some had lapsed, others were still in force and enforced. The need for guidelines in the form of manuals was as great in the late eighteenth century as it had been in Elizabeth I's reign. In 1755 the first edition of the Rev. Richard Burn's *The Justice of Peace and Parish Officer* was published, a work which in various revised versions became accepted for the rest of the century as the most authoritative and complete manual for justices.

The mere passing of laws, however, is no guarantee of their effective execution. That depends on several things, including the beliefs and attitudes of the

---

[57]   J. Childs, *The Army of Charles II* (London, 1976), 75–6, 87; C. Walton, *The History of the Standing Army AD 1600–1700* (London, 1894), 712.

[58]   In 1720 establishments which also distilled were made exempt from compulsory billeting – a regulation which surely must have encouraged inns and alehouses to distil their own gin!; 1689, 1 William and Mary, Session II c4; 1701, 1 Anne, Session II c16.

[59]   London, PRO, WO 40: Petitions against billeting; C. Clode, *Military Forces of the Crown: Their Administration and Government* (London, 1869); D. L. Powell, 'Billeting in Surrey in the Seventeenth and Eighteenth Centuries', in *Surrey Archaeological Collections*, vol. 27 (London, 1914).

population, conflicting policies, and the success or failure of the legislature to publicize the statutes. But perhaps most of all it depends upon the abilities, intentions and interpretations of those entrusted with enforcing and keeping the law. In the late eighteenth century the most important people responsible for this were the justices of the peace, the excise officers, the parish and borough officers, and the licensees themselves.

Public Houses, Clientelism and Faith: Strategies of Power in Early Modern Toggenburg*

Fabian Brändle

'Toggius ratione ducitur' ('The Toggenburg should be governed by caution')[1] was a favourite catch-phrase of the prince-abbots of Saint Gall, the overlords of Toggenburg in the eastern part of Switzerland.[2] In fact, the prince-abbots (*Fürstabte*) of Saint Gall had quite a few difficulties in ruling over their Toggenburg subjects. Especially the Reformed subjects of the valley opposed the overlord's policy of re-Catholicizing his territory. As a result, the prince-abbots had to build their power on Catholic clients and their notorious hostility towards their Reformed countrymen. The allocation of inns and taverns to Catholics was one important means in the battle for souls and power.

This essay will first present some information on the complicated history and constitution of the valley, and then will examine the authorities' strategies to confessionalize the public houses as well as the resistance against these measures. The article concludes with some thoughts on the results of the prince-abbots' public house politics.

In 1468, abbot Ulrich Rösch purchased the county (*Grafschaft*) of Toggenburg from the highly indebted Lords of Raron. An alliance, the so-called *Verlandrechtung* with Glarus and Schwyz, guaranteed some weighty political

---

* I want to thank Kaspar von Greyerz, Tobias Hug, Christian Koller, and Bruno Wickli for reading this text. Errors are, of course, the author's only.
[1] A. Müller, *Lichtensteig: Geschichte des Toggenburger Städtchens* (Lichtensteig, 1978), 115.
[2] The history of Toggenburg in the early modern period still rests on two books of the nineteenth century that document the confessional gaps of that century. The former monk Ildefons von Arx had a strongly pro-Catholic position, whereas the liberal Karl Wegelin wrote his history from the perspective of the Reformed Toggenburgers. I. von Arx, *Geschichten des Kantons St Gallen. Nachdruck der Ausgabe von 1810–1813* (St Gall, 1987); K. Wegelin, *Geschichte der Landschaft Toggenburg* (St Gall, 1830). See also H. Edelmann, *Geschichte der Landschaft Toggenburg* (Lichtensteig, 1956).

rights to the subjects.[3] Over the following decades, however, the new sovereigns tried to restrict the highly developed political autonomy of Toggenburg's chartered body (*Landschaft*).[4] The resistance of the Toggenburgers against this 'process of territorialization' (*Territorialisierungsprozess*) was culminating during the Reformation, when many of them turned Protestant, embracing the ideas of their compatriot Huldrych Zwingli of Wildhaus, the well-known Reformer of Zurich.[5] The subjects ultimately gained independence from their sovereigns. Toggenburg remained an independent republic until 1538, when the Catholic cantons of the Swiss Confederacy restituted the valley of the Thur to the prince-abbot. Nevertheless, the Reformed confession was tolerated, having dominated in the alpine part of the valley (the 'Upper District' or *Oberamt*), where a wealthy elite of cattle-breeders, supported by Zurich and the other Reformed cantons, powerfully opposed the prince-abbot. The 'Lower District' (*Unteramt*) remained strongly Catholic, whereas there were some bi-confessional parishes in which confessional disputes belonged to every-day life.[6]

To claim that the Reformed confession was tolerated does not mean that there was not any repression against it. The prince-abbot had the important right of installing and dismissing the Reformed ministers (the *Kollaturrecht*). He favoured Catholic *Landleute*, men with full citizenship, whenever he was able to do so. During the seventeenth century, especially after the surprising military victory of the Catholic cantons against the Protestants in 1656 (in the first War of Villmergen), the governmental pressure on the Protestants increased; discontent among the Reformed populace was growing steadily as well.[7] The repertoire of the subjects' political agency was very broad, including

---

[3]   A very useful book on the complicated constitution of the Swiss Confederacy is H. C. Peyer, *Verfassungsgeschichte der alten Schweiz* (Zurich, 1978).

[4]   P. Blickle, *Landschaften im Alten Reich: Die staatliche Funktion des gemeinen Mannes in Oberdeutschland* (Munich, 1973), 16–26, 469–75, 552–41.

[5]   For the tradition of resistance in Toggenburg see P. Blickle, 'Bäuerliche Rebellionen im Fürststift St Gallen', in idem (ed.), *Aufruhr und Empörung? Studien zum Widerstand im Alten Reich* (Munich, 1980), 215–95; B. Wickli, *Politische Erfahrung und die 'reine Demokratie': Politische Kultur im Toggenburg zwischen Ancien Régime und Regeneration* (MA University of Zurich, 1998). On the Reformation, see G. Egli, *Die Reformation im Toggenburg* (Zurich, 1955).

[6]   On the many quarrels and conflicts between the members of the two denominations, see, for example, L. Vogel, *Das evangelische Nesslau von der Reformation bis 1806* (Nesslau, 1991); O. Frei, *Evangelisch Alt St Johann: Ein Gang durch seine Geschichte* (Wädenswil, 1961); W. Hofer, *Ebnat-Kappel: Aus der Geschichte von Kirche und Gemeinde* (Ebnat-Kappel, 1994).

[7]   Although strongly pro-Catholic, the theological dissertation of Johannes Duft provides a lot of material on the process of confessionalization (*Konfessionalisierung*): J. Duft, *Die Glaubenssorge der Fürstäbte von St Gallen im 17. und 18. Jahrhundert: Ein Beitrag zur Seelsorgegeschichte der katholischen Restauration als Vorgeschichte des Bistums St Gallen*

petitions and complaints (*gravamina*) to the brethren-in-faith in Zurich, political assassinations, and finally, open rebellion, as when an alliance of Catholic and Reformed subjects achieved independence from the prince-abbot in the early eighteenth century.[8] In the following third Swiss civil war, the Reformed cantons gained a victory over their Catholic opponents in 1712. Toggenburg remained an independent republic until 1718, when it was restored to the prince-abbot once again in the Treaty of Baden. The Protestants obtained nearly full religious rights and were guaranteed at least some political participation.

Without any army and lacking the support of a truly professionalized bureaucracy, the authority (*Herrschaft*) of the prince-abbots was always rather weak.[9] It was necessary to create a system of clients, building on powerful local families and their social networks. Clientelism, widely spread across the paternalistic oligarchies and 'democracies' of the Swiss Confederacy, had been a practice of power in Saint Gall since the late fifteenth century.[10] After the Reformation, the maxim of the prince-abbots was the principle of 'divide and conquer'. The notorious patronizing of Catholic families in the Upper District in all aspects of political, economic, and religious matters aimed at generating a loyal clientele, as well as an ever-alert opposition to the mighty and prosperous Protestants, who were always willing to denounce anti-Catholic activities. In this way, the prince-abbots hoped to re-Catholicize the Upper District by fostering converts and creating Catholic footholds.[11] These measures, however,

---

(ThD Freiburg i.Ü., Lucerne, 1944); Z'Graggen considers the *Herrschaftsintensivierung* to begin under the reign of *Fürstabt* Bernhard Müller (1595–1630): B. Z'Graggen, *Tyrannenmord im Toggenburg* (Zurich, 1999), 191. During the seventeenth century, there were at least twenty-four different conflicts between the *Obrigkeit* and the Reformed Toggenburgers: I am grateful to M. Heiniger and D. von Matt for this information from their unpublished paper, 'Wahrhaftiger und grundlicher Entwurff' (University of Zurich, 1976/1977).

[8] J. Hässig, *Die Anfänge des Toggenburger- oder zweiten Villmergerkrieges 1698–1706* (Ph.D. University of Bern, 1903); A. Mantel, *Über die Veranlassung des Zwölfer- oder zweiten Villmergerkrieges: Die Toggenburgerwirren in den Jahren 1706–1712* (Ph.D. University of Zurich, 1909).

[9] On the administration of the *Fürstäbte* see P. Stärkle, 'Der St. Gallische Hofstaat zur Zeit der Territorialherrschaft', in *Rorschacher Neujahrsblätter* 56 (1966), 35–46.

[10] U. Pfister, 'Politischer Klientelismus in der frühneuzeitlichen Schweiz', in: *Schweizerische Zeitschrift für Geschichte* 42 (1992), 28–68; P. Robinson, *Die Fürstabtei St. Gallen und ihr Territorium 1463-1529* (St Gall, 1995), 305–314.

[11] According to the prevailing tendency in German scholarship of the 1980s, the (finally successful) processes of confessionalization and social disciplining went hand in hand during the early modern period to create obedient, disciplined, and pious subjects. See, for example, E. W. Zeeden, *Die Entstehung der Konfessionen: Grundlagen und Formen der Konfessionsbildung im Zeitalter der Glaubenskämpfe* (Munich and Vienna, 1965), 7–12; H. Schilling, 'The Reformation and the Rise of the Modern State', in J. D. Tracy (ed.), *Luther and the Modern State in Germany* (Kirksville, 1986), 21–30. For Catholic territories, see W.

also touched upon basic human dispositions such as sociability,[12] thus provoking, as historians of popular culture such as Norbert Schindler have pointed out, obstinance and resistance.[13]

The right of licensing taverns and alehouses, the so-called *Täffry*, was a princely prerogative (*regalium*) of the prince-abbots.[14] For the relatively small tax of two or three gulden, a prospective keeper could get a licence for catering to guests commercially for one or several years. An inn (*Taverne*) had to provide full meals, space for sleeping, and stables for horses, whereas the guests of the much smaller taverns (*Schenkhaus, also Wirtshaus*) were offered only snacks as well as wine, cider, and beer.[15]

The authorities strictly limited the number of inns and taverns. Disobedient keepers were heavily fined and even dismissed, while the hosts of unlicensed public houses (*Winkelwirte*) were prosecuted, often with the help of their licensed and jealous rivals. The fief (*Lehen*) of a tavern was very lucrative, indeed. Along with impressive and prestigious buildings, it generally included a respectable piece of land. It comes as no surprise, then, that many innkeepers became very wealthy.[16] They were often engaged in the lucrative wine trade as well as in regional networks of credit. Wealthy and always knowing what was going on, innkeepers became part of the rural elite, finally obtaining most of the leading communal offices such as *Ammann* (the Swiss equivalent of standard German *Amtmann*, a high-level official similar to a mayor) and captain of

---

Reinhard, 'Gegenreformation als Modernisierung? Prolegomena zu einer Theorie des konfessionellen Zeitalters', in *Archiv für Reformationsgeschichte* 68 (1977), 226–52.

[12] On the concept of sociability, see M. Agulhon, 'La sociabilità come categoria storica', in *Dimensioni e problemi della ricerca storica* 1 (1992), 39–47.

[13] N. Schindler, 'Spuren in der Geschichte der "anderen" Zivilisation: Probleme und Perspektiven einer historischen Volkskulturforschung', in R. van Dülmen and Norbert Schindler (eds), *Volkskultur: Zur Wiederentdeckung des vergessenen Alltags (16.–20 Jahrhundert)* (2nd edn, Frankfurt a. M., 1987), 13–77.

[14] M. Gmür (ed.), *Die Rechtsquellen des Kantons St Gallen. Erster Teil: Offnungen und Hofrechte, Zweiter Band: Toggenburg* (Aarau, 1906), 23.

[15] A similar distinction between the different types of public houses was made in early modern England. P. Clark, *The English Alehouse: A Social History 1200-1830* (London, 1983), 5. For the various forms of hospitality see H. C. Peyer, *Von der Gastfreundschaft zum Gasthaus: Studien zur Gastlichkeit im Mittelalter* (Hannover, 1987).

[16] Heiniger and von Matt, 'Wahrhaffter Entwurff', 13–14; F. Brändle, 'Zwischen Volkskultur und Herrschaft: Wirtshäuser und Wirte in der Fürstabtei St Gallen, 1550–1795' (M.A. University of Zurich, 1997), 85–93; idem, 'Toggenburger Wirtshäuser und Wirte im 17. und 18. Jahrhundert', in F. Brändle, L. Heiligensetzer and P. Michel (eds), *Obrigkeit und Opposition: Drei Beiträge zur Kulturgeschichte des Toggenburgs aus dem 17./18. Jahrhundert* (Wattwil, 1999), 33–8.

the guard (*Hauptmann*).[17] Although the government opposed innkeepers attaining such high posts and attempted (without success) to forbid it, the innkeepers' socio-political position remained very high. In normal years, the tavern keepers made their fortune as well – at least, there is some evidence that they were also part of the upper strata of the rural population.

Both the inn- and tavern keepers had to swear an oath of allegiance to the prince-abbot, and to denounce all crimes and subversive acts taking place in and outside their establishments.[18] What is more, in the seventeenth century, they were required to sign a contract (*Bestallung*) that included even more detailed directions than the ordinances.

Like the authorities of their Swiss neighbour states, the prince-abbots of Saint Gall aimed to strengthen control over popular culture, focusing much of their energy on public houses, which were favoured sites for early modern sociability, including social drinking and oral communication.[19] They published numerous mandates[20] where the many sins of the 'devil's altar' were severely condemned.[21] These mandates had to be displayed in public houses. In 1683, Prince-Abbot Gallus Alt condemned drunkenness as 'the mother of all mischief, for blasphemy, slaying, incest, insults and other harm were the very

---

[17] On the prominent role of publicans in Swiss history, see F. A. Stocker, 'Die Wirthe in der Schweizergeschichte als Politiker', in idem (ed.), *Vom Jura zum Schwarzwald: Geschichte, Sage, Land und Leute*, vol. 4 (Aarau, 1887), 286–312.

[18] Publicans had to swear the oath of allegiance (*Aydt der Tafern-Würthen*) beginning in 1525: Gmür, *Rechtsquellen*, 149.

[19] The collective drinking of alcohol, according to theorists of social drinking, aims at promotion of local solidarities. See, for example, D. Horton, 'The Functions of Alcohol in Primitive Societies', in *Quarterly Journal of Studies on Alcohol* 4 (1943), 190–311; T. Brennan, 'Social Drinking in Old Régime Paris', in: S. Barrows and R. Room (eds), *Drinking: Behavior and Belief in Modern History* (Berkeley, 1984), 61–86. On the various meanings of public houses for rural and urban popular culture, see Brändle, 'Volkskultur,' 22–58; idem, 'Toggenburger Wirtshäuser', 8–20. The older cultural history has produced studies rich in material, among them T. von Liebenau, *Das Gasthof- und Wirtshauswesen der Schweiz in älterer Zeit* (Zurich, 1891).

[20] In the Stiftsarchiv of St Gall, I have found printed public house mandates (*Wirtshausmandate*) regulating pub culture in the name of *gute Polizei* etc. for the years of 1652, 1660, 1668, 1692, 1700, 1722, 1753, 1762, 1770, 1776, 1781, 1792, and 1794. St Gall, Stiftsarchiv, Rubr. 42, Fasz. 10 and Rubr. 85, Fasz. 17 and Fasz. 21. See also W. Müller, *Landsatzung und Landmandat der Fürstabtei St Gallen: Zur Gesetzgebung eines geistlichen Staates vom 15. bis zum 18. Jahrhundert* (St Gall, 1970), 270–74; and I am grateful to A. Andermatt and Liselotte Schug for access to their unpublished paper, 'Die Wirtshausmandate als Spiegelbild von Sitte und Moral in Stadt und Landschaft St Gallen im 17. und 18. Jahrhundert' (University of Zurich, 1993).

[21] B. Ann Tlusty, *Bacchus and Civic Order: The Culture of Drink in Early Modern Germany* (Charlottesville, 2001), 10.

result of it.'[22] To be sure, the Protestant ministers also joined in the pious battle against the sinful public house culture.[23]

As we know, taverns and alehouses were common centres for the discussion of popular politics. They were, as Swiss historian Beat Kümin puts it, the actual symbols of communalism.[24] Sometimes, even revolts were planned in these favoured sites of the popular 'public sphere' (*Öffentlichkeit*), often enough in the notorious backrooms.[25] The rebels passed a resolution ritually, by swearing an oath and drinking wine together. In fact, the unruly Reformed folk of the Upper District made use of public houses as 'social sites' several times.[26] The *cause célèbre* was the conspiracy of the entire Protestant elite of the large village of Nesslau against the highly-decorated official (*Statthalter*) Hans Ledergerw in 1621. According to Bruno Z'Graggen, the rather sophisticated plan to assassinate Ledergerw was elaborated in the backroom of Josef Scherrer's alehouse in Sidwald, a market-village next to Nesslau.[27]

There were many 'secret assemblies' of the Protestants in the seventeenth century,[28] although the *Stanser Verkommnis*, a contract made by the ruling elites to pacify the restless people of the Swiss cantons, had forbidden them in the late Middle Ages. There is some evidence that the Protestants sang their psalms, an important means for creating their identity, in public houses, show-

---

[22] Drunkenness is the 'Mutter allen Unheils, dann darus Gotteslesterliche reden, totfähl, blutschanden, scheltungen und anders Unheil entspringen': Wegelin, *Geschichte*, 269. For the perception of drunkenness see the overview of H. Spode, *Die Macht der Trunkenheit: Kultur- und Sozialgeschichte des Alkohols in Deutschland* (Opladen, 1993), 55–82.

[23] Brändle, 'Volkskultur', 66–73; idem, 'Toggenburger Wirtshäuser', 8–20.

[24] B. Kümin, 'Rathaus, Wirtshaus, Gotteshaus. Von der Zwei- zur Dreidimensionalität in der frühneuzeitlichen Gemeindeforschung', in *Geist, Gesellschaft, Kirche im 13.–16. Jahrhundert. Colloquia mediaevalia Pragensia 1* (Prague, 1999), 249–62. See also B. Scribner, 'Mündliche Kommunikation und Strategien der Macht in Deutschland im 16. Jahrhundert', in *Kommunikation und Alltag in Spätmittelalter und früher Neuzeit: Internationaler Kongress Krems an der Donau 9. bis 12. Oktober 1990* (Vienna, 1990), 184–97.

[25] Brändle, 'Volkskultur,' 17–18, 48–53. For early modern Switzerland with its numerous revolts, see, for example, M. Merki-Vollenwyder, *Unruhige Untertanen: Die Rebellion der Luzerner Bauern im Zweiten Villmergerkrieg (1714)* (Ph.D. University of Zurich, Lucerne, 1995), 36–41; A. Suter, *Der schweizerische Bauernkrieg von 1653: Politische Sozialgeschichte–Sozialgeschichte eines politischen Ereignisses* (Tübingen, 1997).

[26] On the concept of 'social sites' as spaces without intense governmental control and as 'training areas' of resistance see J. C. Scott, *Domination and the Arts of Resistance: Hidden Transcripts* (New Haven, 1990), 122–3.

[27] Z'Graggen, *Tyrannemord*, 40.

[28] We know of eight 'secret assemblies' in the *Oberamt* during the seventeenth century alone. Heiniger and von Matt, 'Wahrhafftiger Entwurff', 35–6; Duft, *Glaubenssorge*, 379.

ing their Catholic neighbours their courage and faith in public.[29] In 1657, for instance, Heinrich Wälli yelled a Protestant hymn in front of an alehouse in Lichtensteig.[30] In other instances, Protestants agitated against the Catholics and cursed their overlord, sometimes while drunk. In the year of 1677, for example, Abraham Anderegg of Wattwil mocked the Catholic pilgrims who were heading to the famous pilgrimage site of Einsiedeln, saying that they were adoring small, useless statues of mud as well as little Mary (*Marialin*).[31] The Catholic members of the ruling elite were, as we have already seen, well aware of the various dangers resulting from public house culture. It was up to them to take action.

In 1654, Gallus Alt, a headstrong man of Counter Reformation ideals, became the new prince-abbot. Only seven years later in 1661, he initiated a conference in the newly built baroque monastery of Neu Saint Johann, the Catholic base in the upper part of Toggenburg. This had been built, rather cynically, with the help of the confiscated goods taken from the Reformed conspirators against Hans Ledergerw. The participants' aim was to discuss new ways of encouraging conversions in the Upper District. A conversion, it must be added, was not only the winning of a single soul. It was a spectacular event that could be used for confessional propaganda.[32] In a memorandum, the illustrious group of clergymen and high office-holders drew up a list of suitable measures for encouraging conversions. Money was considered to be the most effective means. In article eight of the memorandum, it was stipulated that Catholics would be given preference whenever a licence of a tavern, alehouse or mill was to be granted.[33]

As early as 1622, the contracts between authorities and keepers, the so-called *Bestallungen*, had begun to contain confessional clauses. Hans Kuontz of Tegerschen in the Lower District was licensed on condition that he remain a

---

[29] Brändle, 'Volkskultur', 46–8; idem, 'Toggenburger Wirtshäuser', 15–18. On the relations between hymns and Protestant *mentalité*, see the survey of M. Jenny, 'Kirchenlied', in *Theologische Realenzyklopädie* 18 (1994), 602–29.

[30] P. Bösch, 'Die Beziehungen zwischen dem Toggenburg und Zürich seit der Reformation bis zum Ende des 17. Jahrhunderts', in *Zeitschrift für Schweizerische Geschichte* 12 (1932), 375.

[31] St Gall, Stiftsarchiv, Band 1478, 145r.

[32] Duft, *Glaubenssorge*, 178–81, 287–96, 389–98. There were special grants to support converts financially. Another measure was the remission of heavy fines and even the death penalty. In Wildhaus, as an example, Pfarrer Heinrich Michael Schwarz was able to make 50 conversions during the late seventeenth century. He endowed the enormous sum of 4000 gulden to continue his work after his death. Duft, *Glaubenssorge*, 291.

[33] Ibid., 297: 'Wenn Wirtschaften und Mühlen als Lehen vergeben werden, sollen Katholiken begünstigt werden.' Article 7 said that the influence of Protestant personalities should be diminished.

Catholic. One of his duties was to deliver wine to the chapel of his village.[34] Thirty-seven years later, in 1659, Jacob Bridler of Sidwald, in the neighbourhood of the Benedictine monastery of Neu Saint Johann, obtained a licence for an alehouse and a tannery on condition that he did not hand it over to an 'unCatholic hand' (UnCatholische Hand).[35] As Werner Vogler and Heini Oberli have pointed out, the licensing of the Sidwald alehouse, together with the representative monastery, was part of an overall attempt to create a strong Catholic base in the unruly Protestant heart of Toggenburg.[36] Bridler was a successor of Josef Scherrer, one of the conspirators against Hans Ledergerw in 1621, so this licence had, of course, its symbolic dimension. The Sidwaldian keeper and tanner, who also became an important office-holder (Hofammann), had to be rich enough to support his Catholic brethren with financial aid. Their economic dependency on the rich Protestant elite would be weakened, as historian Johannes Duft put it, by installing some prosperous Catholic publicans able to offer credit facilities.[37]

The prince-abbots themselves showed a great deal of interest in public house politics, as the notes in their diaries prove. In 1683, a 'brave convert' was allowed to open a new alehouse,[38] and four years later, Prince-Abbot Coelestin Sfondrati gave directions to the Landvogt (prefect, or governor) in Lichtensteig concerning the tavern in the Hummelwald, a strategically important area on the Ricken pass, just on the road to the closely allied Catholic canton of Schwyz. Sfondrati ordered the purchase of the entire building after a Protestant had gone bankrupt. He considered it to be important to have a Catholic publican at this outpost.[39] Finally, in the year 1697, the only Catholic inhabitant of Brunnadern, who was the keeper of a public house, was given direct financial support to maintain this last religious bastion.[40]

Fostering Catholic people was one tactic, dismissing Protestants another. In 1603, the Protestant mayor and keeper of the Rössli (Little Horse Tavern) in Flawil, Jörg Steiner, was fined heavily because of his many intolerable 'excesses'. After not paying the horrendous sum of ten pounds, he was prohibited from having guests in the future. Members of the Catholic families

---

[34]   J. G. Hagmann, Tegerschen und Degersheim (Breslau, 1922), 51.
[35]   The Bestallung is fully printed in W. Vogler and H. Oberli, 'Pinten und Tavernen im oberen Toggenburg', in Toggenburger Annalen 14 (1987), 56.
[36]   Ibid.
[37]   Duft, Glaubenssorge, 383–8.
[38]   Ibid., 386.
[39]   St Gall, Stiftsarchiv, Band 271, 5: 'Ist auch H. Landtvogt zu Liechtensteig ein gewißeß Wirtshauß mitten in dem Hummelwald, und bishero von den un Catholischen beseßen, und so faillements halber feil worden, zu beziehen, anbefohlen worden. Dise Mittel sind assigniert worden auff die Dispensations Gelter.'
[40]   Duft, Glaubenssorge, 386.

of Murer and Brack replaced Steiner until the year 1712.[41] Hans Caspar Scherrer of Sidwald, a prosperous member of the most distinguished Reformed family in the area, encountered a similar fate in 1683. As three public houses were considered to be too many in this village, Scherrer's licence was not extended.[42] And in 1697, the Reformed tavern keeper of the Star at Magdenau in the Lower District, one of the last Protestant inhabitants of the village, was replaced by a Catholic.[43]

Whereas Protestants seemed to be punished strictly according to the mandates, the authorities were much more tolerant with Catholic publicans. In 1672, the inhabitants of Mosnang in the Lower District protested against the Catholic judge Anthon Brändle and his many faults and crimes. After this, Brändle lost his concession, only to be reinstalled as a judge and publican some months later.[44] In 1683, Jacob Grob in the Hummelwald, also Catholic, was accused of committing many bad deeds (comparable to the 'excesses' of the Protestant Jörg Steiner). But, as the source tells us, 'there must be some patience with him because he is a brave convert.'[45] In the same year, an order was given to replace Hans Jacob Kuontz of Brunnadern only if a more decent Catholic could be found in this small village.[46]

The Protestants were, of course, frustrated about these developments. In their eyes, the authorities were robbing them of their most useful social sites. In their complaints to Zurich of 1680, the Reformed Toggenburgers claimed that 'Reformed public houses had been removed everywhere, and that, as a consequence, there were no more than four or five in the whole district.'[47] In 1702, they protested again, complaining that the Catholics now owned all the public houses.[48] In a pamphlet published during the revolt of 1709, the Protestants repeated their argument, adding that the few remaining Reformed keepers were

---

[41] A. Hofmann, *Das 'Rössli' zu Flawil 1712–1962* (Flawil, 1962), 6.

[42] H. Frank, *Politik, Wirtschaft und Religion in oberen Toggenburg 1650–1690* (Nesslau, 1990), 51.

[43] Duft, *Glaubenssorge*, 386f.

[44] St Gall, Stiftsarchiv, Rubr. 105, Fasz. 1, Nr. 7. Anthon Brändle was, to be sure, no ancestor of mine.

[45] St Gall, Stiftsarchiv, Band 1670, 94. 'Man vermeint, weil er ein guoter *Convertit*, daß mit ihme Geduld zu haben.'

[46] St Gall, Stiftsarchiv, Band 1670, 95. 'Wan man ein Catholische hete, wäre Ursach gewesen, disem die Wirtschaft zu nemmen.'

[47] Zurich, Staatsarchiv, A 339.3: 'Man stellt allenthalben die Evang. Wirtsheüsser ab, also das im gantzen Land nicht mehr über 4 oder 5 sind.'

[48] Duft, *Glaubenssorge*, 387.

not allowed to serve any meat during Lent.[49] The ban on selling meat during Lent had a symbolic dimension, for the Protestants wanted to follow Huldrych Zwingli's famous precedent of eating meat on Good Friday in 1522. They had protested against this prohibition already in 1673.[50]

The rigorous practice of confessionalization and attempts to intensify power over the whole Toggenburg population during the late seventeenth century (*Herrschaftsintensivierung*) caused more and more resistance from members of both confessions, finally leading to the great rebellion that started in 1699. It is one of history's ironies that the Catholic publican of Wattwil, Johann Maggion, played a key role at the beginning of this rebellion. The Toggenburgers of both confessions were holding 'secret meetings' in Maggion's house.[51]

In the hot phase of the rebellion, after the first republican assembly of all citizens (the *Landsgemeinde*) of 1703, the Toggenburgers openly violated the governmental mandates by selling wine wherever and as long as they wanted. Officials of the *Landvogt* von Besenval who tried to stop these rituals of rebellion were ridiculed and driven away, and the ostentatious drinking and dancing just went on.[52] To cite another example, the Grape, the well-known inn of Ulrich Steger of Lichtensteig, was a rebel stronghold, where the Reformed Toggenburgers met their allies from Zurich and jailed their pro-abbot opponents.[53]

Even in the worst phase of confessional hatred, however, some inter-confessional contacts in public houses continued. As the Reformed minister Alexander Bösch wrote in his autobiography, his son Alexander the Younger celebrated his wedding, together with no fewer than ninety-eight guests, in the house of the Catholic publican and judge Hans Martin Oettli in 1678. In this year, Caspar Scherrer still held his tavern in nearby Sidwald, but the Bösch family preferred to be entertained by a Catholic.[54]

In the Treaty of Baden of 1718 between the Swiss cantons of Bern and Zurich on the one hand, and the prince-abbot of Saint Gall on the other, the Protestant

---

[49] Zurich, Zentralbibliothek, Alte Drucke, 18 446: 'Die Wirthschaften werden den Evangelischen besten theils entzogen, und denen die solche behalten, aufgeburdet, die Catholische Fasttag zubeachten.'

[50] Zurich, Staatsarchiv, A 339.3, pt. 15.

[51] Hässig, *Anfänge*, 41.

[52] Ibid., 177.

[53] Ibid., 172; F. Brändle, 'Republik und Glaube: Symbolische Handlungen der Aufständischen während der "Toggenburger Wirren", 1700–1709', in *Toggenburger Jahrbuch* 2 (2002), 53-70.

[54] L. Heiligensetzer (ed.), *Alexander Bösch: Liber familiarium personalium: Lebensbericht und Familiengeschichte des Toggenburger Pfarrers Alexander Bösch (1618–1693)* (Basel, 2001), 135.

Toggenburgers reached an equal distribution of inns as well as taverns.[55] When a *Täffry* was allocated, confession was no longer an issue. The confessional clauses, as a result, disappeared from the inn contracts (*Bestallungen*).[56] We can imagine the frustration of the abbot's chancellor in Lichtensteig who complained about the increasing number of public houses in possession of unloved Protestants. After compiling a detailed register of taverns and alehouses for every parish, recording the name, confession, and office of the publican, the chancellor demanded that both confessions should have eighteen public houses each in the bi-confessional villages. In reality, however, the Protestants owned no fewer than twenty-seven.[57]

There are some indications that equal distribution favoured a more confession-orientated sociability. In the bi-confessional city of Lichtensteig in 1740, two rival Catholic candidates for a seat on the urban council were looking for support – in fact, they were spending more than 200 gulden to buy votes. To enter Reformed public houses, they had to engage Protestant 'brokers' paying for wine and food in the name of their ambitious patrons. The source tells us that there was strong confessional segregation. Guests of both confessions mingled in only one establishment, the representative *Rathausstube* (the official communal public house located in the town hall).[58]

There were, however, some signs of religious toleration as well. In 1759 or 1760, Protestants in the bi-confessional village of Saint Peterzell asked for a tavern of their own. The *Landvogt* refused the concession; but in 1762, after weighing the advantages and disadvantages of a Protestant tavern, the Catholic priest of the village finally opted to allow it, on the grounds that it was much better for the Reformed villagers to hold meetings in a room of their own than to be disturbing the mass all the time.[59]

The prince-abbots of Saint Gall and their officials were well aware of the importance of public houses as political meeting points for the rebellious Reformed subjects of the Upper District. As a result, they used the right of granting licences for taverns and alehouses, the so-called *Täffry*, as an important source of power. In the later seventeenth century, Catholics were systematically favoured in the granting of licences. The newly confessionalized

---

[55] *Die eidgenössischen Abschiede VII, II, 1712–1743* (Basel, 1860), 1388.

[56] Vogler and Oberli, 'Pinten', 56–7.

[57] St Gall, Stiftsarchiv, Rubr. 85, Fasz 17. 'die Reformierten aber haben 27. Da doch alle diese Orth *mixtae religionis*, mithin wan sie so strikte zue observieren ist, die Catholischen und Reformierten jeden Theil 18. haben an solchen mixten Orthen.'

[58] For a broader analysis of this spectacular case of corruption, see F. Brändle, 'Wahltag war vor dem Zahltag! Korruption in Lichtensteig im Jahre 1740', in: *Toggenburger Jahrbuch* 1 (2000), 33–48.

[59] St Gall, Stiftsarchiv, R 113/F1. I am grateful to Jost Kirchgraber for this reference.

public houses were intended as Counter Reformation strongholds, run, if at all possible, by converts. Catholic client keepers had to undermine the wealthy Protestant elite by providing credit to their poorer brethren. The notoriously poor Catholic population of the area was to become more independent of Reformed patrons. At the same time, the position of the leading Reformed families like the Scherrer of Nesslau was severly weakened. Indeed, only one or two Protestants were able to hold on to their public houses until 1700.

The Reformed Toggenburgers were well aware of losing their 'social sites' and protested several times against this fatal development. I would argue that the successful confessionalization of public houses during the late seventeenth century was one main reason for the powerful uprising of 1699. The rebellious Toggenburgers celebrated their victory over the prince-abbot by ignoring detested official mandates and much-hated restrictions. The Treaty of Baden then brought the principle of equal distribution of public houses in 1718. This equal distribution led to a more confession-oriented sociability. The Protestants, it can be said, finally succeeded in defending the right to have their own 'social sites'.

Taverns in Nuremberg Prints at the Time of the German Reformation[*]

Alison Stewart

During the sixteenth century, representations of taverns and inns increased in both prominence and number within the visual art of northern Europe. From Hieronymus Bosch to Pieter Bruegel, painters and designers of prints made images employing taverns and inns as the setting for religious and secular subjects.[1] Bosch's panel painting of a travelling merchant, variously titled the *Wayfarer*, *Peddler*, and the *Prodigal Son*, from ca 1510 (Figure 2), includes one of the earliest renderings of the tavern or inn in European art.[2] Traditional interpretations of the work's subject as the Prodigal Son underscore the religious and moralizing meanings both painting and inn have held within the discipline of art history.[3]

The Prodigal Son 'wasting his substance in riotous living' (Luke 15:13) undoubtedly offered fuel for visual thought in such imagery.[4] In Bosch's painting, the man with tattered clothing, bandaged leg, and basket on back walks to the right while looking back over his shoulder toward the inn, with what may be longing, even regret. Bosch's inn stands in a partial state of disrepair. The roof

---

[*] Research for this essay was supported by the Department of Art & Art History and the Hixson-Lied College of Fine and Performing Arts at the University of Nebraska-Lincoln. Parts of this essay appeared earlier in my 'Paper Festivals and Popular Entertainment. The Kermis Woodcuts of Sebald Beham in Reformation Nuremberg' in *Sixteenth Century Journal* 34 (1993), 301–50.

[1] For Netherlandish images of taverns in religious settings, see E. M. Kavaler, *Pieter Bruegel: Parables of Order and Enterprise* (Cambridge, 1999), especially 152, 154, 185, and 189; K. Renger, *Lockere Gesellschaft: Zur Ikonographie des Verlorenen Sohnes und von Wirtshausszenen in der niederländischen Malerei* (Berlin, 1970). Renger identifies many inn scenes as representations of the Prodigal Son.

[2] For Bosch, see W. Gibson, *Hieronymus Bosch* (New York, 1973), 103–4; C. de Tolnay, *Hieronymus Bosch* (Basel, 1937), figure 88; P. Reuterswärd, *Hieronymus Bosch* (Stockholm, 1970), figure 38.

[3] On the Prodigal Son, see Renger, *Lockere Gesellschaft*, and W. Stechow, 'Lusus Laetitiaeque Modus', in *Art Quarterly* 35 (1972), 165–75; For late sixteenth- and early seventeenth-century paintings, see Stechow, 'Lusus'.

[4] Stechow, 'Lusus', 165.

Figure 2: Hieronymus Bosch, *The Wayfarer*. Oil on panel, ca 1510-20 (Courtesy Museum Boijmans Van Beuningen, Rotterdam).

and windows are riddled with holes and one window shutter hangs precariously from a hinge.

Art historians have interpreted Bosch's inn as an emblem of moral degeneration based on its physical decay,[5] yet the fabric of the building appears intact. In the doorway of the inn the man fondling the breast of the woman and the man urinating around the corner support the moralizing interpretation. In addition, the pigs eating from the trough in front of the doorway appear to identify the man at the centre of Bosch's painting as the Prodigal Son – seen, for example, in Albrecht Dürer's engraving of the subject from ca 1496.[6] Art historians have, in sum, viewed the tavern – and its more ambitious counterpart, the inn – within sixteenth-century Northern art as a locus of negative behaviour whose representation elicited a moralizing interpretation from the viewer.

This essay expands this traditional moralizing and negative approach to public houses by investigating images of taverns designed by Sebald Beham, a pupil of Dürer in Germany. Published in Beham's home town of Nuremberg between 1528 and 1535 as woodcut prints, the works have as their subject kermis (*Kirchweih*), which was centred around a tavern or inn in the sixteenth century.[7] Kermis was the most popular peasant festival during the late Middle Ages and Reformation period and it celebrated the anniversary of either a church's consecration or saint's day. In Beham's kermis images, the exterior of a tavern provides the setting for celebrating by peasants and a few members of other social classes. In this essay, Beham's *Large Kermis* woodcut (Figure 3), the physically largest and most complex example of the theme, will be explored for the variety of meanings and associations the tavern held in sixteenth-century Germany and that reach beyond art history's traditional moralizing approach. I argue that art historians need to consider a wider range of sources and associations when considering the tavern, including those relating to eating and drinking, social gatherings, and peasant festivals. Only then will tavern and kermis be viewed neutrally if not joyously.

For Beham, I would suggest, the tavern becomes the setting and symbol for celebrating and drinking, and for the body with its various historical meanings.

---

[5]   Renger, *Lockere Gesellschaft*, 90; Gibson, *Hieronymus Bosch*, 103.

[6]   This print is reproduced in W. L. Strauss (ed.), *The Illustrated Bartsch*, vol. 10 (New York, 1980), 25 (no. 28).

[7]   Here I investigate the exteriors of taverns. Beham's *Spinning Bee* woodcut from ca 1524 illustrates a tavern interior as does Erhard Schön's *Peasant Wedding Celebration* from 1527. For illustrations, see M. Geisberg, *The German Single-Leaf Woodcut: 1500–1550*, rev. and ed. W. L. Strauss (New York, 1974), nos 154 and 1171; for discussion, A. Stewart, 'The First Peasant Festivals: Eleven Woodcuts Produced in Reformation Nuremberg by Barthel and Sebald Beham and Erhard Schön, ca 1524 to 1535' (PhD Columbia University, 1986), 254–331 and 226–64.

Rather than one moralizing meaning, the tavern had a complex range of meanings that requires understanding the historical and social setting of the images' making, Reformation Nuremberg. Beham's tavern and kermis images are integrally linked to the new institution of the Lutheran religion in Nuremberg, officially adopted by the city in March 1525 after several years of gradual acceptance. The tavern in Beham's Nuremberg prints becomes a multivalent image whose various associations add to the richness and complexity of meaning for Beham's kermis prints. The tavern thus serves as an important focal point and nexus of meanings.[8]

In this essay, then, taverns and inns are discussed within the context of kermis and drinking, and a complex range of contemporary responses to these social practices. Emphasis will be placed on what we can learn about taverns from contemporary documents, and the attitudes toward taverns and drinking reflected in legislation issued by the city of Nuremberg, in proverbial expressions, and in carnival plays. The role of the clergy at kermis and taverns will also be discussed, as will Erasmus's *Book of Inns*; proverbs and carnival plays; animal symbolism; early modern drinking practices; the four effects of wine; and scatological humour. Because drinking at taverns brought with it expulsion from both the upper and lower body, a re-thinking of another art historical response, revulsion, is encouraged and contrasted within a contextual reading of scatological imagery (in accordance with attitudes of the time). In this way, Norbert Elias's 'civilizing process' and ideas by other writers on German literature, including the literary figure of Grobianus, will be evaluated.

In the German kermis prints, a prominently placed building can be identified as a tavern by the presence of a pole hung with flag or sign, cloth or pitcher. In the *Large Kermis*, Beham places a pole with cloth and covered beaker in a window-like opening over the tavern's door. Cloth and vessel indicate that food and drink are served at the tavern; the cloth appears to be a tablecloth like the one on the table before the tavern's doorway. In addition three closely related kermis woodcuts employ a circle, or a circle inscribed with an x, indicating the availability of wine.[9] In Bosch's *Wayfarer*, a sign with duck or swan, attached to the side of the building, probably refers to the tavern's name. Nearly a half century later (ca 1568), Bruegel's *Peasant Kermis* painting (now

---

[8]   For ambiguity of meaning, see E. Muir, *Ritual in Early Modern Europe* (New York, 1997), 14; for multivalency, Stewart, 'Paper Festivals'.

[9]   W. Treue and K. Goldmann (eds), *Das Hausbuch der Mendelschen Zwölfbrüderstiftung zu Nürnberg: Deutsche Handwerksbilder des 15. und 16. Jahrhunderts* (Munich, 1965), text vol., 115; H. Bauer, *Tisch und Tafel in alten Zeiten: Aus der Kulturgeschichte der Gastronomie* (Leipzig, 1967), 137; Stewart, 'Paper Festivals', figures 2 and 6–8.

in Vienna) makes use of a similar flag over the front door.[10] Bosch's and Bruegel's Netherlandish paintings appear to draw on the northern European cultural tradition that also gave rise to Beham's German *Large Kermis*.

A tavern dominates the centre of Beham's *Large Kermis*, before which at least a dozen people talk, drink, and embrace. Above the tavern at left, a castle looms large before the horizon, a possible reference to Nuremberg's imperial castle, or *Burg*, and to the emperor to whom the city of Nuremberg was directly responsible. Like Bosch's inn, the tavern here has fallen into disrepair and thus can be seen to exist in a state of moral degeneration for its guests. But the tavern is not singled out for decay; the similar dilapidated condition of several secular buildings behind it casts doubt on such a moralizing interpretation. Just as cracks on the tavern could have indicated moral decay to morally driven viewers, they could also have pointed to rural poverty or simply to the building's advanced age to many others. More certain is the fact that Nuremberg's town councillors, the town government, viewed taverns as breeding grounds for undesirable behaviour at the time the kermis woodcuts were made. In 1528 the council commanded residents of Nuremberg to go to church and hear the sermon early on Sundays and feast days, and it discouraged residents from visiting taverns and drinking, gambling, and engaging in frivolities and laziness.[11] The council also forbade dancing in 1532 at all times of the day at taverns and inns, and knives (*Stechmesser*) were banished from such locations for butchers and their journeymen because of resulting injuries and deaths.[12] Council members expressed concern that taverns and inns were the site of discussions by Sacramentarians, a religious group more radical than Nuremberg's own Lutheran religion and not allowed in Nuremberg, and by insurrectionary individuals at the time of the Peasants' War.[13]

---

[10] For Bruegel's kermis painting, see W. Gibson, *Bruegel* (New York and Toronto, 1977), 163, figure 116; R.-M. and R. Hagen, *Pieter Bruegel the Elder c. 1525–1569: Peasants, Fools and Demons*, translated Michael Claridge (Cologne, 1994), 79 (in colour). For Netherlandish prints of the subject pre-dating Bruegel's painting, see Kavaler, *Pieter Bruegel*, 188–90; H.-J. Raupp, *Bauernsatiren: Entstehung und Entwicklung des bäuerlichen Genres in der deutschen und niederländischen Kunst ca. 1470–1570* (Niederzier, 1986), 246–9.

[11] *Mandate ... wider die Wiedertäufer* (n.d. [1528]); Nuremberg, Staatsarchiv, Rep. 63² Titel III: Nürnberger Mandate, no. 19a. Gambling and excessive drinking are mentioned in connection with taverns in Nuremberg, Stadtarchiv, Rep. A6: Mandate, 1529, f. Diiir, although no specific occasion for these problems is included. For texts of both, see Stewart, 'First *Peasant Festivals'*, 215 n. 217 and 218.

[12] Nuremberg, Stadtarchiv, Rep. A6: Mandate (8 April 1532). For kermis, see Nuremberg, Staatsarchiv, Rep. 63–1a: Nürnberger Mandate, Bd. A, no. 86 (26 May 1548).

[13] Nuremberg, Staatsarchiv, Rep. 63–1a: Nürnberger Mandate, Bd. A, no. 29 (19 January 1532); L. P. Buck, 'The Containment of Civil Insurrection: Nürnberg and the Peasants' Revolt, 1524–1525' (Ph.D. Ohio State University, 1971), 54.

Figure 3:   Sebald Beham, *Large Kermis*. Woodcut, 1535 (Courtesy Ashmolean Museum, Oxford).

Yet, it is important to keep in mind that these views are those of the authorities constituting Nuremberg's official culture, which, although governing all of Nuremberg society, comprised but a small fraction of the population. The tavern undoubtedly served a greater function in society than as centre of gambling, stabbing, and as a meeting place for religious and social radicals. In fact, the functions of public houses across England and Europe were broader and more positive, including the provision of space for people to gather in general and at kermis and other carnival-like celebrations, and for conducting commerce.[14] Public houses also served as sites for the performance of carnival plays inside and outside Nuremberg.[15] Socially, German taverns and inns were broadly based, and included women among innkeepers. Public houses came in larger and smaller sizes, the latter visited by poor and common folk.[16] The cracked facade of the tavern in Beham's print, then, might point to the low economic status of the innkeeper and village.

Peter Burke views such taverns and inns as a public setting that transmitted popular culture, while Peter Stallybrass and Allon White link tavern and popular festivals in the expression 'the tavern and the popular festive scene'.[17] Although Burke's discussion centres on the English inn, alehouse or beer cellar, many of the activities that went on in these institutions (card playing, cock fights, and the game of ninepins) are similar to those of their German relatives, thereby validating a comparison.[18]

At Nuremberg, the council issued a variety of printed mandates that offer insights into the council's views on taverns and what it believed took place there. In 1530 council members stated that at the occasion of kermis gangs and crowds were creating disturbances at taverns and inns. According to the town fathers, innkeepers offered prizes for the largest group on the skittles or ninepins field, or on fields where games of chance were played. In Beham's *Large Kermis* at right, a skittles field, game of chance below the Maypole, and crowds can be seen. In order to reduce noise and violence, the council commanded that public houses not be visited at kermis in large groups with drums and fifes.[19]

---

[14] P. Stallybrass and A. White, *The Politics and Poetics of Transgression* (Ithaca, 1986), 30.

[15] D. Wuttke (ed.), *Fastnachtspiele des 15. und 16. Jahrhunderts* (Stuttgart, 1973), 402.

[16] M. Wiesner, *Working Women in Renaissance Germany* (New Brunswick, N.J., 1986), 133.

[17] Stallybrass and White, *Politics*, 198.

[18] P. Burke, *Popular Culture in Early Modern Europe* (London, 1978), 109.

[19] 'mit grossen hauffen/auch Trummeln vndd pfeyffen zubesuchen': Nuremberg, Stadtarchiv Nürnberg: Mandate (23 August 1530); and Nuremberg, Staatsarchiv: Nürnberger Mandate, vol. A, 52, no. 24: 'Tentz vf dem Land'.

Nuremberg authorities also condemned excessive drinking (*zechen*) at kermis both in this decree and in another mandate of 1537.[20]

The varied views of taverns and inns and the variety of activities taking place at them point to a broad and popular audience that frequented taverns. In fact, according to the artist-writer Joachim von Sandrart in the seventeenth century, Beham himself owned his own inn at Frankfurt late in life (although recent studies lend no credence to such ownership).[21] In any case, taverns like the one Beham showcases in his *Large Kermis* would likely have also served as an indoor site for hanging and viewing prints with the kermis theme.[22]

Nuremberg's public houses provided services far beyond those indicated in the town's council records. We have seen that food and drink were served at Nuremberg taverns. For German inns and taverns in general the availability of wine or beer was indicated by the display of drinking vessels made of iron, by bush or twigs, and by paintings on wood or tin hung before the building. In Beham's *Large Kermis*, the pole extending from the window specifically denotes the sale of wine as does the circle inscribed with cross in his *Kermis (Erlangen)* and its two related kermis woodcuts.[23] In the *Large Kermis*, the availability and importance of wine are underscored by the grape vine growing against it on a trellis.

The tavern and table before it form the centre of activity in Beham's *Large Kermis* woodcut (Figure 4). Behind the rectangular table sits a man who, judging from his dress, is probably learned; he is accentuated by the tall arched doorway above his head. He sits behind a rectangular table reminiscent of *Last Supper* imagery, such as Leonardo da Vinci's painting from 1498–99. The placement of a round tray at centre, however, visually links Beham's woodcut to northern European imagery of the Last Supper theme, including Dirck Bouts's painting from ca 1467 and Dürer's Lutheran-inspired woodcut from 1523.[24] Beham may have deliberately inserted such visual references as a play on earlier Last Supper images, including those by his teacher Dürer. The core component of the Last Supper, the sacrament and its nature, had earlier been

---

[20] For the mandate of 1537, see Nuremberg, Staatsarchiv: Nürnberger Mandate, vol. A, 116, no. 49 (17 September 1537).

[21] M. Carroll, 'Peasant Festivity and Political Identity in the Sixteenth Century' in *Art History* 10 (1987), 294; S. Goddard, *The World in Miniature: Engravings by the Little Masters, 1500–1550*, exhibition catalogue (Spencer Museum of Art, University of Kansas, Lawrence, 1988), 222.

[22] Stewart, 'Paper Festivals', 347–8.

[23] Treue and Goldmann, *Das Hausbuch*, text vol., 115; Bauer, *Tisch und Tafel*, 137.

[24] For illustrations of Bouts's and Leonardo's *Last Suppers*, see L. Goldscheider, *Leonardo da Vinci* (New York, 1959), plate 73, and J. Snyder, *Northern Renaissance Art: Painting, Sculpture, the Graphic Arts from 1350 to 1575* (New York, 1985), colour plate 25.

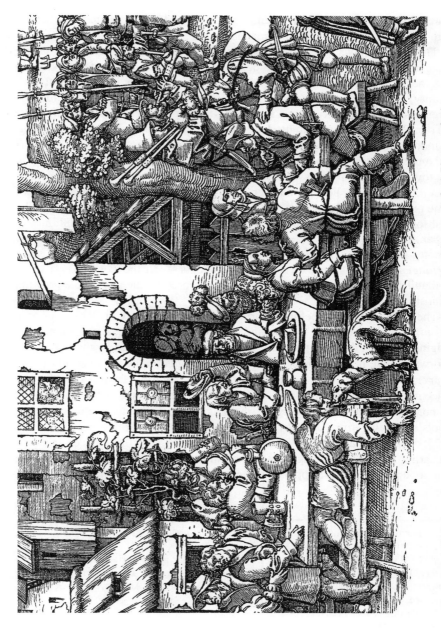

Figure 4: Sebald Beham, *Large Kermis*, detail of centre (courtesy Ashmolean Museum, Oxford. Photo: author).

widely debated at Nuremberg taverns and inns, leading the council to prohibit such discussions there.[25]

Beham offers a wide variety of activities before the tavern. At the left end of the table, a man dressed in slashed clothing appears to call the peasant holding a beaker to military service, a function lansquenets from villages served in the sixteenth century.[26] Judging from the horrified expression on the peasant's face, it is possible that the lansquenet has just informed the peasant of his conscription (or some equally unwelcome news). The male peasant between them, who wears a pointed peasant hat and who places one hand on each of their shoulders, appears to be attempting to reconcile them. To the right, a couple in profile embraces enthusiastically before the grape vine, while the man behind them serves as go-between with the viewer. His gesturing hand and beaker suggest that the wine he holds, produced from grapes and vines like those behind him, contributed to the couple's loving attitude. Another couple embraces within the darkness of the tavern's doorway – reminiscent of Bosch's imagery in Figure 2 – and another man seated on the bench before the table places one arm around his companion's waist. She gently touches his shoulder and returns his gaze in a manner now recognized for the sixteenth century as indicating visual intimacy.

Beham underscores the importance of wine and its amorous effects through the trellis and the embraces of these three couples. He includes other effects of wine as well. The man carrying a box or container over his shoulder, at the right end of the table, has been identified as a peddler,[27] and he offers dice to a peasant man and a more formally dressed woman who show little interest in the offer. In Beham's time, giving in to the lures of betting on dice was believed to be a common result of the enjoyment of wine, as were amorous embracing and vomiting. Gambling was enjoyed across the social classes, even by such well respected members of Nuremberg's community as Albrecht Dürer. Playing cards and coins were found behind wainscoting in Dürer's home, a discovery that not only indicates the enjoyment of gaming in Nuremberg, but also suggests the necessity of hiding evidence of it from the authorities. Gambling was forbidden during the sermon on feast days by Nuremberg's authorities in 1528.[28] Because kermis was considered to be a feast day in Nuremberg, the authorities would have deemed gambling inappropriate and impermissible, at least during the church sermon.

---

[25] Buck, 'Containment', 54; H. Moeller, *Die Bauern in der deutschen Litteratur des 16. Jahrhunderts* (Berlin, 1902), 101 n. 41.

[26] R. W. Scribner, *For the Sake of Simple Folk: Popular Propaganda for the German Reformation* (Cambridge, 1981), 31, 40.

[27] Renger, *Lockere Gesellschaft*, 89.

[28] M. Mende, 'Der Maler mit dem Silberblick', in *Merian* 6 (1981), 70; Nuremberg, Staatsarchiv, Rep. 63–2 Titel III Nr. l9a: Nürnberger Mandate, 1528.

The fact that the time on the church clock at left indicates eight hours after sunrise, thus after the sermon and in the afternoon, may mean that this was not a problem here – nonetheless, despite its popularity at kermis, members of Nuremberg's elite may well have considered the use of dice unacceptable in the context of a church holiday. Patrician council members who were responsible for penning legislation, along with members of the clergy, might have hoped to reduce the presence of gambling at kermis even while acknowledging its existence.

Seated before the tavern of Beham's *Large Kermis* are men from several social classes who can be identified by their clothing. In the sixteenth century, class determined clothing and ordinances attempted to keep an individual's dress class-appropriate.[29] As noted above, a learned man, presumably a member of the clergy, sits before the tavern door; at left, a peasant greets him. They are accompanied by a man dressed as a prince at right. The prince's social position, indicated by his brocaded shirt, wide neck chains, and plumed hat, can be seen in a woodcut by Jost Amman.[30] The prince touches the clergyman's arm and shoulder suggesting animated talk, friendship, or persuasion. As the peasant raises his hat in respect or greeting, he offers a tumbler of drink to the clergyman, who wears a thick coat with lapels and the standard scholar's headdress of flat hat with short sides. The hat appears similar to one worn by the male dancer at far right and by the bishop of Freising in a portrait from ca 1528.[31]

The face of this clergyman is similar to Martin Luther's, as depicted in Hans Brosamer's woodcut from 1530.[32] This print, along with numerous painted portraits of Luther, made the Reformer's features known to the populace. But the clergyman in Beham's *Large Kermis* could have been seen less as a portrait of Luther than as a general likeness of a member of that religious group for whom the consumption of alcoholic drinks was common among the rural clergy, in particular at kermis. The inclusion of a pastor before the tavern at Beham's *Large Kermis* carried various associations depending on the viewer.

Clergy regularly attended kermis. Documents indicate that several members of the clergy and a judge sat together at an Austrian kermis in 1525, and members of the clergy were given money for drinking (*zechen*) at kermis in Lower

---

[29] For clothing ordinances in Nuremberg, see J. Baader (ed.), *Nürnberger Polizeiordnungen aus dem XIII. bis XV. Jahrhundert* (Stuttgart, 1861), 65–7, 95–112.

[30] J. Amman, *Trachtenbuch* (Nuremberg: Hans Weigel, 1577), fol. Br.

[31] *Portrait of Philipp van der Pfalz, Bishop of Freising* by Barthel Beham: J. Kettlewell, *The Hyde Collection Catalogue* (Glen Falls, N.Y., 1981), 72–3.

[32] For Brosamer's *Luther*, see Geisberg, *German Single-Leaf Woodcut*, no. 423.

Franconia, closer to Nuremberg, in 1535.[33] Members of the clergy (ministers, preachers, and chaplains) in Nuremberg's neighbouring territory of Brandenburg-Ansbach-Kulmbach were also asked in 1536 if they held kermis. This question suggests that members of the clergy may have still sponsored kermis, or at least attended it themselves in their own village, if not in other villages.[34] The same authorities told the Catholic clergy some thirty years later that they should not go to another village's kermis, thereby underscoring the authorities' intention to limit kermis visits (and possibly the clergy's reluctance to give them up).[35]

Members of the clergy who visited taverns at kermis were probably local rural lower clergy, and not the more prominent and socially conservative members of Nuremberg's urban upper clergy, who vocally criticized and condemned kermis as a secular celebration. In general, pastors were viewed as representatives of social authority and usually possessed greater learning and social status than did parishioners. The prominent placement of such a cleric at the centre of the *Large Kermis* underscores his authority as the local rural pastor, whom contemporaries saw as an extension of the state and reinforcer of moral and social order, as Bob Scribner observed.[36]

At kermis as well as more generally, alcohol consumption was considered a normal part of a clergyman's life. Parishes included wine as one of a pastor's benefits, and clergymen drank alcohol on a daily basis.[37] In Mögeldorf the pastor also ran the tavern, much to the discontent of the council. In 1524 the Nuremberg council instructed Mögeldorf's pastor to stop selling alcohol or the bottom of his barrels would be smashed.[38] But the presence of clergy imbibing at kermis could also have been understood by council members as an indication that Bacchus – more than God or the anniversary of the church's consecration – was being celebrated. For others, however, including peasants, drinking at kermis, even by the clergy, was considered a normal and acceptable practice.

---

[33] G. Franz, *Quellen zur Geschichte des Bauernkrieges* (Darmstadt, 1963), vol. 2, 338 no. 161; K.-S. Kramer, *Bauern und Bürger im nachmittelalterlichen Unterfranken: Eine Volkskunde auf Grund archivalischer Quellen* (Würzburg, 1957), 71.

[34] E. Sehling (ed.), *Die evangelischen Kirchenordnungen des XVI. Jahrhunderts*, vol. 11 pt 1 (Tübingen, 1961); pt 26, 321–1: 'Item darnach soll gefragt werden der pfarrer [prediger, caplonen] desselben orts, wie hernach volgt: ob er kirchwei und hagelfeier halte'.

[35] Sehling, *Kirchenordnungen*, pt 8, 357, 'Kapitelsordnung 1565/1578': 'Es soll kein priester zum andern auf die kirchweihe gehen, weder an der rechten noch an der nachkirchweihe'.

[36] Scribner, *Simple Folk*, 57–8, and n. 63. See Stewart, 'Paper Festivals', 332–3, for more on rural clergy.

[37] F. Blanke, 'Reformation und Alkoholismus', in *Zwingliana* 9 (1953), 18, 76.

[38] Nuremberg, Staatsarchiv: Ratsverlässe 700, fol. 3v (13 Feb. 1524): 'Den pfarer von megeldorff sagen das er seins schenckens abste, wie nicht, so wird mon den fessern die poden auss schlahen.'

Perhaps for this reason, Luther and his followers were berated by their opponents for falling short of cleansing ordinary people of the kind of excesses that kermis encouraged. One such opponent was Sebastian Franck, who especially accused Luther of failing to curb widespread drinking. In his *On the Horrible Vice of Drunkenness* from 1528, Franck complains that being drunk has become the Bible for many Lutherans, and that fasting and abstaining – what he recommends as a cure for drunkenness – are considered sinful and papist.[39] Franck despised Luther (who returned the sentiment). Luther claimed that Franck's radical spirit was blown into his ear by his wife, Ottilie, Beham's sister.[40] If Lutherans were viewed as drunkards by Franck and other Spiritualists, the presence of a minister at the centre of the *Large Kermis* might raise the question of whether Beham was criticizing religious men from Nuremberg (i.e., Lutherans) for drinking at all in 1535, no matter how common the practice. On the other hand, although Beham does show the pastor across the table from a drunk peasant, thus in his presence, he does not actually depict the pastor drinking.

In the polemical battle for Protestant support, criticism of Lutherans' excessive drinking appeared in print as early as 1525 outside Nuremberg, where it was not limited to Franck. The Anabaptist Ludwig Hätzer railed against Luther's concept of 'evangelical freedom' that praised Satan and boozing.[41] Luther himself believed that many of his followers misunderstood his concept of 'evangelical freedom' as granting *carte blanche* to the expression of the basest of needs. This failure to comprehend the true meaning of Luther's words is considered one way in which the Reformation indirectly encouraged excessive drinking.[42] Surely the presence of a pastor at kermis in Lutheran Nuremberg may have indicated to Luther's opponents that kermis celebrators in Nuremberg were drunken Lutherans, or at least that the pastor shown gave tacit approval to such drinking. Keeping in mind, however, that the definitions of 'drunkenness' or alcohol abuse in early modern Germany were quite different and more nuanced than they are today, the presence of a pastor in Beham's print could carry a double meaning: at once pointing up the normalcy of kermis drinking, and at the same time, indicating that it fit the description of the Reformer and his 'well-known fondness for beer and wine'. Luther approved of moderate drinking, which to him could include occasional inebriation, or intoxication, as distinct from more habitual drunkenness (including drunkenness

---

[39]   Blanke, 'Reformation und Alkoholismus', 80.
[40]   *D. Martin Luthers Werke: Kritische Gesamtausgabe* 58/1 (Weimar, 1883–1948), 219; H. Weigelt, 'Sebastian Franck', in *Gestalten der Kirchengeschichte* 6 (1981), 120.
[41]   Blanke, 'Alkholismus', 80–81, cites Hätzer's *Von den evangelischen Zechen* of 1525.
[42]   Blanke, 'Alkholismus', 80–81.

on a daily basis). Thus, Luther condemned only habitual drunkenness, not the occasional indulgence.[43]

But it must be remembered that the *Large Kermis* was published at Nuremberg, the Lutheran stronghold of south Germany, and that most of the individual printed images, or impressions, of the woodcut from the sixteenth century were required to be identified with both the location of Nuremberg and the publisher's name. For the *Large Kermis* that meant Albrecht Glockendon within Beham's lifetime, and Hans Weygel in the second half of the sixteenth century.[44] It seems unlikely, therefore, that a woodcut circulating widely in Nuremberg would be viewed as blatantly critical of the town's religious leader, Martin Luther.

If impressions of the print were distributed outside the imperial city, as I believe they were, then Luther's critics could have seen a likeness of Luther in the face of the pastor seated in the midst of drinking before the tavern. Like John Calvin, Franck supported greater moderation in drink and criticized Luther's 'fondness for beer and wine.' But in the sixteenth century, particularly in Lutheran Nuremberg, total abstention from drink was a new approach that had not yet become part of the cultural vocabulary. Whereas Calvin, Martin Bucer, and Ulrich Zwingli demanded a strict moral code (perhaps Franck and Beham as well) in which the outward behaviour was to conform to one's inner piety, Luther's theology stressed rather the individual Christian's personal relationship with God. That relationship with God included the enjoyment of one of His best gifts, wine and beer.[45]

In 1523, over a decade before the publication of Beham's *Large Kermis*, Erasmus of Rotterdam published his *Book of Inns* (*Diversoria*) and his own account of what must have been a large German inn, judging from the nearly 100 people from all social classes he said gathered in its dining room. According to Edward Muir, 'dining rituals' can serve as markers of social identity. Erasmus's account of the inside of a German inn demonstrates Muir's point. When Erasmus describes the eating habits he observed in the inn, he describes those of a rich mix of old and young, men and women, adults and children, nobles and peasants. They ate food from a communal dish into which each person dipped a piece of bread, ate, and re-dipped. This mixing of hands, bread,

---

[43] B. A. Tlusty, 'Defining "drunk" in early modern Germany', in *Contemporary Drug Problems* (Fall 1994), 427–51, esp. 437–8, 443–6; idem., *Bacchus and Civic Order: The Culture of Drink in Early Modern Germany* (Charlottesville, 2001), 48, 72–4.

[44] For the various states and impressions of Beham's *Large Kermis*, see Stewart, 'First Peasant Festivals', 400–401.

[45] Tlusty, 'Defining "drunk"', 437, 438, 445.

even saliva in the dish used by all resulted for Erasmus in what Muir calls 'the undisciplined mixing of classes, functions, and bodily processes'.[46]

Here Erasmus views the inn as the site of distasteful experiences involving the mixing of bodily fluids. Erasmus's view is an elite one involving social distancing and attitudes that reveal the 'civilizing process' Norbert Elias proposed fifty years ago. According to Elias, Erasmus, other humanists, and members of the secular authorities attempted to effect a social transformation in which the rough customs and manners of ordinary people – i.e. most people – would be smoothed and cleaned up, and made more like those of the elite, who attempted to induce the change. To be civilized meant no more picking one's teeth and nose, defecating, or vomiting before others.[47] To be civilized meant privatizing one's bodily processes.

Humanists often employed animals to label undesirable human behavior with what Muir called animal-human opposition. Erasmus called the impatient youthful eater a 'wolf' in his *Manners for Children* from 1530: 'Some people put their hands in the dishes the moment they have sat down. Wolves do that … .'[48] The dog was also often employed as an emblem of the indiscriminate eater or imbiber. In Italy, Giovanni della Casa condemned slothful eaters in his *Galateo* from 1558 when he described those 'lying like swine with their snouts in the soup, not once lifting their heads and turning their eyes, still less their hands, from the food, puffing out both cheeks as if they were blowing a trumpet or trying to fan a fire, not eating but gorging themselves … .' As Muir observed, this mixing of animal and human 'threatened the whole system of distinction made through manners'.[49]

When humanist-writers and print designers in Germany employed animals in their sixteenth-century visual and textual discourse to underscore human's animal-like habits, both pigs and dogs became popular emblems for gluttony. [50] By including these animals before a centrally located tavern, Beham marked the building within the humanist tradition as a place where inordinate imbibing took place. In the *Large Kermis*, such drinking led to the vomiting of one peasant from a bench probably from wine, judging from the nearby grape vines and grapes. The drunken man appears as 'drunk as a swine' (*voll wie ein schwein*), thus visualizing an expression seen also in sixteenth-century woodcuts. The pig alone served as an emblem of gluttony from the Seven Deadly Sins in prints

---

[46] Muir, *Ritual*, 127–8.

[47] N. Elias, *The History of Manners: The Civilizing Process* (New York, 1978).

[48] Muir, *Ritual*, 128, here citing Elias, *History of Manners*, 89.

[49] Muir, *Ritual*, 127. On drunkards as animals, see Tlusty, *Bacchus*, 54–5, 59–62, 65–7, 74–5.

[50] A. Bömer, 'Anstand und Etikette nach den Theorien der Humanisten', in *Neue Jahrbücher für das klassische Altertum, Geschichte und deutsche Literatur und für Pädagogik* 14 (1904), 223–42, 249–85, 330–55, 361–990.

such as Hans Burgkmair's woodcut from 1512 and Jörg Pencz's engraving from ca 1540.[51]

The pig also functioned as an emblem for the popular sixteenth-century notion of the effects of wine on the drinker. In 1528 Erhard Schön, Beham's collaborator and contemporary, published a woodcut with the subject of the four effects of wine.[52] Schön visually outlines the different reactions to wine drinking in keeping with contemporary ideas on the four humours or temperaments. The consequences of drink range from reacting as sanguine as a lamb, to as choleric as a bear or as phlegmatic as a pig. Schön shows one phlegmatic man vomiting and two others defecating. Collectively they act like the kind of four-legged pig Schön shows lapping up what the drunkard emits.

The pig here serves as emblem for both swinish behaviour in general, and for the phlegmatic temperament in particular. Because of their excess bodily fluids, phlegmatics were believed to lose control of their bodily functions when drunk.[53] The accompanying text by Hans Sachs, Nuremberg's poet-cobbler, describes such effects of drink on the phlegmatic drinker under the third characteristic of wine: overeating and excessive drinking (*fressen, schlampen*), drunkenness (*trunken und stüdvol*), filthy language (*Erst lat er die sew glocken klingenn*), staggering, lying in filth (*bsult sich im kot, wie ein schwein;* and *Ligt etwan ein wil inn eym mist*), belching and farting like a pig (*gröltzt und fartzt er wie ein saw*), and urinating in bed (*villeicht pruntzt er auch in das pett*).[54]

Approximately 1528 Beham designed his *Kermis at Mögeldorf* woodcut, a wide, frieze-like image that begins with a small tavern-like building, bearing a pole with circle and what appears to be a bush. In front of the building a pig consumes filth beside a man who vomits from a bench. Both man and pig serve here as emblems of gluttony probably for the men and women who eat, drink, and celebrate at a wide table, at right.[55] Shawm and bagpipe players provide music for some fifteen couples who dance to the right.

In the *Kermis at Mögeldorf* Beham informs that too much drinking and celebrating can result in the kind of swinish behaviour shown in the print. This moralizing message suggests that one response to the activities shown could have been revulsion and avoidance of such behaviour. In a printed sermon on sobriety from 1539, Martin Luther states that a drunkard should be represented

---

[51] On Burgkmair's gluttony print, see Stewart, 'Paper Festivals', figure 3. On Pencz's, see Stewart, 'First *Peasant Festivals*', figure 40. Cornelis Anthonisz's *Demon of Drink* woodcut (ca 1540) shows a person with beer barrel torso and head of a pig: Stewart, 'Paper Festivals', figure 4.

[52] Reproduced in Stewart, 'Paper Festivals', figure 11.

[53] Tlusty, 'Defining "drunk"', 430; idem, *Bacchus*, 54–5, 59–60.

[54] A. von Keller (ed.), *Hans Sachs* 4 (Tübingen, 1870), 237, 240–43.

[55] For illustrations of Beham's *Kermis at Mögeldorf* woodcuts from ca 1528 and 1534, see Stewart, 'Paper Festivals', figures 2 and 5.

in the form of a pig.[56] Less censorious responses to such images of expulsion, however, were also possible. Pigs were highly visible and ordinary in urban settings beginning in the sixteenth century.[57] The pig in Beham's *Kermis at Mögeldorf* could have been understood in a number of ways including, but not limited to a commonplace animal, emblem of too much drink, and symbol for the sin of gluttony.

But it is important to remember that the potentially moralizing details of men vomiting and sometimes defecating before a tavern functioned on another level that mixed moralizing attitudes with entertainment and delight. German carnival plays enjoyed a long tradition of delighting in scatology as a vehicle for the comic, what Johannes Merkel calls 'faecal comic'.[58] Calling attention to such expulsion while joking about it is what Sidney Shrager has seen as both a moralizing element and what he calls 'scatological satire'.[59] More recently, Barbara Correll merges moralizing and pleasurable approaches by referring to the scatological antics of the scandalous figure Grobianus as the 'peepshow of civility'.[60] Correll underscores that scatology can both call attention to undesirable behaviours while delighting in them, as part of what she sees as the civilizing process explained by Norbert Elias.[61]

For Elias, society's elite and authorities encouraged manners and social graces across class boundaries, advancing what Elias calls the changing 'shame frontier'. By bringing the effect of drink on the body before a broad audience in his kermis prints, Beham called attention to social problems, attempted to cleanse society of them, and delighted in them as well.[62]

In approximately 1528 Hans Sachs penned a carnival-play like text that appeared above Beham's *Kermis at Mögeldorf* woodcut; a copy of the woodcut was published in 1534 with slightly altered text. The text describes peasants at kermis in colourful terms. The peasants are boisterous, earthy, and eager for

---

[56] 'Sauffteüfel ... vnd durchausz eytel Sewleben füret//Das/wenn man es malen solt//so muszt man es ainer Saw gleich malen.' Martin Luther, *Wider Völlerey vnd Trunckenhait, Ausz der Epistel S. Petri* (Augsburg: Valentin Othmar, [1539]), fol. Aiiiiv.

[57] Stallybrass and White, *Politics*, 44–59.

[58] J. Merkel, *Form und Funktion der Komik im Nürnberger Fastnachtspiel* (Freiburg im Breisgau, 1971), 192–201. On the related literary tradition in France and what Andrew Cowell calls the 'comico-realist' literary tradition, see his *At Play in the Tavern: Signs, Coins, and Bodies in the Middle Ages* (Ann Arbor, 1999), 1.

[59] S. Shrager, *Scatology in Modern Drama* (New York, 1982), 75–95.

[60] Eckhard Bernstein singled out this expression in his review for the *Scholars of Early Modern Studies* directory, 34 (2000), 99, of B. Correll, *The End of Conduct: Grobianus and the Renaissance Text of the Subject* (Ithaca, 1996).

[61] Correll, *The End of Conduct*, 107.

[62] For an examination of additional images that simultaneously express social critique and carnivalesque humour, see Tlusty, *Bacchus*, 58–68.

drink, love, and a fight. There is an abundance of food and enough drink to cause the intoxication of several peasants who vomit as a result. 'Liendl from Ganckhofen, Drank until he was blind drunk' (stanza 9) and Eselsmüller from Potenstein 'was the biggest glutton at the table, With Gretel Meyer he rummaged about, And hugged her until she threw up' (stanza 19).[63]

Drink serves a similar role in both text and woodcut. The text encourages gluttonous, drunken behaviour, loud and uncontrolled noises, and amorous, if not adulterous encounters. 'Wine was drunk in large quantities, Such that many sank under the bench, On this side there was great belching and vomiting, Yelling, singing, shouting, shrieking' (stanza 3). The viewer also learns that Distaff Christen, who dances with Liendl from Ganckhofen, 'probably farted (*fisten*) thirteen times' (stanza 9). Bodily functions of several kinds are repeatedly included in Sachs's *Kermis at Mögeldorf* text.[64]

Sachs also includes sexuality, aggression and fighting, and anticlerical humour, with the text alone informing that fighting forces the kermis to end, much as it could have in the *Large Kermis* (at right). Sachs's text must be read in the original German if its humorous aspects are to be best appreciated. The colourful language adds to the humorous, almost farcical tone of the text. Better read aloud in the custom of the time than silently in the modern manner of reading, the rhymed couplets were undoubtedly read out loud to many listeners in public places. These included any place where the woodcuts could be hung on walls over wainscoting, yet low enough to be read. The tavern within a kermis print was thus experienced through looking and listening, if not looking and reading.[65] The tavern was entertainment, and it recreated the entertainment of kermis.

---

[63] Geisberg, *German Single-Leaf Woodcut*, vol. 1 (Barthel Beham), 144–49,
Stanza 9:
> Vnd der pösz Liendl von ganckhofen
> Der het sich gantz plindt vol gesoffen
> Der dantzet mit der Spindel Cristen
> Die het wol dreytzemal gefisten.

Stanza 19:
> Vom Potenstain der Esels miller
> Der war am dysch der gröst Füller
> Mit mayer Gred auch vmhin nülpt
> Vnd hertzet sie das sie ergülpt.

[64] Ibid., Stanza 3:
> Der Weyn wart also knollet druncken
> Das jr vil vnther Penck suncken
> Sich huben grosz gröltzen vnd Speyen
> Ein Kallen/singen/Juchtzen/schreyen.

[65] For reading practices in the sixteenth century, see my 'Paper Festivals', 347–8.

Beham also showcases before the tavern a man lying on a bench in the *Large Kermis* where he vomits a full stream onto the ground, as a dog eagerly samples the fresh issue. Beham underscores the effects of wine for this drinker through trellis and grapes. But here, too, Beham links the emblem of vomiting man and dog with drunkenness in other ways. The man and dog together visualize the contemporary proverb, the 'drunken matins' (*die truncken Metten*), which ironically refers to the vomit of a drunkard as singing in church. The expression is included in both visual and textual form on the title page with woodcut illustration to a pamphlet entitled *A New Song. The Song is Called the Drunken Matins*, which was printed at Nuremberg in the 1530s.[66] Sebastian Franck explains the expression in his book of proverbs from 1541: the drunken matins results from drinking so much that Bacchus throws the drinker under a bench where the drinker begins to sing the drunken matins with long notes (a euphemism for vomiting). The result is that all dogs and pigs run to the drinker and gobble the song and the matins he produces. Franck calls such singing of the drunken matins debauchery.[67]

Beham's image of a drunken man can be seen to have functioned on at least three levels – as visualizations of the third (phlegmatic) effect of wine, the sin of gluttony, and a proverbial expression. So understood, the bread placed over the drunkard's head in the *Large Kermis* appears to ironically stand in for a halo. The moralizing association of gluttony for the proverb appears to parallel the kinds of meanings understood by humanists and civic and local authorities in early sixteenth-century Germany who believed drinking was such a widespread social problem that they rallied against it. Franck summed up such attitudes when he stated that, 'More people die from excessive eating and drinking than from the sword'.[68]

Taverns were clearly the locus of a variety of experiences that viewers interpreted according to their own subjective set of responses. Such responses ranged from enjoyment and laughter to earnest moralizing and revulsion. On one hand, Beham's print emphasizes the shared outlook of the population at

---

[66]   *Ein newes Lied: Das lied ist die truncken Metten genant/Ist manchem guten gsellen wol erkant* (Nuremberg: Hans Guldenmund, ca 1530s). The title page woodcut is illustrated in Stewart, 'Paper Festivals', figure 12.

[67]   Sebastian Franck, *Sprichwörter* (Frankfurt am Main: Christian Egenolff, 1541), part 2, fol. 148v: 'O das ist dann ein grosse ehr ... under die banck wirfft, dz er anfahet die truncken mettin mit den langen noten zu singen, dasz all hund vnd sew zulauffen, vnd sich des gesangs vnd der mettin frewen.' On the drunken matins expression, see Stewart, 'Paper Festivals', 340–43.

[68]   'Es sterben mehr leut von fressen vnnd sauffen, dann vom schwerd'. K. Christoffel, *Durch die Zeiten strömt der Wein: Die wunderbare Historie des Weins* (Hamburg, 1957), 226; Franck, *Sprichwörter*, part 2, fol. 162.

large, especially the rural one that enjoyed kermis because of its potential for drink and other secular delights centred around taverns. At the same time, Beham's work also emphasizes the views of Nuremberg's small elite, comprising city clergy and council members, who viewed kermis as unchristian and heavy drinking as unfavourable at such religious festivals where the church, not the tavern, should predominate.

The kermis prints designed by Beham and his German contemporaries, and the images of taverns within them, served manifold purposes and reached large audiences. Descriptive, entertaining, and moralizing, the kermis woodcuts created in Nuremberg codify and perpetuate a world of celebration, conflict and aggression, and of occasional excessive drinking. The iconographic strategies outlined here indicate that Sebald Beham intentionally created prints that drew on society and its festivals, at the same time undergoing reevaluation and attempts at reform, as a slow and ongoing process spurred by the Lutheran Reformation at Nuremberg. Such festivals and social practices were centred around the tavern and were still alive, thriving, and extremely popular, despite criticisms. It is the prevalence and popularity of those tavern- and inn-centred festivals, as well as contemporary criticisms of them, that we see in the prints themselves, works that have helped stretch our understanding of the meanings and functions of tavern and inn in the sixteenth century.

Inns and Taverns of Western Sussex, England, 1550–1700: A Documentary and Architectural Investigation*

Janet Pennington

'If you love good roads, conveniences, good inns, plenty of postilions and horses, be so kind as never to go into Sussex.' [1]

Horace Walpole, dilettante English novelist and connoisseur, wrote the above in 1749 after a visit to Midhurst, Petworth and Arundel in western Sussex. Contemporary writers complained bitterly of bad travelling conditions in the county, 'a land desolate and muddy', and of poor accommodation: 'the George, [at Rye, is] a dirty, sea-port inn with a wretched stable ... I do not believe that in the county of Sussex there are any such excellent inns ... .' [2] How easy is it to discover whether this had always been the case?

The regional history of inns and taverns in England is a much neglected area of research even though many of the inn buildings still exist as our well-known pubs. Of the few pioneering scholarly articles and the many popular works on the subject, none are wholly regional in concept.[3] This article will fill that gap

---

* I am most grateful to Joyce Sleight and Dr Andrew Foster for comments and suggestions, and particularly to Sue Rowland who so expertly produced the maps.

[1] Chichester, West Sussex Record Office, MP 423, Miscellaneous Papers. A letter from Horace Walpole to George Montagu, 1749.

[2] W. Blaaw (trans.), 'Extracts from the "Iter Sussexiense" of Dr John Burton', *Sussex Archaeological Collections* 8 (1856), 254; D. Souden (ed.), *Byng's Tours, The Journals of The Hon. John Byng 1781–1792* (1991), 70, 82.

[3] General histories include W. A. Pantin, 'Medieval inns', in E. M. Jope (ed.), *Studies in Building History* (London, 1961), 166–91; A. Everitt, 'The English urban inn, 1560–1760' in idem (ed.), *Perspectives in English Urban History* (London, 1973), 91–137; J. A. Chartres, 'The place of inns in the commercial life of London and Western England 1660–1760' (Ph.D. Oxford University, 1973); P. Clark, *The English Alehouse, A Social History 1200–1830* (London, 1983); B. Cox, *English Inn & Tavern Names* (Nottingham, 1994); J. Hunter, 'Legislation, royal proclamations & other national directives affecting inns, taverns, alehouses, brandy shops & punch houses 1552–1757' (Ph.D. University of Reading, 1994).

by using a combination of research methods to examine the inns and taverns in one region of England over a 150 year period (approximately 1550–1700).

Historically, the inn was always a place for travellers. It offered food and drink, accommodation and paid hospitality of the best kind, including secure overnight stabling for horses and wheeled vehicles. Taverns were only allowed to operate in towns, supplying wine as well as food. They were not intended to offer accommodation but in practice many did. From 1553, anyone selling wine for consumption on the premises needed a licence, so an inn with a wine licence was technically also a tavern, which caused problems of definition.[4] A third class of drinking establishment co-existed uneasily with inns and taverns – the alehouse – which catered primarily to the lower social classes.[5]

This article will show how the perceived idea of the English inn and tavern stands up to scrutiny in part of Sussex, a coastal county in the south-east of the country. Historically it was administered from two centres, Chichester in the west and Lewes in the east. From 1865 this was gradually formalized and until 1974 the boundary between west and east more or less divided the county in half.[6] Most of the area to the west of this boundary has been examined, taking a line northwards from the port of New Shoreham as an eastern boundary. There are seven towns of which Chichester, the regional capital, is a small cathedral city. They all show evidence of having been urban inn centres during the period.

England is fortunate in having a good survival of medieval and early modern inn buildings in the streets of its provincial towns and country villages. Many Sussex inns have survived the vicissitudes of war and town planning. They served a local and travelling public in a variety of ways, often over many centuries. As time passed, many buildings were adapted to suit changing needs and customs.

At the beginning of the period there were about twenty urban inns in the region and eight wine licences. By 1626 there were eighteen urban wine licences, most of which were probably held by the inns, of which there were about fifty. By 1700 the number of inns in the towns had increased to around sixty-five, although some of the original number had ceased to function and new inns had taken their place. It is difficult to give figures for the rural inns in

---

[4]   Hunter, 'Legislation', 87.

[5]   Clark, *The English Alehouse*, 173–4. In 1617, Sir Giles Mompesson, a Member of Parliament and courtier of King James I, was granted a patent to license inns. He was impeached in 1621 due to his corrupt methods and the patent withdrawn, but thereafter inns increasingly applied for alehouse licences. Clark's research has clarified the function of the alehouse in contrast to that of the inn and tavern.

[6]   J. Godfrey, 'Local government in the 19th and 20th centuries', in K. Leslie and B. Short (eds), *An Historical Atlas of Sussex* (Chichester, 1999), 126–7. The Local Government Act 1888 established elected county councils for East and West Sussex.

LOCATION MAP

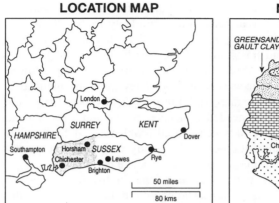

NATURAL REGIONS

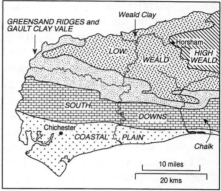

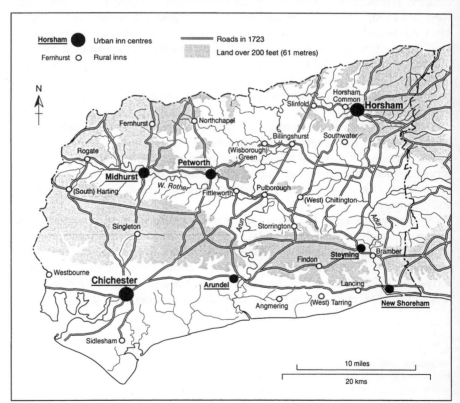

Figure 5: Map of land features and inns in Sussex

the early period as documentation is sparse, but there were probably about ten, of which four held wine licences between 1555–85. By 1700 there were approximately thirty. There were several hundred alehouses, both licensed and unlicensed, some of which had become inns by 1700.[7]

The rapidly expanding area of London lay to the north. From 1550–1600 the population of the capital nearly doubled, from ca 120,000 to ca 200,000. In 1650 it was around 375,000 and by 1700 approximately half a million.[8] Its proximity was the reason for many journeys to and from Sussex, which was well-placed to provide grain, beef, mutton and fish, as well as labour. Iron and timber were some of the heavier goods transported, which caused deterioration of the roads. Wool was exported across the Channel, legally and illegally. Merchants, politicians and the militia crossed the region. Nor should the aristocracy travelling for pleasure and business to the continent and London be discounted. Overseas visitors landed at Sussex ports and needed to find accommodation, hire horses and employ guides.[9] The inns of the region supported their journeys.

Sussex was a largely agricultural area containing oak woodlands, with some iron and glass industry, but the underlying geology – mainly clay, sandstone and chalk – caused endless problems for travellers. Sussex roads were notorious for their impassability throughout the period and became worse as wheeled transport proliferated. In the reign of Henry VIII (1509–47) the county was known for its 'dyrt and myre'; pack-horse trains were easier to use than wagons. In the mid-seventeenth century London coachmen charged by the mile for journeys into all the counties around the capital, except for Sussex, which was 'better measured to its advantage by days journeys than by miles'.[10] This

---

[7]   Kew, Public Record Office (PRO), E351/3153, Pipe Rolls; E176/1/172, Exchequer: King's Remembrancer: Vintners' Fines; E163/17/22, Miscellanea of the Exchequer; Chichester, West Sussex Record Office, EP1/33/1678 Henry Mersher, Probate Accounts; J. Pennington, 'The Inns and Taverns of Western Sussex, 1500–1700: A Regional Study of their Architectural and Social History' (Ph.D. University of Southampton, 2002).

[8]   R. Finlay and B. Shearer (eds), 'Population growth and suburban expansion' in A. L. Beier and R. Finlay (eds), *London 1500–1700. The Making of the Metropolis* (London, 1986), 48.

[9]   Ibid., 244; J. Thirsk and J. P.Cooper (eds), *Seventeenth-Century Economic Documents* (Oxford, 1972), 575, 590; W. C. Cooper, 'Smuggling in Sussex', in *Sussex Archaeological Collections* 10 (London, 1858), 69–77; H. Cleere and D. Crossley, *The Iron Industry of the Weald* (Leicester, 1985), 161, 166–8; P. Brandon and B. Short, *The South East From AD 1000* (London, 1990), 161–8, 232–3; T. P. Hudson (ed.), *The Victoria History of the County of Sussex* (hereafter *VCH*) vol. 5, pt 1 (Oxford, 1997), 32–4; M. Howard, 'Tudor and Stuart great houses', in Leslie and Short, *Historical Atlas*, 54–5; C. N. Sutton, *Historical Notes of Withyham, Hartfield and Ashdown Forest* (Tunbridge Wells, 1902), 208–9.

[10]   'Extracts from the journal and account book of the Rev. Giles Moore, rector of Horstead Keynes, Sussex, from the year 1655 to 1679. With remarks by Robert Willis Blencowe Esq.', *Sussex Archaeological Collections* 1 (1848), 104 n.

affected the growth of the inns, and purpose-built taverns were few and far between. However, merchants and farmers managed to serve the capital, and travellers crossed the region to the coastal ports. Inns were the pivot around which communication and travel revolved.

A government survey of inns and alehouses for the county taken in 1686 can be used to give an illustration of the town hierarchy, which holds good throughout the period, even though no distinction can be made between the two classes of drinking establishment (Table 1). The towns emerge in three distinct groups. Chichester and Horsham, important administrative towns for the south and north of the region, not surprisingly led with the highest figures for beds and stabling. Horsham had 144 more stablings, as extra horses were needed to cope with the bad roads crossing the surrounding clay soils; wet weather also caused travellers to stay there longer. Midhurst and Petworth, situated in the middle of the clay, were on through routes to London, and each held the country seat of a powerful landowner. On or near the coast the ports of Arundel and New Shoreham were on a par with Steyning, a former port near an important river estuary crossing.

Table 1: The regional town hierarchy, 1686

Towns	Guest beds	Stabling
Chichester	84	221
Horsham	83	365
Midhurst	53	118
Petworth	45	122
New Shoreham	28	44
Arundel	26	50
Steyning	25	48

Source: Kew, Public Record Office, WO/30/48/7788, War Office, Miscellanea: Inns and Ale-houses, fos 437–43; P. Clark & J. Hosking, *Population Estimates of English Small Towns 1550–1851* (Leicester, 1993), 147–53.

It should be remembered that inns in the countryside, though smaller, were just as essential as their urban counterparts. Twenty-one rural inn sites can be identified, situated at bridges, crossroads and in small villages, many in difficult territory (see Figure 5). Some of the inns might have been mistaken for alehouses, but documentary evidence shows that, though small, they were functioning as inns.

A pattern began to emerge from the seven towns. In most cases, the earliest established inn in each was named after England's popular patron saint, George.[11] This was the inn greeting pilgrims and merchants travelling from London and those going to the local 'big' house where the landowner had his country seat. Most of the towns also had clusters of inns in and around the market areas, taking advantage of regular trade and annual fairs and offering safe accommodation and stabling for merchants and their wares. There were smaller inns at city gates or end-of-towns, in a good position to offer fields for cattle or pack-horse trains.[12] The commonest inn names, such as George, Swan, and Crown usually belonged to the oldest buildings. Others, such as Half Moon, Red Lion and White Horse, were linked to patronage and land owner-ship.

The sources for inn history are quite overwhelming. The region considered here comprises many large agricultural estates, with associated towns and villages, that have changed hands only a few times since the Norman Conquest in 1066. The thousands of manuscripts contained in these estate archives are mostly held at the West Sussex Record Office, Chichester. They contain not only deeds and conveyances of properties, but one of the best collections of maps in any English Record Office.[13] All this documentation reveals travel net-works and inn sites, as well as names of innkeepers and sometimes building details.

Some of the most interesting sources available are the Chichester diocesan records, from which I examined seventy-three innkeeping probate inventories for the region covering the years 1579–1710 (plus one from the Public Record Office).[14] Many have associated wills, though unfortunately only two have probate accounts, and there are no surviving inventories for New Shoreham's innkeepers.[15] Of the named occupations in the inventory preambles, thirty are

---

[11] See S. Riches, *St. George. Hero, Martyr and Myth* (Stroud, 2000), for the importance of St George in English life from the early twelfth century. The earliest known English church wall paintings of St George, ca 1080–1120, are in Sussex (ibid., 20).

[12] See Everitt, 'The English urban Inn', 98–100, 108 for examples; also R. Morgan, *Chichester. A Documentary History* (Chichester, 1992), 167, 177, 182, 187, 191.

[13] K. C. Leslie & T. J. McCann, *Local History in West Sussex. A Guide to Sources* (2nd revised ed., Chichester, 1975); F. W. Steer (ed.), 'A catalogue of Sussex estate and tithe award maps', *Sussex Record Society* 61 (Lewes & Chichester, 1962); F. W. Steer (ed.), 'A Catalogue of Sussex Maps', *Sussex Record Society* 66 (Lewes & Chichester, 1968).

[14] T. J. McCann, *West Sussex Probate Inventories 1521–1834, A Catalogue* (Chichester, 1981). These four microfiche list 11,740 probate inventories and associated wills. Kew, PRO, PROB4/10679, Probate Inventories.

[15] Chichester, West Sussex Record Office, EP1/88/43. This lists 1,230 probate accounts, 1572–1711, alphabetically by surname and parish; occupations were not always noted in the accounts. Two innkeepers have been identified: EP111/9/1/1678, John Scott of Chichester;

described as innholders or innkeepers, and twelve as victuallers. There are three vintners. Twelve have no stated occupation, and contents reveal that a merchant, an alderman, seven yeomen and two gentlemen were running inns, as well as four widows and two tradesmen. The goods valued in the inventories often reveal evidence of dual occupation such as farming, fishing and milling.

There are many known pitfalls in inventory analysis. Even when a will survives, the financial status of the deceased is never certain unless there is also a probate account.[16] Only a few of the wills have been helpful – the deceased's inn is rarely mentioned and unless the occupational status is listed in the pre-amble, it is not often possible to tell that the testator had been involved in the trade. Bearing this in mind, together with an uneven documentary survival rate, the inventories still reveal important evidence relating to room use, furnishings, guest status, new building work and dual occupation, from which inn typology and function can be deduced.

A neglected but vital source for the English inn and tavern is the building itself. Fortunately, Sussex still has early inn buildings, though some have been refronted or undergone major alterations. Of approximately sixty-five inns functioning in the seven towns during the mid-seventeenth century, twenty-four buildings survive, plus parts of another two. Thirteen are still functioning as pubs. When inns have ceased trading or been demolished, documentation and maps survive to pinpoint their former sites. There are also name indicators such as Red Lion Street in Midhurst, George House in Petworth, Crown Yard in Arundel and Star Lane in New Shoreham.

A good example for examining architecture, function and change over time is the Spread Eagle at Midhurst, which is still in operation (Figure 6). Midhurst is situated on the river Rother in the Weald Clay. The inn stands opposite the market house and to the modern visitor is perceived as a typical English country town inn. It is well known in the area, specializing in conferences and corporate entertaining, as well as catering for wedding parties and overseas visitors.

The inn comprises three builds. The earliest range is timber-framed, situated on the corner of West and South Street by the Market Square. The second build is a large southern brick range, with stone dressings; a third brick range adjoins the western side.

EP1/33/1678, Henry Mersher of Midhurst. EP1/29/106/228, Richard Pryce of Horsham has part of an account included in his inventory.

[16] See M. Spufford, 'The limitations of the probate inventory' in J. Chartres and D. Hey (eds), *English rural society, 1500–1800. Essays in honour of Joan Thirsk* (Cambridge, 1990), 139–74, and C. Gittings, 'Probate accounts: a neglected source', *The Local Historian* 21, no. 2 (Chichester, 1991), 51–9; P. Spufford (ed.), *Index to the Probate Accounts of England and Wales*, 2 vols (London, 1999).

Figure 6: The Spread Eagle Inn, Midhurst (Photo: author).

The date 1430 is firmly attached to the inn, at least in its literature, though it is not evidenced architecturally. If there was an inn or alehouse on the site in the early fifteenth century, it was not the Spread Eagle – its timber-framing identifies it as a mid-sixteenth-century building.[17] The front facing the market place is jettied, indicative of high status. The name originated with Sir Anthony Browne, who inherited Cowdray House at Midhurst in 1542.[18] The crest displayed on his coat of arms is a spread eagle, and two of his nearby manors also used this for their inn signs.[19] A Roman Catholic during the reign of Protestant Queen Elizabeth I, Browne was a powerful man in court and government circles. His son granted space for a market house at Midhurst in 1552, and this is a likely date for the building of the Spread Eagle, which he possibly financed.[20]

Mary Hudson, the occupier from at least 1614, when she held a wine licence, was still there in 1637, possibly longer.[21] While she was presumably selling wine, she may also have been keeping an inn. By 1646 the Courtney family had arrived and a large stable range was built at the Spread Eagle soon afterwards.[22] Some of the other service buildings have disappeared, but their lay-out can be seen on the 1875 Ordnance Survey map for the town. This shows a central entrance between the north and south ranges, and a rear exit from the northern courtyard.[23] Henry Courtney's inventory, taken 6 June 1673, describes him as an innholder. It reveals a building with five bed chambers, a garret, kitchen, brewhouse, and two cellars, one for beer and the other for wine.[24] There is reference to a balcony chamber. A 'shuffle board' room indicates the popular game played there. There were three named rooms – the Crown, Eagle Room, and Angel Chamber – another indication of a high status building. The beer cellar had a capacity for 7,000 pints at the time of

---

[17]   L. F. Salzman (ed.), *VCH*, vol. 4 (Oxford, 1953), 74–5. I am grateful to Dr A. Hughes of Horsham for advice on architectural interpretation.

[18]   Howard, 'Tudor and Stuart great houses', 54–5.

[19]   Buckinghamshire Record Office, D/X 648, 'S[i]r Giles Mompesson, his first Accompt, Sussex', which lists the Spread Eagle at Lodsworth in 1617; Chichester, West Sussex Record Office, Add. Ms. 14,859, Additional Manuscripts, Spread Eagle at Fernhurst 1772.

[20]   Salzman, *VCH*, vol. 4, 74.

[21]   Kew, PRO, E 163/17/22, Miscellanea of the Exchequer; M. Balfour, *The Spread Eagle Hotel* (Chichester, 1980), 11–12.

[22]   Balfour, *The Spread Eagle*, 12; the stable range bears a datestone inscribed in 1650 which may well be relevant.

[23]   Chichester, West Sussex Record Office, Ordnance Survey, 1st Edition, 25" Series, Sheet 21:XB1.

[24]   Ibid., EP 1/29/138/72, Probate Inventories. All references to the contents of the Spread Eagle under Henry Courtney come from this source.

Courtney's death, and the wine cellar held Spanish and French wines valued at £124 (about £8500 in today's currency).[25]

Courtney was also farming, some of his land leased from the Browne family. With over thirty acres of arable crops, forty sheep, six cattle and six pigs, he could have provided malt for his brewhouse, hay and oats for guests' horses, milk for butter and cheese, and lamb, beef and pork for dinner. He had hops for brewing beer. There were sacks of corn and wool in the garret over the balcony chamber in the inn. These may have been his own, securely stored at the top of the house, or possibly trade samples. The reference to a balcony probably indicated a galleried chamber overlooking the inn yard, where his black mare was stabled. The bedchamber for his wife and himself was probably the heated balcony chamber with a curtained bed. It doubled as a 'bed-sitting room' with six upholstered chairs and a display cupboard for glasses and cups.

The named rooms had coloured themes; it was blue and red in the Crown where there was some furniture. The only identifiable guest chamber, the Eagle Room, had a four-poster bed with red curtains and valance, and two red rugs. The room was heated and had a window curtain – the only one listed – and a looking glass, two tables and enough seating for at least eight people. The Angel Chamber was being used for storage of linen – twelve pillow slips, twelve towels, six table cloths, ninety-six napkins and thirty sheets – valued at nearly £12. Inventories reveal that other establishments functioning as inns usually had comparable numbers of sheets and napkins; thus eating and drinking were probably more important here than accommodation. If the Spread Eagle had been an inn in 1673, ninety-six napkins would have been accompanied by a similar number of sheets.[26] There were also silver drinking cups worth £4, and two silver claret cups, indicating the nature of some of the French wine. The wine and linen suggest that the Spread Eagle was functioning as a tavern under Henry Courtney, despite the appraisers' description of him as an innholder. There is no accommodation listed for living-in servants, as there would have been for an inn.

Twenty-six flagons and twelve chamber pots are an additional indicator of what was going on here – drinking, and plenty of it. A pewter still provided distilled spirits, and wine and beer were being consumed in great quantities at the Spread Eagle in the mid seventeenth century. In the evening a pair of great pewter candlesticks and two pairs of little ones threw some light on the scene.

---

[25] Bank of England, *Equivalent Contemporary Values of the Pound: A Historical Series 1270–1995* (London, 1995).

[26] See Chichester, West Sussex Record Office, Probate Inventories: EP1/29/183/033, J. Cowlstocke of Steyning, 1633, 60 napkins, 60 sheets; EP1/29/106/209, S. Brian, Horsham, 1686, 120 napkins, 100 sheets; EP1/29/008/200, T. Goodgroome, Arundel, 1690, 24 napkins, 24 sheets; EP1/29/106/281, H. Waller, Horsham, 1702, 72 napkins, 72 sheets.

The large hearth housed a jack to turn the spits, and there was a bench and a high-backed settle by the fire; the five flitches of bacon would have hung from the ceiling. The brewhouse was large, the contents valued at £22, and included one great and one small copper furnace as well as a great tun and six brewing coolers. The washing was also done there. Beer may well have been supplied to other outlets. Courtney's will included instructions for forty shillings and a twenty gallon barrel of beer to be given to the poor of Midhurst on the morning of his burial.[27]

Henry Courtney's son William was the occupier in 1695, by which time the large southern range had been built and the Spread Eagle was functioning as an inn, but still supplying wine. In 1694 it could sleep at least twenty-five people in nine named chambers. A new garret was listed. Four chambers and the parlour had window curtains. There were now seventy sheets, seventy-two napkins and twenty-four towels. As well as beer, there was canary, and white and red port wine on offer.[28]

After William Courtney died his widow married the grandson of a former landlord. By 1716 the lease was conveyed to Henry Pruet, and his grandson William was there in 1760, having taken over from his father John. In 1730 the inn buildings and stock were insured with the Sun Insurance Company of London for £1000.[29] The stability and experience of these innkeeping families must have contributed greatly to the success of the Spread Eagle.

The early inns, like the Spread Eagle's first build, were of timber-framed construction, built of oak grown in the clay regions of Sussex, their frames infilled with plastered wattle and daub. Brick became cheaper and more desirable throughout the seventeenth century; local flint and sandstone were also used. Some urban inns had gated entrances, either at the side and often chambered over later on, or made through the building by taking out a ground floor section. Gateway chambers are listed in inventories for Midhurst, Petworth, Arundel and Steyning during the period, and at a rural inn at South Harting. Some still survive, as at the former Crown at Arundel and the Chequer at Steyning.

The inns are easily identifiable in their urban settings. Not only do their signs call attention to their situation, but they can still be distinguished by their yards and former service buildings. The sites are often noticeable for the space around the main inn building. The yards are now usually car parks, and the service buildings, once barns, blacksmiths' shops, brewhouses, coachhouses, malthouses, ostlers' accommodation and stables, have either been replaced or

---

[27] Chichester, West Sussex Record Office, STCI/25, Sussex Testamentary Collection, Chichester Archdeaconry, fol. 95.

[28] Ibid., EP1/29/138/132, Probate Inventories.

[29] Balfour, 'The Spread Eagle', 15.

are in other use. The 1875 series of Ordnance Survey maps is useful in delineating an inn's curtilage, and service buildings can usually be identified. Many urban inns organized a rear exit to avoid traffic problems in confined yards once wheeled vehicles became commonplace, and some of these are still in use.

A photographic record of the inns and service buildings has been invaluable in identifying former use, together with on-site sketches and the recording of architectural features inside and out. It has been possible to visit first floors and roof interiors of many buildings for recording purposes. The roof structure of timber-framed buildings in the region changed over time and the experienced eye can give an approximate date of construction.[30]

Horsham stone or slab, a flaggy sandstone outcropping in the vicinity, was widely used for roof covering in the region; clay roofing tiles were also common. A steep pitch indicates a former thatched roof. Chimneys were added to end walls or inserted into hall houses, mostly during the seventeenth century, when the opportunity was taken to add first floor rooms to the hall, giving extra chambers for an inn's guests.

Unlike mainland Europe during the period under investigation, England did not seriously suffer from property destruction caused by war with overseas countries. However, the years 1642–60 saw the English Civil War and its aftermath. While no battles of national significance took place in Sussex, both Chichester and Arundel were besieged by parliamentary forces, having previously been garrisoned by royalist troops. There was a fight at Bramber bridge near the White Lion inn, resulting in several deaths.[31] Some destruction of property did take place and inns must have been commandeered to billet men and horses.[32] There was much administrative disruption during this period, and documentary sources for inn history are scarce. Only five innkeeping inventories survive for these nineteen years, but there are glimpses of inn life in the region from other sources. Some of the larger inns were being used as meeting places by the parliamentary County Commissioners.[33] In 1653 traveller and poet John Taylor commented on the empty frame of a Sussex village inn sign, at the Kings Arms, Billingshurst, on the London to Chichester road. The sign had been shattered by 'shot and flame'. He wrote: 'For arms are of no use without a Head', wryly referring to the execution of King Charles I four years

---

[30] See for example J. Warren (ed.), *Wealden Buildings: Studies in Kent, Sussex, and Surrey* (Horsham 1990). As a member of the Wealden Buildings Study Group, and the Vernacular Architecture Group, I owe particular thanks to Dr A. Hughes and other group members for help and advice.

[31] M. Howard, 'Civil War', in Leslie and Short, *Historical Atlas*, 58–9.

[32] A. Fletcher, *Sussex 1600–1660: A County Community in Peace and War* (Chichester, 1980), 270–71; Morgan, *Chichester*, 54.

[33] Fletcher, *Sussex 1600–1660*, 325–6.

earlier.[34] In 1658 the innkeeper of the Dolphin inn, Chichester, was one of the ringleaders in a plot to restore Charles II to the throne.[35] With the restoration of the monarchy in 1660 the administrative situation stabilized and documentary sources for the region's inns improve.

Communications were vital for the continued prosperity of Sussex inns and their keepers. Two cartographers, John Ogilby and Richard Budgen, produced maps that have been invaluable in assessing routes and inn sitings for the region.[36] Ogilby's 1675 series of road maps in strip form can still be followed today, though some parts are now bridleways or footpaths.[37] Three of his Sussex maps guided travellers from London to the ports of Chichester, Arundel and New Shoreham. He showed alternative routes in some parts where flooding or the difficult clay soils would have caused problems. Richard Budgen lived in Sussex and his 1723 survey resulted in the first proper county road map. The scale is nearly one inch to the mile; no inns are marked, but the map is accurate enough to plot them.

The rivers were a great problem to early travellers, and still are in times of flood. The headwaters of the Western Rother, Arun and Adur rise and inter-mingle in the Weald Clay. It can be seen from the Natural Regions section of Figure 5 that the town of Horsham, situated at the western end of a sandstone ridge projecting into the clay, was well-placed to receive visitors crossing this difficult area which explains the large stabling facilities noted in 1686. The Post Office in England was founded in 1635, but fifty-five years later Horsham had no postal facilities within six miles. Lawyer William Cowper, the future Lord Chancellor of England, stayed there in 1690 but had to write to his wife after he had returned to the safety of Surrey, saying 'I have come off without hurt, both in my going and return through the Sussex ways, which are bad and ruinous beyond imagination. I vow 'tis a melancholy consideration that mankind will inhabit such a heap of dirt for a poor livelihood. The country is a sink... .'[38]

This goes some way towards explaining why the rural inns were so im-portant. They are a complete contrast to their urban counterparts. Most were

---

[34] J. B. Caldecott, 'John Taylor's tour of Sussex in 1653', *Sussex Archaeological Collections* 81 (1940), 23.

[35] Fletcher, *Sussex 1600-1660*, 313.

[36] D. Kingsley (ed.), 'Printed maps of Sussex 1575–1900', *Sussex Record Society* 72 (Lewes, 1980–81), 57–63, 358–60.

[37] Ibid., 358–60.

[38] C. Thomas-Stanford, *Sussex in the Great Civil War and Interregnum 1642–1660* (London 1910), 6; J. Greenwood, *The Posts of Sussex: The Chichester Branch, 1250–1840* (1973), 51. Greenwood states 'less is known about the postal arrangements of Horsham than any other town in West Sussex', though a post had commenced in 1678, but presumably foundered.

small, with only one or two guest chambers, but their importance to the early modern traveller in the region cannot be overstated. The rider stumbling along the notorious Sussex roads with their broken-down bridges and uncertain ferries might not have minded too much if he had had to sleep in coarse sheets on a flock bed, rather than between the best Holland linen on the feather bed that would have been available in a town inn.

Some of these rural inns probably provided smuggled wines and spirits at a cheaper price than many licensed premises.[39] However, in 1570 and 1585 a wine licence was held for an inn or tavern at Bramber, a decayed village situated at the foot of a crumbling Norman castle.[40] Almost certainly the White Lion, this small inn was near an important river crossing. The village, an ancient borough, returned two Members of Parliament. The franchise accompanied burgage tenure and the White Lion, as an 'ancient' house, owned a vote; it grew in size and importance in consequence.[41] One of its innkeepers, Robert Cox, who died in 1624, was also a barber and the inn had two guest chambers that could accommodate about six people. Stores of bacon, mustard and butter were listed, with thirty-two sheets and twenty-eight napkins. A 'paire of tables' provided for the game of backgammon. Cox's inventory is one of the few to mention a lavatory – euphemistically described as a 'howse of office' – situated in the stable.[42]

There were no major improvements in the region's roads and few of the rural inns grew in size, though two had a new chamber towards the end of the period.[43] Many of the inventories show their occupants farming and fishing as well as working as blacksmiths, carpenters, grocers and husbandmen. Not only rural innkeepers diversified. Some of the smaller town innkeepers acted as bakers, barbers, brewers, gaolers, millers, saddlers and wheelwrights. Many of these skills would have been very useful for travellers as well as the local inhabitants.

No strong documentary evidence emerges to show the interaction of the urban inns with the markets, despite the undoubted growth of trade and com-

---

[39] M. Waugh, *Smuggling in Kent & Sussex 1700–1840* (Newbury, 1998, rev. and updated edn), 92, 100, 104, 121, 126, 140, 161, 163; while these rereferences are for the early eighteenth century, there is no reason to suppose that inns were any the less involved in smuggling wine and spirits during the seventeenth century.

[40] Kew, PRO, E 351/3153, Pipe Rolls; E 176/1/169, Exchequer: King's Remembrancer: Vintners' Fines; E 163/17/22.

[41] T. P. Hudson (ed.), *VCH*, vol. 6 pt 1 (Oxford, 1980), 202, 204, 211–12. Burgage is a tenure in an ancient borough held of the Crown or the lords of the borough.

[42] Chichester, West Sussex Record Office, EP1/29/004, Probate Inventories; S. Dean 20, Storrington Deanery; J. Pennington, 'Bramber Castle Hotel or the White Lion Rediscovered', in A. Noble (ed.), *Bramber. Glimpses of a Village* (Bramber, 1996), 28–33.

[43] Chichester, West Sussex Record Office, EP1/29/176/045, EP1/29/029/103, Probate Inventories.

merce. Everitt gives many examples of the importance of innkeeping and trade, some inns specializing in, say, the wool, leather or grain trades, and it could be expected that this also happened in Sussex.[44]

The city of Chichester was a port. Though it did not have its own harbour, there were wharves and landing places at nearby coastal villages. Five inns were recorded in the city in 1574, six in 1604 and more than a dozen within the walls by 1670, others clustering outside the four city gates. In the seventeenth century grain and cloth exports brought increased prosperity and nearly 300 merchants were recorded.[45] One of them was certainly running an inn in the 1630s and it could be expected that merchants met at inns to dine and conduct business. Carriers, probably working from specific inn yards, must have gone to and from the various landing places.[46]

Chichester formerly had another reason to attract travellers – as pilgrims – which might be one of the reasons why inns are recorded there earlier than the other towns. Soon after 1253 there was a shrine in the cathedral to a former bishop, Richard of Wych (ca 1197–1253), canonized in 1262. St Richard was a revered local saint, bishop of Chichester from 1244 until his death in 1253; until the mid sixteenth century many visitors came to pay homage at the shrine and all needed accommodation.[47] The city inns were well positioned to offer this, and inn-owning ecclesiastical authorities profited. There is little evidence that cathedrals regularly extended free hospitality to non-noble pilgrims, and the middle-class traveller would have expected to pay for his lodging.[48]

The first known record of an innkeeper in Chichester is ca 1250, though the inn is not named.[49] The George, documented from 1487, was owned by the Dean and Chapter, sited opposite the Cathedral in West Street. By 1649 it had been replaced by a new inn on the site named the Dolphin, which in 1670 had twenty-three hearths and was owned by a Chapter Clerk. The White Horse in South Street, mentioned in 1533, was owned by the Vicars' Choral, who had extra cellars across the street. A shop on the site of the Swan in East Street had been owned by one of the Chantries in the early fifteenth century and the inn had appeared before 1527. Other inns opened and closed, but the Swan and the

---

[44]   Everitt, 'The English urban Inn', 104–9.

[45]   Morgan, *Chichester*, 43, 52–4.

[46]   Chichester, West Sussex Record Office, EP1/29/541/043, Probate Inventories; Morgan, *Chichester*, 89. Edward Salloway, merchant of Chichester, had been running the Swan inn in East Street, probably the best inn in the city, when he died in 1638.

[47]   D. Jones, 'The Cult of St. Richard of Chichester in the Middle Ages', *Sussex Archaeological Collections* 121 (Lewes, 1983), 79–86. Jones states that the cult of St Richard persisted in Chichester until the Reformation and even revived in Queen Mary's reign (85).

[48]   B. Nilson, *Cathedral Shrines of Medieval England* (Woodbridge, 1998), 184.

[49]   L. Fleming (ed.), 'The Chartulary of Boxgrove Priory', *Sussex Record Society* 59 (Lewes, 1960), 178.

Dolphin jostled for position of prime inn throughout the last half of the seventeenth century, the Swan suffering because of its age. It underwent a refronting and reordering in the early eighteenth century.[50] The top inns had no need of diversification, but they had to keep up with the times.

Chichester's shifting inn hierarchy is echoed by Horsham, where the medieval Red Lion was gradually superseded by the Kings Head, first documented in 1665 and possibly purpose-built.[51] Horsham was an important stopping-off place for travellers coming to and from London and going on to the ports of New Shoreham or Brighton. As a borough, it returned two Members of Parliament. Until 1624 they were nominees of the absentee landowners, the dukes of Norfolk, but thereafter local landowners tended to predominate. Properties on burgage plots had a vote and these included nearly all of the inns of Horsham.[52] By splitting buildings into several tenancies, the votes per property were illegally increased and the inns prospered at election times when bribery and corruption were rife.

Nearly all the inns were situated around the large market area, which grew in size throughout the seventeenth century, and not only to take advantage of the commercial activities. The county gaol was there too, and military stores were housed in the town. Assize courts and quarter sessions also took place in Horsham, though usually only in the summer, presumably due to problems of access during bad winter weather.[53]

Four inventories show new rooms and chambers being added to Horsham inns during the seventeenth century. In 1611 one of these was the Red Lion, strategically placed on the corner of West Street and the market place.[54] Recent building work has uncovered evidence for jettying on these two sides, a high status feature.[55]

Midhurst and Petworth are quite a contrast to Horsham. The landowners were often in residence and both Cowdray House at Midhurst and Petworth House had a George inn near their entrance gates. The Browne family of Cowdray House probably owned the Angel, situated close to their gates. The towns were also located on through routes between London and the ports of Chichester and Arundel. In Petworth the early inns had all been replaced by other buildings by 1900. The Crown closed in 1673 and was divided into several houses, the George was divided into several tenements by 1760 and the

[50]   Morgan, *Chichester*, 70, 89–90, 112.

[51]   A. Hughes, *The King's Head. Horsham's Best-Known Inn* (Horsham, 1998).

[52]   For a comprehensive list of the inns of Horsham and other Sussex locations, along with earliest identifiable dates, see Pennington, 'Inns and Taverns of Western Sussex', Table 4.

[53]   T. P. Hudson (ed.), *VCH*, vol. 6 pt 2 (Oxford, 1986), 133–4, 172, 189.

[54]   Chichester, West Sussex Record Office, EP1/29/106/002, 041, 224, 237, Probate Inventories.

[55]   I am grateful to A. Hughes for this information.

Great White Hart had become a private house by 1779. As these inns declined, a new inn named the Half Moon, possibly built in the first half of the seventeenth century, prospered. Named after the badge of a local landowning family, the Percy's of Petworth House, it dominated the market square until the end of the nineteenth century. The Swan, also in the square, managed to survive a rebuilding in 1899 but closed at the end of the twentieth century. Both towns had at least five inns around their market areas by the mid-seventeenth century.[56] Four of the Midhurst inns continue to trade under their seventeenth century signs.[57]

Steyning, Arundel and New Shoreham show a similar pattern of three or four market inns at any one time. Arundel was a river port, four miles inland, and its castle loomed over the George Inn, which was owned by the dukes of Norfolk.[58] The Sherleys of Wiston House, a mile to the west of Steyning, owned the Chequer inn which was on a prime site in the middle of the small market town; they may also have owned the George.[59] New Shoreham was a sea port, but a great storm shattered the town in 1703. This event, combined with the increasing traffic on the coastal road, has resulted in the disappearance of the early inns, such as the George, the Dolphin, the Kings Head and the Fountain; part of the Star may remain as a shop.[60]

Innkeeping functions have been fully described by Everitt, and many of the same activities of regional administration took place in Sussex inns. Heated first floor chambers doubled as meeting rooms, furnished with numerous tables and chairs, with maps and pictures on the walls and curtains at the windows. The inns served as venues for manorial and coroners' courts, amongst many other activities. The Red Lion at Horsham was owned by an innkeeping vintner in the first decade of the seventeenth century, and could accommodate over thirty guests. It had several chambers that could double up as meeting rooms, with tables and plenty of seating. One such room had curtains at its three windows.[61] Agents for the king – 'His Majesty's Escheators' – met there in 1644,

---

[56] G. M. A. Beck, 'Some Petworth inns and alehouses', in G. H. Kenyon, 'Petworth Town and Trades 1610–1760', pt 3, *Sussex Archaeological Collections* 99 (Lewes, 1961), 136–44.

[57] Chichester, West Sussex Record Office, M.Dean.30, Midhurst Deanery. Innholder Richard Bishop's will shows that in 1641 the Swan was in North Street, but Pigot & Co.'s *Royal National & Commercial Directory & Topography of the Counties of Kent, Surrey, Sussex* (London, 1839, facsimile edn, 1993), 267, shows that a Swan Inn had been functioning in the market square since at least 1839.

[58] Arundel Castle Archives, MD 535, Miscellaneous Documents.

[59] J. Pennington, *The Chequer Inn, Steyning: Five Centuries of Innkeeping in a Sussex Market Town* (Lancing, 1990), 5; Chichester, West Sussex Record Office, Wiston Archives MS 2485.

[60] Hudson, *VCH*, vol. 6 pt 1 (Oxford, 1980), 146–7.

[61] Chichester, West Sussex Record Office, EP1/29/106/002, Probate Inventories.

collecting revenues from estates where owners had died without known heirs.[62] In 1687 depositions in a law suit were taken at the Kings Head and by 1690 the Red Lion was in five separate tenancies, fast sliding down the social scale.[63]

An inn sign was very much part of the building's identity. It reflected social status, and travellers may have expected that the larger the sign the better would be the inn. A hierarchy of inn signs and their supporting brackets and posts emerges from the documentation of the region, and contemporary illustrations reveal their forms. Some inns had a gallows sign. This was a large wooden beam supported over the whole width of the road by a stout post on either side, from which the sign, and possibly a carved and painted wooden bunch of grapes (indicating that wine was available), was suspended. The grapes were sometimes above the beam in their own bracket. This elaborate inn sign would have signalled to the traveller that the inn was of the better sort. At Horsham in 1622 the landlady of the Anchor inn was fined because her sign was rated as an 'obstruction' and the Red Lion had 'a sign and posts' in 1637.[64] In 1604 it was reported to a Chichester court that 'the sign of the White Horse is very much decayed and not well to be discerned by reason of the weather ... which hath washed away the colour of him.'[65] The innkeeper presumably had to repaint it.

There is evidence for the build-up of innkeeping dynasties within the region throughout the period and multiple ownership of inns can also be seen. John Oliver held a wine licence in New Shoreham in 1585; in 1636 Thomas Oliver held wine licences for an inn in Steyning, and eight others for inns or taverns in east Sussex.[66] An amusing example from the neighbouring region can be seen when diarist John Byng commented in 1788 that his 'host's name at Winchelsea was Bray, the same at Battle, and so is our host at Horsebridge; all relations. We like asses have been braying about for these four days'.[67]

One innkeeping family was connected with the Musket Gun inn at Findon from 1619 or earlier to at least 1800. Thomas Lasseter was running a small inn, as well as making muskets, in 1619. William Lasseter-French insured the much enlarged inn with the Sun Fire Office in 1798. In 1725 John Lasseter was a maltster in Findon and at least nine family members were blacksmiths there throughout the period. The inn had a brewhouse; in 1722 the cellars held 4,000

[62] Chichester, West Sussex Record Office, Holmes, Campbell & Co. MSS. 1022.

[63] Arundel Castle Archives, HO 16–67, Title deeds of Red Lion; in 1791, 'much split up for votes'.

[64] A. Hughes, *Down at the Old Bull and Bush* (Horsham, 1997), 6; Chichester, West Sussex Record Office, Probate Inventories, EP1/29/106/059.

[65] Morgan, *Chichester*, 112.

[66] PRO, Exchequer: King's Remembrancer: Vintners' Fines, E 176/1/172; Caldecott, 'Sussex Taverns', 68. John Oliver was keeping the Black Rabbit near Arundel in 1804.

[67] Souden, *Byng's Tours*, 81.

pints of beer and nearly 2,000 pints of wine. As a pub, it continues to trade under the sign of the Gun.[68]

Innkeeping was a skilled occupation and those who married wisely prospered and built up their trade. Family members who were prepared to spread their abilities over several linked occupations contributed to the longevity of the successful innkeeping dynasties within the region, as at the Gun and the Spread Eagle. Many widows also ran inns, some staying for a long time, others disappearing from the written record, perhaps into judicious marriages with other innkeepers.

Across the region the inns, both urban and rural, tripled in number over the 150 year period. In 1550 Sussex was well known for its terrible road system. Few dedicated taverns seem to have been operating at this time, as accommodation for travellers and their transport was the major consideration. By law taverns were not allowed to provide guest beds, although some licensed vintners ran inns. By the early-seventeenth century this was more common in the towns than in the countryside, though several rural inns provided wine for much of the period. The urban inns were relatively small compared to Everitt's late-seventeenth century Northampton inns, where the Bull had thirty-six rooms in 1672 and the George forty-one in 1698.[69] The largest inns in west Sussex in 1670 may have been the Dolphin at Chichester, with twenty-three hearths (the number of rooms is unknown) and the Great White Hart at Petworth, which had twenty-six rooms.[70] The Red Lion at Horsham had twenty-four rooms in 1611, but these inns were the exceptions.[71] Most of the urban inns for which inventories survive show an average of three to eight chambers – this also included sleeping accommodation for the innkeeper, his family and servants. Rural inns supplied two guest chambers on average, but often kept good cellars and varied food.

Inns built in the fifteenth and sixteenth centuries were falling on hard times by the end of the period. Changing commercial needs may also have led to some closures. As the seventeenth century progressed the inn hierarchy within the region began to break down. Soon after 1660 new inn names began to appear as new buildings were erected. The old medieval timber-framed inns needed repairs, and may well have been seen as old-fashioned, travellers expecting modern comforts such as heated chambers with lockable doors that did not have to be shared with strangers. One major cause of change was the difficult travelling conditions; as wheeled transport improved, the roads in the

[68]   J.Pennington, 'The Gun Inn, Findon, West Sussex', *West Sussex History* 60 (Chichester, October 1997), 25–9.

[69]   Everitt, 'The English urban Inn', 124, 127.

[70]   Morgan, *Chichester*, 70; Chichester, West Sussex Record Office, EP1/29/ 149/145, Probate Inventories.

[71]   Chichester, West Sussex Record Office, EP1/29/106/002, Probate Inventories.

region worsened. The rise in carriages and iron-shod wheels caused even more difficulties in the Sussex clay.

As travel deteriorated, and the need for it quickened, the inns of the region were in a dilemma. The population was rising, London was growing in size and more people were travelling. They all depended on the inn. The bad state of the roads in the region meant that travellers often had to stay longer than they might have wished if the weather worsened. The inns benefited from this and their numbers rose, though by 1700 there were still very few really large establishments.[72] It was not until the mid-eighteenth century that Turnpike Acts were implemented in Sussex, driven by the rise in popularity of sea-bathing at Brighton and other nearby seaside resorts.[73] The region's inns began to increase in size and multiply in number, though not, unfortunately, in time to impress Horace Walpole.[74]

---

[72] Bier and Finlay, *London*, 244; J. Pennington, 'Inns and Alehouses in 1686', in Leslie and Short, *Historical Atlas*, 68–9; J. Farrant, 'Growth of Communications 1720–1840', in Leslie and Short, *Historical Atlas*, 78–9.

[73] Chichester, West Sussex Record Office, MP 867, Miscellaneous Papers – Turnpike Trusts. County Reports of the Secretary of State, no. 3, Sussex (London 1852). Under a Turnpike Act a defined stretch of road came under the jurisdiction of a trust which maintained it from tolls collected to defray expenses; S. Berry, 'Urban Development 1750–1914', in Leslie & Short, *Historical Atlas*, 92–3.

[74] Chichester, West Sussex Record Office, MP 423, Miscellaneous Papers. Walpole reported that he had set up his staff and finished his pilgrimages for 1749, as 'Sussex is a great damper of curiosity.'

The Public House and Military Culture in Germany, 1500–1648

B. Ann Tlusty

According to local chronicles, when the mercenary captain Schertlin von Burtenbach entered the city of Augsburg during the Schmalkaldic War in 1546, he was accompanied by four thousand men, all of whom were quartered in the city and its environs.[1] A year later, the victorious emperor Charles V entered the city 'with great strength of troops.'[2] What would this many soldiers, many of whom were accompanied by their wives and children, mean to a city with a population of between thirty and forty thousand? Where did they stay and how did they get on with the local populace?

Since Michael Roberts published his theory of an early modern 'military revolution' in 1956, historians have debated the extent to which this period represents a turning point in the development of the professional military corps that gradually replaced local defence systems.[3] The establishment of a standing army was an important step in the process of centralization and in the development of national identity, both of which attended the rise of absolutism. Studies of this process, however, tend to concentrate primarily on institutional aspects such as military organization, competing jurisdictions, improvements in technology, recruitment and financing of troops, and so on, and to pay little attention to parallel socio-cultural factors that also affected defence decisions.

Recent work that targets the social history of war has begun to correct this imbalance, initially by focusing attention on the primacy of the human needs of the soldiers as a factor affecting military decisions. Frank Tallet for example sees logistics, or the provisioning of troops, as a more crucial problem than the dangers faced in battle. Military leaders since antiquity had known that troop efficiency was tied to sufficient provisions, and by the seventeenth century, this

---

[1]   W. Zorn, *Augsburg: Geschichte einer deutschen Stadt* (Augsburg, 1972), 188.

[2]   'mit starker Truppenmacht.' Ibid., 190.

[3]   Roberts's argument appears more recently as 'The Military Revolution', in M. Roberts (ed.), *Essays in Swedish history* (Minneapolis, 1967); see also J. Black, *A Military Revolution?* (Basingstroke, 1991); C. Rogers (ed.), *The Military Revolution Debate* (Boulder, CO, 1995).

was a major impetus in the development of standing national armies backed by state-controlled financing.[4]

Food for the soldiers, however, was only part of the problem. Soldiers also needed shelter to survive, particularly in winter. The public inn or tavern provided the obvious solution to both problems, for the provision of food, drink, and lodging in return for money was the basic form of economic exchange that defined the innkeeper's trade.[5] Paralleling other forms of hospitality, the function of quartering soldiers was gradually taken away from private householders and assumed by inns over the course of the sixteenth century. Inns and taverns also furnished soldiers and military recruiters with space for both professional and social activities. Even the state financing of military operations was partially dependent on public houses, for they provided a significant amount of revenue in the form of taxes on alcohol sales.

This paper will explore the role of inns and taverns in defence systems and in the lives of soldiers in Germany from the sixteenth century through the Thirty Years' War (1618–1648), primarily on the example of the imperial city of Augsburg and its environs. The importance of the inn to the highly mobile early modern soldier was related to its designation as a public form of household. Civic leaders after the Reformation placed increasing emphasis on the household as the key to the social discipline of their subjects. Control of the household and responsibility for its peaceful and productive functioning lay in the hands of the family head, and the sanctity of the home was protected by the traditional right of household peace (*Hausfrieden*).[6] An innkeeper, as master of his household, was also responsible for what went on within his house, and could be held partially responsible for fights and injuries, illegal gambling, blasphemies, or even the conversations that took place on his premises. Nonetheless, as 'public' (*öffentliche*) spaces, inns were more subject to control by the authorities than private households. With the late medieval shift from private to public hospitality, territorial and town officials slowly took over the role of controlling and protecting travellers, and in turn controlling the houses

---

[4]   F. Tallet, *War and Society in Early Modern Europe, 1495–1715* (London, 1992), 53–5, 62–3; R. Asch, *The Thirty Years War: The Holy Roman Empire and Europe, 1618–48* (New York, 1997), 152–5. For an overview of recent trends in German military history during the early modern period, notably the recent attention to socio-cultural factors, see the review article by P. H. Wilson, 'War in Early Modern German History', in *German History* 19, no. 3 (2001), 419–38.

[5]   All public houses in Augsburg were required by law to provide beds and stables in order to be licensed to seat guests for food or drinks; thus the terms 'inn' and 'tavern' might be used interchangeably.

[6]   H. C. Peyer, *Von der Gastfreundschaft zum Gasthaus: Studien zur Gastlichkeit im Mittelalter* (Hannover, 1987), 34–51, 67.

in which they stayed.[7] Only in a public house could the city government regulate the amounts and types of food and drink that could be served, the hours during which hospitality was available, and the sorts of facilities guests could expect. This aspect of control increased the suitability of inns for recruiting and military quartering.

Tensions between soldiers and local residents also played out in tavern settings. Inns and taverns had a role in the process of constructing the distinct soldier identities that would ultimately drive a cultural wedge between the military sector and the civilian populace. At the same time, segregation of soldiers from civilians strained relations between urban and rural populations, as soldiers were increasingly expelled from the civic community and forced on the villages.

The relationship between public houses and soldiers in many cases began at the outset of the soldier's military career, with his recruitment. The combination of public space and alcoholic drinks offered by the inn was particularly convenient for military recruiters. As was the case with many kinds of contracts, the fact that the recruitment occurred in a public place made witnesses easy to find. The innkeeper himself sometimes signed recruiting contracts as an official witness.[8] Persons wishing to enlist not only received an immediate cash payment (*Laufgeld*) from the recruiter, but also a drink afterwards to seal the contract. The offer of cash and drink was naturally irresistible to some tavern patrons, particularly those who were broke, unemployed, and already under the influence of alcohol. Tavern visitors who contracted to enlist while in a drunken state could get out of the contract by returning the *Laufgeld*, for the actual enlistment, or swearing in, did not take place until the recruit appeared at the muster at a time and place designated by the recruiter.[9] However, if the recruit

---

[7]   Stadtarchiv Augsburg (hereafter StadtAA), Ratsbücher no. 16 1529–42, 49; Schätze no. ad 36/8, 27; Zucht- und Policey-Ordnung 1537, fol. A4; Staats- und Stadtbibliothek Augsburg (hereafter SStBA), 4° Cod.Aug.132, fol. 38v; Peyer, *Von der Gastfreundschaft zum Gasthaus*, 34–51, 67; N. Schindler, *Widerspenstige Leute: Studien zur Volkskultur in der frühen Neuzeit* (Frankfurt, 1992), 250; A. Erler and E. Kaufmann (eds), *Handwörterbuch zur deutschen Rechtsgeschichte*, 8 vols (Berlin, 1967), vol. 1, 2022–3.

[8]   StadtAA, Militaria 53, Werbungen 1578–1716.

[9]   The *Laufgeld* was normally one gulden in the 1590s, but was raised to six gulden during the Thirty Years' War: J. Kraus, *Das Militärwesen der Reichsstadt Augsburg 1548–1806* (Augsburg, 1980), 188. Based on prices for wine and beer in 1589 and 1602, one gulden would have been sufficient for nearly 4 litres of wine or over ten times as much beer: see StadtAA, Chroniken 10, Siedeler Chronik 1055–1619, 173, 284; U. Dirlmeier, *Untersuchungen zu Einkommensverhältnissen und Lebenshaltungskosten in oberdeutschen Städten des Spätmittelalters (Mitte 14. bis Anfang 16. Jahrhundert)* (Heidelberg, 1978), 570. For persons who enlisted while drunk and later returned the *Laufgeld*: StadtAA, Urgichten (hereafter Urg.),

had spent the money in the meantime and was unable to return it, then failure to appear for the muster could lead to arrest and possible punishment.[10]

The primary concern of local councils in military matters was of course local defence, and thus civic authorities in Augsburg did not tolerate recruitment of local citizens by foreign powers in their inns. The penalty for enlisting to a foreign power was loss of citizenship.[11] Foreign recruiters, however, did operate in Augsburg inns along with local and imperial military representatives, for local citizens were not the only source of new recruits. Strangers from outside the city sometimes reported the intention to enlist as their reason for coming to town.[12] Their activities would most likely have been welcomed by local innkeepers, who would be certain to profit from the combination of hosting travellers and providing drinks for recruits. In fact, some were not above allowing recruiters to advertise their presence by displaying military hardware outside the tavern door.[13]

Once the soldiers had been mustered, military leaders were immediately faced with the challenge of providing them with sufficient food and housing. For this, they depended primarily on local resources. Soldiers during the sixteenth and seventeenth century could rarely expect to be paid regularly, or at a rate sufficient to cover living expenses. Instead, they supported themselves by exacting food, shelter, and contributions from the local populace, or by resorting to plunder. Normally, the households in which soldiers were quartered had to provide provisions, usually in the form of food and supplies, but sometimes also as cash contributions. Provisions ordinances that listed these requirements were designed both to ensure that soldiers were treated in accordance with their rank, and to limit exploitation of their hosts.[14] Cooperation in these matters was often

Hans Dietrich, 15 May 1590; Michael Jeckle, 30 Sept.–12 Oct. 1591; Matthäus Naterer, 1592; Georg Eberle, 10 Oct. 1594; Elias Köln, 9 May 1590.

[10] Even more serious was signing up twice and accepting two payments from different recruiters, which constituted fraud (*Betrug*) and was punishable by banishment even after the money had been returned. StadtAA, Urg., Hans Dietrich, 15 May 1590; Hans Mair, 6 Aug. 1592; Matheus Funck, 5 Aug. 1594.

[11] An exception was made for recruiting for imperial forces, since Augsburg, as an imperial city, was officially under the Emperor's jurisdiction (Kraus, *Militärwesen*, 96).

[12] See for example StadtAA, Urg., Michel Jeckle, 30 Sept. 1591; Hans Mair, 6 Aug. 1592; Matthäus Naterer, 1592; Hans Büler, 25–6 Jan. 1594.

[13] P. Burschel, *Söldner im Nordwestdeutschland des 16. und 17. Jahrhunderts: Sozialgeschichtliche Studien* (Göttingen, 1994), 106.

[14] J. Theibault, *German Villages in Crisis: Rural Life in Hesse-Kassel and the Thirty Years' War, 1580–1720* (Boston, 1995), 138; E. Landsteiner and A. Weigl, "'Sonsten finden wir die Sachen sehr übel aufm Landt beschaffen....'" Krieg und lokale Gesellschaft in Niederösterreich (1618–1621)', in B. von Krusenstjern and H. Medick (eds), *Zwischen Alltag und Katastrophe: Der Dreißigjährige Krieg aus der Nähe* (Göttingen, 1999), 229–71, esp.

the best policy. Providing for the soldiers was expensive, but resistance usually meant that the soldiers would be given permission to plunder at will.

During most of the sixteenth century, soldiers in Augsburg were billeted in pairs or with their families in private homes. Some were also put up in inns, which also served as homes for the innkeeper and his family. Sharing living quarters with local families for as long as a year or more, these soldiers and their families were thus integrated into the daily life of the local residents. This is not to suggest that they formed happy multiple-family groups. Certainly friendly relations between the soldiers and their hosts were possible; but such relationships are difficult to evaluate, for peaceful families leave few records behind. To most local citizens, however, the soldiers with their mobile lifestyle, even if they were travelling with wives and children, must have carried a taint of suspicion and disorder from the outset. Households without houses, the vagabond-like soldier families were particularly threatening to the metaphor of the orderly household fostered by civic leaders during the post-Reformation period. Soldiers thus remained 'outsiders' and tended to be unwelcome guests under the best of circumstances. Unmarried soldiers especially, who were usually quartered in pairs, were inclined towards rowdy and unruly behaviour.

In reading the statements of witnesses and defendants involved in altercations with soldiers, it is possible to identify a pattern. Most householders in either defending their actions or discrediting those of their adversaries used a vocabulary that represented the soldiers as a threat to the household. During the so-called 'armoured Imperial Diet' of 1548, for example, Augsburg craftsman Simon Schwert became irritated when he came home drunk and found 'several soldiers sitting about his oven none of whom had been presented to him'.[15] Although the group had apparently been invited by a soldier quartered in his house, Schwert justified provoking them with insults by characterizing them as intruders at his hearth. Perhaps most typical was the household squabble that broke out between weaver Hans Heiss and his unwelcome guest Hainrich Imveld after Heiss tried to put out the fire upon which Imveld's wife was cooking. According to Heiss, the soldier's wife had too much wood on the fire.[16] The accusation that the soldiers wasted wood and other household provisions was a common one, as were arguments over the control of keys and locked doors.[17]

234; StadtAA, Militaria 57, 1645. Officers were afforded amounts sufficient to support their entire entourage.

[15] 'etlich lanndtsknecht vmb seinen offen herumb gesessen, vnd doch ime khainer eingefurrt gewest', StadtAA, Urg., Simon Schwert, 23 Jan. 1548.

[16] Heiss attacked both the soldier and his pregnant wife with a javelin. StadtAA, Urg., Hans Heiss, 11 Aug. 1548.

[17] Landsteiner and Weigl, 'Krieg und lokale Gesellschaft', 257–8.

At stake in these squabbles was dominion in the household. In formulating their arguments, householders drew on traditional notions of household peace and patriarchal control. The intrusion of these outsiders threatened to undermine order in the household and corrupt the morals of its members.[18] At stake, too, was the dominion of civic authorities; just as the presence of additional men in the household undermined the authority of the family patriarch, the presence of a separate locus of power and discipline in the city in the form of military authority threatened the power of local governors. Household dominion and civic power were related both on a practical and on a metaphorical level. Civic government especially after the Reformation was based on an image of patriarchal discipline and control, with the city council acting in the role of city fathers. They based their vision of a godly community on the model of an orderly household.[19] The unruly soldiers threatened to destroy this ideal on both levels, for fights breaking out between soldiers and citizens represented a greater problem than the normal sorts of swordplay common in early modern city streets. What began as a household squabble could escalate to a confessional or political dispute, and a soldier being killed as a result might have political ramifications. The council's sensitivity to this danger is evident in an ordinance issued in 1547, in which city fathers demanded 'patience' in putting up with the unwelcome visitors and warned sharply against any form of resistance. Provocative or rebellious behaviour on the part of the citizenry, they warned, would lead to the city's ruin, and 'drown [it] in blood';[20] elsewhere they cautioned that actions that encouraged 'quarrelling and ill-will between citizens and the soldiers' could easily lead to 'havoc and pandemonium'.[21]

The disgruntled citizenry did not accept the burden of quartering without complaint. In fact, Augsburg's townspeople flooded the city council with countless petitions, seeking every possible avenue of relief. Again, their arguments were shaped to appeal to concern for orderly households and productive crafts. Some invoked moral concerns, complaining that the men of the house often had to be out and the women were left alone with single soldiers. Others complained of space problems, noting that they were sleeping

---

[18] Tallett, *War and Society*, 166.

[19] According to Agrippa von Nettesheim (1486–1535), the household serves as metaphor for the state ('Das Haus ist ein Bild des Staates'): H. C. Agrippa von Nettesheim, *Die Eitelkeit und Unsicherheit der Wissenschaften und die Verteidigungsschrift* , ed. F. Mauthner (Munich, 1913), 300.

[20] 'dardurch dise Stat ... gewisslich im plut ertrinckhen vnnd verterben muest'. StadtAA, Anschläge und Dekrete no. 23, 21 Feb. 1547. Relations with soldiers were particularly tense during the politically charged years of the Augsburg *Interim* (1548–55).

[21] 'Hans Erhart von Augspurg hat zwischen Burgern vnnd den knechten, villerlay Rumor, Zankh vnnd widerwillen angericht, daraus leichtlich vnrat vnnd auffrur het ensteen mög[en]'. StadtAA, Urg., Hans Erhart, 25 Mar. 1548.

three to a bed even before the soldiers arrived and the only space left was the shop room, leaving them unable to practice their crafts. Many complained about the costs of wasted provisions and damage for which they were not paid, suggesting that their household could end up in financial ruin and their families would be forced to seek poor relief from the city.[22]

As disruptive as soldiers could be in private homes, it appears that those billeted in pairs and small groups caused fewer problems for their hosts than larger groups stationed together in public houses. For Augsburg's publicans, hospitality was a matter of ordinance; all those who wished to serve drinks at tables were required by law to provide beds and linen for overnight guests and stables for their horses. A list of quartering costs that has survived from the Imperial Diet of 1550–51 allows a statistical look at the difference between quartering in inns and private households. Based on a sample of half of the entries in the list, 1,399 soldiers and family members were quartered in 553 private homes, for an average of 2.5 per household. Twelve of these were listed as including children. An additional 130 soldiers and their families, three of which included children, were quartered in sixteen public inns, for an average of eight per inn.

The concentration of soldiers in larger groups seems in turn to have increased the potential for disorder. Innkeepers were over ten times more likely to report both costs from damages and incidents of violence than private citizens.[23] It is of course possible that this statistic is inflated by the innkeeper's professional experience in keeping accounts. Innkeepers may well have been more savvy about reporting the costs of damage than private citizens, although the public inn had not by 1551 become so separate from the household as to account for a disparity this great. Unfortunately for the city's innkeepers, however, the threat posed by soldiers to the private household must have seemed more pervasive than the danger posed by rowdy tavern comportment. Over the course of the sixteenth century, soldiers were gradually moved out of the private households and into public institutions, including both permanent military quarters and inns. The result was to create a firmer boundary between the soldiers and the local populace.

The process of isolating soldiers from the populace began in Augsburg with the construction during the 1580s of permanent military barracks. In 1582 the first wing of the so-called *Zwinger* (or barbican)[24] was erected on the city wall.

---

[22]   StadtAA, Militaria 55, Landquartierwesen 1518–1638.

[23]   StadtAA, Schätze 137e, Einquartierbuch 1551. 62.5 per cent of innkeepers claimed damages averaging 15.5 gulden each, and 25 per cent complained of violent incidents; by comparison, 5.4 per cent of other citizens claimed damages averaging 5.2 gulden each, and 2.2 per cent reported violence.

[24]   The *Zwinger* was so named because of its location in the barbican, the area between the city's inner and outer fortifications.

The *Zwinger* was expanded between 1585 and 1597 to a total of 274 apartments. The apartments were originally built as a residence for permanent
members of the local guard, who had formerly been housed in mean huts along
the wall, but it was later used to quarter soldiers from outside the city as well.[25]
The *Zwinger* even contained its own tap house, with wine available to the soldiers at a reduced tax rate. Unlike other publicans in the city, the landlord in the
Zwinger tap house was also allowed to extend credit to his customers. These
measures may have been intended as an incentive for soldiers to stay away
from the local taverns (and out of brawls with local citizens).[26]

The numbers of troops recruited in and around the city during the Thirty
Years' War, however, far exceeded the capacity of the city's barracks. By this
time, quartering in private homes was apparently no longer considered an option except in extreme situations. This development was not unique to
Augsburg, but paralleled billeting decisions elsewhere in Europe.[27] Innkeepers,
whose houses were considered public, were unable to raise effective objections
to the forced billeting of soldiers in their homes. At the beginning of the war,
the large numbers of newly recruited soldiers were quartered exclusively in
public inns, nearly all of them outside the city walls in the surrounding villages.
This remained the solution of choice for Augsburg's authorities throughout the
war – whenever possible, troops were quartered in public houses, preferably
outside the city. In addition, new military apartments were added to the city
walls in 1619, according one chronicler, 'so that the citizenry would not be too
burdened by the troops'.[28] Thus the city was successful, for the time being, in
keeping distance between professional soldiers and the local populace. During
this phase of the war, quartering in the city was generally limited to high-
ranking officers, who were put up either in the finer inns or the homes of the
local elites.

Of course, the quartering of common troops in country villages also had its
problems. Based on complaints by the innkeepers of Oberhausen (a village just
outside Augsburg's walls), soldiers billeted in village inns proved to be most
unpleasant company. Innkeepers complained that they kept other guests out of
the inns, either refusing to allow them in or frightening them off with their disorderly behaviour, and that they threatened the wives and families of their hosts

---

[25] Kraus, *Militärwesen*, 198; G. Grünsteudel, G. Hägele, and R. Frankenberger (eds),
Augsburger Stadtlexikon (2nd edn, Augsburg, 1998), 953.

[26] StadtAA, Militaria 196, 1603. Money to repay debts to the *Zwinger* tap-house could be
withheld from the soldier's pay.

[27] See for example J. Hunter (England) and H. Heiss (Tyrol) in this volume.

[28] 'Damit aber das Kriegs-Volck der Burgerschafft nicht allzu beschwehrlich fallen
möchte'. P. von Stetten, *Geschichte der Heil. Röm. Reichs Freyen Stadt Augspurg aus
Bewährten Jahr-Büchern und Tüchtigen Urkunden gezogen*, 2 vols (Frankfurt a. M. and
Leipzig, 1743), vol. 1, 833–4.

as well. One publican insisted that he 'could not be sure of life and limb' as long as the soldiers were in his house; another, that a soldier had beaten his crippled daughter.[29] Others told stories of soldiers wrecking inn property, injuring other customers, cursing, gambling, and committing all manner of 'sins and blasphemies'. The introduction of tobacco in the seventeenth century led to an even greater threat – soldiers, the innkeepers complained, were smoking in the stables in a state of drunkenness, and were certain eventually to burn down their stables, inns, and yards.[30] Chronicles and other accounts from throughout Germany suggest that this was hardly an isolated problem; in fact, some historians have suggested that during the Thirty Years' War, more damage occurred as a result of quartering than from any other form of military action.[31]

To make matters worse, collecting payment for the expenses incurred by quartered soldiers proved extremely problematic for the innkeepers. Theoretically, publicans should have been paid for feeding and lodging soldiers from moneys collected as war contributions. War financing, however, was in a transitional phase during the sixteenth and seventeenth centuries. Ordinances regulating provisions and payments for quarters were difficult to enforce, and the responsible parties were often far away. Many innkeepers complained that soldiers simply refused to pay, or paid only 'as much as suits their pleasure'.[32] One innkeeper petitioned to the War Commission in 1619 for reimbursement after soldiers left secretly during the night without paying their bill of five hundred gulden, leaving an additional four hundred gulden in damages, and stealing much of his silver, linens, and other property besides.[33] Based on this and many other bills, the soldiers spared no expenses at their meals and drinking bouts. Officers in particular often chose expensive imported wine and drank vermouth or brandy with their breakfast. On many days they invited guests and held banquets, consuming amounts equal to five or six days' ordinary board at one meal.[34]

Village innkeepers rarely seemed to receive satisfaction for unpaid bills. The War Commission found plenty of excuses to refuse bills, claiming they were submitted too late or included inflated charges.[35] When the soldiers were

---

[29]   StadtAA, Militaria 34, Werbungen 1624–1745, 1632; Militaria 55, Landquartierwesen Contributionsamt 1518–1638, 1561.

[30]   StadtAA, Militaria 34, Werbungen 1624–1745, 1632.

[31]   Landsteiner and Weigle, 'Krieg und lokale Gesellschaft', 234.

[32]   '...nit, wie dann die verordneten taxier herrn taxiert, betzallt, sonnder sovill und was sy gelust ires gefallens geben'. StadtAA, Militaria 55, 1551.

[33]   StadtAA, Militaria 55, 1619.

[34]   StadtAA, Militaria 55. Foods consumed are not itemized in any of the bills. For similar descriptions from elsewhere in Germany, see for example *Die Chronik des Johann Philipp Mohr*, ed. Christian Waas, in *Die Chroniken von Friedberg in der Wetterau* (Friedberg, 1937), 243–53; Reginbald Moehner, *Reisetagebuch* (SStBA, 4° Cod. Aug.83), fols 1v–5v, 101v.

[35]   StadtAA, Militaria 55; Militaria 59.

imperial troops, their hosts often reported that they did not know to whom they could turn with their claims, and even when they applied to the appropriate authorities, the processing of the claim could take years.[36] Some innkeepers went into debt themselves in order to keep the inn running, and ultimately were forced to close their doors permanently.[37]

For Augsburg and its surrounding villages, however, the most devastating phase of the war was yet to come. In March of 1632, between nine hundred and thirteen hundred Bavarian troops entered the city in a short-lived attempt to provide additional defence against the advancing army of King Gustavus Adolphus. They were routed and replaced a month later by several Swedish regiments with a total troop strength estimated at between two and four thousand men. The Swedish troops arrived under the command of the Swedish king himself, who was welcomed as an avenging angel by many of Augsburg's Protestant citizens.[38]

Space limitations do not permit a detailed description of the complicated shifts in confessional politics that attended the fortunes of war during the years that followed; the primary point to be made is that beginning with Gustavus Adolphus's entry into the city in 1632, using quartering as a form of confessional abuse became the rule. Initially, these abuses still tended to target public institutions, although the numbers of soldiers present in the city during the Swedish occupation soon exceeded the capacity of public houses and buildings. Thus Swedish troops began by taking over Catholic schools, the various buildings associated with the Cathedral, and the Catholic welfare settlement known as the Fuggerei, as well as the *Zwinger* quarters.[39] But eventually they also moved into Catholic homes. The ruinous costs of maintaining these troops within the city, too, fell largely upon the unfortunate Catholic citizenry. Military finances by this time were becoming increasingly tied to the government bureaucracy, allowing a greater measure of control from the top. A large portion of the nearly 320,000 gulden spent on war costs in 1633, which made up nearly half of the total city budget, was collected from Catholic householders.[40] When the city again fell into the hands of the

---

[36] As one petitioner put it, payment could be obtained 'only with a great deal of inconvenience and trouble' ('erst mit grosser unglegenhait unnd mühe') (StadtAA, Militaria 34, 1632); another was still trying to get his payment six years after the fact (StadtAA, Militaria 59, 1638).

[37] StadtAA, Militaria 59; Fürstlich und Gräflich Fuggerisches Familien- und Stiftungsarchiv, Kirchheim/Amtsrechnung, 10 April 1634.

[38] B. Roeck, *Eine Stadt in Krieg und Frieden: Studien zur Geschichte der Reichsstadt Augsburg zwischen Kalenderstreit und Parität* (Göttingen, 1989), 687–9.

[39] Roeck, *Eine Stadt*, 731; StadtAA, Chroniken 27a, Chronik von Jakob Wagner 1609–47, 150.

[40] SStBA, 2 Cod°Aug.123 (Singularia Augustana) fol. 33.

Catholics in 1635, the situation quickly reversed, with both the physical and the financial burdens of quartering now falling upon the Protestant members of the bi-confessional city.

Along with financial burdens, the city suffered physical abuse at the hands of both the Swedish and the imperial troops. The extravagant soldier banquets continued, according to one chronicler 'beginning with brandy in the morning and continuing with wine and beer the entire day'. The drunken soldiers then engaged in malicious destruction of gardens and homes, carried off livestock, and left the city in filth and ruin.[41] By 1635, the financial situation in the city was catastrophic. According to a desperate petition from local defence officials on the part of the citizenry, at least 100 households were already in ruin and the survival of the entire city was at risk.[42]

At this point even the elite members of the Lords' and Merchants' societies began to petition for relief from the ruinous costs of contributions. In return for their financial support of the war effort (overwhelmingly extracted from the Protestant members), most of these wealthy citizens were exempted from actually putting up soldiers in their homes. The standard response from the Office of the Quartermaster to their complaints, then, was that his office was operating under the assumption that contributions were preferable to having the soldiers 'in [their] very homes and about [their] necks', but if they would prefer they could take in the soldiers rather than pay the contributions.[43]

Yet the greatest burden of quartering troops within the city continued to fall on the innkeepers, whose houses were by now clearly viewed as public institutions. In 1634, when the Brewer's guild petitioned against their disproportionate burden and requested that more soldiers be put up in private homes, they were rebuffed with the explanation that they 'were all required by their duty and oath to keep public inns and stables'.[44] According to the brewers' petition, they had been promised that they would not be disadvantaged by the presence of troops, but would be properly paid and thus should treat them as they would any other guest.[45] Instead, the soldiers were wasting precious commodities such as oil, wood, salt, and candles, all of which were in short supply during the war, for which they refused to pay. Added to this charge were the usual complaints that they chased off other guests and terrorized the

---

[41] 'vnd ist des eßens vnd trinckhens ... am morgen mit dem brandtwein angefangen, vnd hernach mit dem bier vnd wein den gantzen tag gewehrt'. StadtAA, Chroniken 27a, Chronik von Jakob Wagner 1609–47, 173.

[42] SStBA, 2 Cod°Aug.123 (Singularia Augustana), 1635.

[43] 'gar im Hauß vnnd ob dem Halß zue haben', StadtAA, Militaria 55, 23 July 1633.

[44] 'sie Bierschenckhen all offne würthßsheüser vnd stalungen: auch pflicht vnd aydt halber haben müßen.' StadtAA, Militaria 55, 1634.

[45] 'hatt man vnnß darneben angezaigt, das wür sie anderst nit, alls für frembde Gösst annemen vnd halten, vnd irenthalber khain beschwerdt tragen sollen'. Ibid.

brewers' families and servants, jeopardizing the continued existence of their businesses. Although Protestant brewers were also more heavily burdened than Catholics, their real disadvantage lay less in their confession of faith than it did in their oath of profession.

Based on Augsburg's financial records, however, these urban innkeepers were ultimately more successful than their village counterparts in collecting reimbursement for the expenses of war. Some may even have profited from entertaining soldiers; at the least, they suffered less than many other groups. The Thirty Years' War had a devastating effect on all of Augsburg's society, but innkeepers as a group recovered more quickly than did most other trades. The total number of inns in the city remained fairly consistent despite a drop in the population of over fifty per cent, so that while there was approximately one inn for every 460 inhabitants around 1600, by 1646 the ratio was greater than 1:200. In poorer areas of the city, numbers of innkeepers actually increased, as did their average net worth, a rare phenomenon after the devastation of the war. Several of the brewing families, far from suffering financially, spent the war years expanding their business into larger breweries. By 1646 a number of beerhouses existed that incorporated two or even three buildings.[46] This degree of success in the face of adversity certainly contradicts the assumption that the sixteenth-century attacks on drunkenness died out during the seventeenth century because the common classes could no longer afford the luxury of drinking bouts.[47] Apparently social drinking bouts continued despite the pains of war.

The fact that tavern drinking continued unabated could only have been welcomed by city authorities, for (in the words of Augsburg patrician Markus Welser), 'the daily excesses in boozing [brought] to the city coffers a great and notable profit'.[48] In fact, the contribution made by innkeepers in providing quarters for soldiers paled in comparison to the financial contributions collected in the form of excise taxes on alcohol. These taxes had always been an important source of income. Between 1550 and 1650, taxes on alcohol made

---

[46] B. A. Tlusty, *Bacchus and Civic Order: The Culture of Drink in Early Modern Germany* (Charlottesville, VA, 2001), 43. Net worth is based on collection of property tax, which Roeck has shown to be a reasonable measure of comparative wealth; Roeck, *Eine Stadt*, 52–62; and compare Roeck's tables 56 and 144 (ibid., 486, 938), which show that the mean tax payment of virtually every group in the city decreased between 1618 and 1646.

[47] As claimed, for example, by R. van Dülmen, *Entstehung des frühneuzeitlichen Europa 1550–1648* (Frankfurt, 1982), 209.

[48] 'Der Cammer bey solchem vbermässigen Sauffen ... täglich ein namhafften vnd grossen Gelt einträgt'. Welser's remark was made in connection with the excise tax raise of 1547. M. Welser, *Chronica der weitberühmten Kaiserlichen freien und des H. Reichs Stadt Augsburg in Schwaben* (1595, reprint Augsburg, 1984), 68.

up an average of over fifty per cent of Augsburg's total revenue, making them the city's largest single source of funds – and they gained even more in importance during wartime.[49] A raise in excise taxes on alcohol had helped to finance the cost of peace with the Emperor in 1547,[50] and the same measure in 1596 raised money to support the war with the Turks.[51] When the expenses of the Thirty Years' War became too burdensome, the council again found that there was 'no more comfortable means' by which to offset the costs than to raise the tax once more.[52] The first major tax raise came in 1623, and the income that resulted made up over eighty per cent of the sharp rise in total city revenue that occurred in that year.[53] The tavern keepers, however, found this solution more burdensome than the war, and filed numerous complaints. The following year, the tax was returned to the former rate, although a higher tax on brandy remained in effect.[54] The city was again forced to raise the tax on alcoholic beverages during the Swedish occupation between 1633 and 1635, although by this time the results were less spectacular. Still, the income from alcohol taxes made a quicker and more solid recovery after the siege than did other sources of civic income (for example, property taxes). Innkeepers were aware of the importance of this contribution, suggesting in their complaints that because the soldiers were keeping regular guests away from their houses, the city would suffer as a result of lost excise tax revenue.[55] Their claims were not exaggerated, for excise taxes on alcohol were second only to incurring debt as a means of financing local defence and paying off troops to prevent unrestrained plundering.[56] Even in towns that depended on raises in direct taxes rather than alcohol taxes as a solution to the problem of war expenses – as, for example, in

---

[49] Based on a total of all revenues excluding loans to the city. See Tlusty, *Bacchus*, 176–81. These statistics refer to the account 'Wine Tax' (*Weinungeld*), which included taxes on beer, mead, and brandy as well as wine. Brandy was taxed separately only between 1472 and 1543.

[50] The tax on wine was raised by 50 per cent, so that nearly half the price of a glass of wine was for tax. Tax on beer and mead was also raised, but at a lesser rate (Welser, *Chronica*, 68); 85,619 gulden in alcohol taxes were collected in 1547, an increase of 87 per cent over the previous year (StadtAA, Einnehmerbücher, 1546, 1547). Altogether, the city had to pay 270,000 gulden to the Emperor and his allies, most of which was financed by loans (Zorn, *Augsburg*, 189).

[51] StadtAA, Evangelisches Wesensarchiv no. 458, 212.

[52] 'kein bequemer mittel': StadtAA, Schätze no. 16, 438, Verrueff vnd Anschlag wegen erhohung dess Ungelts, 15 Sep. 1633.

[53] Total revenues for 1623 were 653,554 gulden, 536,772 of which came from tax on alcohol. StadtAA, Einnehmerbücher, 1623.

[54] StadtAA, Ungeldamt MM XVII (fasc. 2).

[55] StadtAA, Militaria 55, 1634.

[56] Roeck, *Eine Stadt*, 733–75; Zorn, *Augsburg*, 217–19. The relative importance of excise tax to city income, as compared to that of the property tax, increased steadily throughout the war years. StadtAA, Einnehmerbücher, 1624–48.

Nördlingen – the alcohol tax continued unabated, remaining a dependable source of city income throughout the worst of the war years.[57]

The soldiers themselves undoubtedly contributed to the health of the drink trade, for their reputation for being less than consistent in paying for their room and board was far exceeded by their reputation as hearty drinkers. The combination of groups of soldiers and readily available alcohol was a dangerous mix. This was especially true as the soldiers were more likely than other citizens to be carrying swords. Early modern men in general were quick to resort to violence in defence of their honour, especially in public places, but military men were under even more pressure to do so. Their profession required not only that they maintain and carry a weapon; they were also expected to know how to use it. Thus tavern fights involving soldiers were a common occurrence. A tragic example of the pressure soldiers and members of the guards could face in tavern situations is provided in the case of Caspar Aufschlager, a guardsman interrogated in 1591 for killing another soldier in a duel that began in an Augsburg public house. Witnesses reported that the victim, Caspar Rauner, had accused Aufschlager of not being 'man enough'[58] to defend himself, and had said that if Aufschlager were an 'honourable soldier' (*redlicher Landsknecht*) he would meet him in the street. A local weaver who was present to hear Rauner's insults also chided Aufschlager with the words, 'I'll hit you in the face myself, if you call yourself a soldier and put up with that'.[59] Thus Aufschlager had no choice but to defend his honour, a decision that was fully endorsed by his guard unit. A petition from his superior officers noted that Rauner had 'not only greatly injured Aufschlager's honour, but especially ... made claims that Aufschlager did not have the manhood or honour to fight'.[60] His actions, they concluded, were entirely in keeping with the expectations of his profession.

Particularly skilful use of a weapon could also win the respect of observers to a fight, as illustrated in the case of an officer identified only as 'the

---

[57] Income from alcohol taxes in Nördlingen ranged from around 35 to 45 per cent of city income in the sixteenth century; during the worst phase of the Thirty Years' War, there was a real rise in the alcohol taxes, although they dropped to 11.6 per cent of receipts as a result of raises in direct taxes. By 1700, excise taxes on alcohol again made up 39 per cent of municipal income. C. R. Friedrichs, *Urban Society in an Age of War: Nördlingen, 1580–1720* (Princeton, NJ, 1979), 146–62; Stadtarchiv Nördlingen, Stadtkammerrechnungen 1565–79, 1634.

[58] 'nit mans genug': StadtAA, Urg., Caspar Aufschlager, 16 Aug. 1591.

[59] 'ich wolt dich selbs in das Angesicht schlagen, wan du woltest ein Landsknecht sein, und solliches gedulden': ibid.

[60] 'Er Rauner, nit allain Jhne auffschlager an seinen Ehren gröblich verlötzt, sondern auch ... Jhme fürgeworffen haben soll, als were er auffschlager, der mannlichait Vnnd Redlichait nit, sich mit ainem Zubalgen': ibid.

Portugaller' recorded in 1596. Descriptions by witnesses of what would by our standards be considered a violent killing expressed awe and admiration for the randy soldier, who dispatched his opponent with such speed that he inflicted seven wounds before his unfortunate rival could draw his weapon.[61] Elsewhere, soldiers were moved to violence when a tavern keeper insulted them with the accusation that they were not real soldiers if they had 'never seen a dead man'.[62] These exaggerated norms of masculine behaviour were particularly likely to come into play in the public house, where tempers were heated with wine and the tavern company provided a supportive audience.

The situation was made even more volatile by the fact that most of the soldiers who shared tables with Augsburg's citizens were foreigners to the city (*Fremde*), and thus outsiders by definition. Local citizens often emphasized this fact by referring to them by their assumed place of origin rather than by name or profession (for example, as Hessians or Prussians). A clear expression of the distance and mistrust that local tavern-goers felt towards their unwelcome visitors is provided by the weaver Jacob Lang, who testified as evidence of his peaceful intentions that before entering an inn in 1548, he was careful to ask if there were any soldiers present, for he did not want any trouble.[63] Soldiers also drew on their foreign status to claim ignorance of local laws and ordinances regulating violent behaviour. Thus a soldier from Kassel, who was accused of violating tradition and local ordinance by continuing a fight after an offer of peace had been made, defended himself by claiming that 'he had just arrived, and knew nothing of the customs of this city or how things are here'.[64]

The soldiers, then, were never viewed as a very orderly group, but their image was worsening by the later stages of the Thirty Years' War. The quartermaster in 1635 described the huge numbers of new recruits arriving every day as 'half-grown boys, old hopeless and used-up vagrant beggars, unemployed trouble-makers, [and] the hungry and poor', who, arriving with a great following of women, children, and other relatives, spend their days in bed and do no service beyond wastefully depleting provisions, 'many eating themselves to death before they once hold a weapon in their hands'.[65] Their dependents were then left to collect poor relief. The depiction of the unruly landsknecht, hardly

---

[61]   StadtAA, Militaria, 192, Georg Pfanner, 3 Feb. 1596.

[62]   'waß wir fur Soldaten sein wolten … heten wol vnnser lebtag khein todten Man gesehen'. StadtAA, Militaria 198, Frevel & Excesse 1584–1758, 13 Aug. 1648.

[63]   StadtAA, Urg., Balthas Laimer, 23 July 1548.

[64]   'er doch … aller erst herkhumen, vnd weder prauch noch gelegenhait diser Stat gewusst'; StadtAA, Urg., Hans Pilgerin and Niklaus (Claus) Lunckmair, 24–6 March 1545.

[65]   'halb gewachßene buben, dann auch alte hailoße auß gearbeitete offene landt: vnnd straß pettler, störyer, erhungerte, [vnnd] mangelhaffte … auß welchen irer vil sich bereith schon zue todt gessen ehe sie ein mahl … ein wöhr in die hand genomen haben'. SStBA, 2 Cod°Aug.123 (Singularia Augustana), 1635.

more than a vagabond, had by this time become a literary topos. The constant use by the authorities of terms such as 'soldiers about the neck' as a threat meant that the cliché of the disorderly soldier was likely to be exaggerated, further enflaming tensions between the occupying troops and the local populace. By this time, too, tensions between the unwelcome guests and their hosts were often exacerbated by confessional differences.

When we examine relations between soldiers and civilians from the perspective of the soldiers, however, these tensions are less apparent. Men at all levels of the military hierarchy attempted to repudiate the tarnished image of their troops, consistently representing their behaviour as honourable, exemplary, disciplined and obedient (as, for example, in the case of the duellist Caspar Aufschlager described above). And according to petitions filed in response to civilian complaints, the abuses of war were not one-sided, for the citizens also took advantage of the soldiers, stealing from them or plaguing them with false charges.[66] The traditions of hospitality normally associated with early modern public houses often did not seem to apply when it came to soldiers. Instead of being provided with beds, they might be expected to sleep on hard benches in the common room, or be sent to the stables to sleep with animals.[67] Innkeepers sometimes went to great lengths to try and trick the soldiers or keep them out of their houses, including strewing their homes with filth, claiming their ovens were broken, or charging inflated rates for food and lodging. Ordinances in Nördlingen published during the Thirty Years' War provide support for such complaints, warning innkeepers to treat soldiers quartered in their inns properly, and in particular to stop insulting them and interfering with their preparation of meals.[68] Numerous accounts represent plundering by soldiers either as a result of desperation in the face of hunger and poverty, or retaliation for poor treatment at the hands of their hosts.[69]

Unfortunately, sources providing the soldier's side of the story are few. But where first-hand accounts by common soldiers can be found, they also tend, not surprisingly, to present a more orderly image of their own comportment than that gleaned from innkeepers' petitions. Soldiers report rewarding good quarters by treating their hosts with respect, leaving their food stores and livestock

---

[66]   StadtAA, Militaria 57.
[67]   Examples in StadtAA, Militaria 34, Werbungen 1624–1745, 1632; StadtAA, Urg. Georg Engelhart and Mathaus Bosch, 21 April–3 May 1593.
[68]   Stadtarchiv Nördlingen, Ordnungen und Decrete 1612–1640, fols 74r–75v, 226v–227r, 230r–v.
[69]   Die Chronik des Johann Philipp Mohr, 243; StadtAA, Militaria 55; Peter Burschel, *Söldner im Nordwestdeutschland des 16. und 17. Jahrhunderts* (Göttingen, 1994), 195–8; Landsteiner and Weigl, 'Krieg und lokale Gesellschaft,' 250; Asch, *The Thirty Years War*, 177.

untouched, and even presenting them with gifts upon departure.[70] They wrote fondly of 'good quarters' (*gute Quartiere*) and sociable times spent with amiable innkeepers, and especially praised landlords who provided them with good-quality food and drink. 'I had a very good innkeeper', reported a Bavarian soldier of his quarters near Halberstadt in 1631, 'who did not serve beef, but only veal, young pigeons, chicken, and birds'. Elsewhere, quarters were highly rated because of the quality and quantity of the wine, the friendliness of the innkeeper, and the availability of cash contributions for the soldiers' pay.[71] Where none of these were lacking, soldiers enjoyed their quarters and, they claimed, treated their hosts accordingly. In fact, studies by military historians suggest that serious abuses were unlikely as long as soldiers were well provided for.[72]

Soldiers and their commanders seemed to define 'orderly' or 'honourable' behaviour differently from their unwilling hosts. Consorting with prostitutes, engaging in duels, and enjoying feasts and drinking bouts that seemed excessive by civilian standards were privileges of military life; whereas theft of inn property, refusal to pay bills, and physical violence directed at the publican and his family were simply reasonable reactions to poor treatment by innkeepers. This reflects more than an attempt by the troops to cover up inappropriate behaviour. By the late sixteenth century, soldiers were operating from a different set of cultural norms. This was partly due to a conscious effort on the part of their military commanders, who at least by the period of the Thirty Years' War were learning that fostering a separate identity and a special honour code among their troops could be an effective motivator in battle.

The growing cultural division between the military and the civilian sector paralleled other forms of increased social stratification over the course of the sixteenth and seventeenth centuries, as evidenced for example by increasingly detailed sumptuary laws (clothing and wedding ordinances) designed to shore up the lines of division between the social orders.[73] The sumptuary laws themselves provided soldiers with an opportunity to express publicly their cultural difference from civilian society. Military men especially flaunted their

---

[70] For example, M. Friesenegger, *Tagebuch aus dem 30jährigen Krieg*, ed. P. W. Mathäser (Munich, 1974), 148–9 (1646).

[71] 'Hier habe ich einen gar guten Wirt bekommen, hat mir kein Rindfleisch gegeben, sondern lauter Kalbfleisch, junge Tauben, Hühner und Vögel'. The soldier (whose identity is uncertain) credited the good quarters with restoring his health after being wounded. *Ein Söldnerleben im Dreißigjährigen Krieg: Eine Quelle zur Sozialgeschichte*, ed. Jan Peters (Berlin, 1993), 139, also 136, 141, 143, 147.

[72] Burschel, *Söldner im Nordwestdeutschland des 16. und 17. Jahrhunderts*, 195–8; Landsteiner and Weigl, 'Krieg und lokale Gesellschaft,' 250; Asch, *The Thirty Years War*, 177.

[73] A. Corvisier, *Armies and Societies in Europe 1494–1789* (Bloomington, Indiana, 1979) 181.

disdain for clothing ordinances, which proliferated during the seventeenth century and restricted styles and materials of garments to a level commensurate with social rank. The soldier's flamboyant clothing – slashed, stuffed, and decorated with colourful plumes and ribbons that bounced and rustled with every step – reflected their distinct sense of masculinity and their disregard for social norms. Their beribboned crotches also accentuated their contempt for sexual convention. In some ordinances, the ineffectiveness of trying to control soldier's clothing was codified with clauses allowing them to dress 'as they deemed appropriate'.[74]

Figure 7: Hans Ulrich Franck, *Soldiers at the Inn*. Folge über den 30-jährigen Krieg, 1656 (Courtesy Kunstsammlungen der Stadt Augsburg).

---

[74] 'wie j[n] gelegen': R. Baumann, *Landsknechte: Ihre Geschichte und Kultur vom späten Mittelalter bis zum Dreißigjährigen Krieg* (Munich, 1994), 40.

Clothes were only one way in which soldiers set themselves apart from the rest of society. They further demonstrated their disregard for sexual norms by common-law marriages and open relationships with courtesans. They also developed their own distinct jargon, mixing technical military terms with creative curses and foreign terms picked up on their travels, calling even more attention to their status as outsiders.[75] The effect of this cultural segregation on social relations can be traced in the make-up of drinking groups in Augsburg taverns; while around twelve per cent of artisan drinking groups during the sixteenth century included soldiers, no such mixed drinking groups were identifiable during the 1640s.[76]

In the interest of order, then, these increasingly marginalized elements needed to be distanced as much as possible from the civic community. The process that began with the construction of soldiers' barracks in 1582 as a means of getting soldiers out of private households continued during the Thirty Years' War, as local authorities fought ever harder to keep soldiers out of the city entirely. By 1639, the city had obtained assurances from the emperor that its citizens would be spared physical quartering in return for adequate contributions.[77]

Despite the emperor's promise, soldiers did return to Augsburg during the final phases of the war, but never in the numbers suffered during the 1630s.[78] When quartering in the city could not be avoided, the pattern established earlier in the war was repeated; the troops were placed first in inns, and then in the homes of the less obedient citizenry. The bulk of the soldiers, however, were kept outside the city walls and housed in the surrounding villages. City leaders used every available argument to keep troops out of the city: their poor citizens had been burdened enough already; their wealthier citizens were already doing their part in the form of cash contributions; and the soldiers would be better off in the villages anyway, where raw feed and open pasture for their animals were readily available.[79]

These economic arguments were underscored by a growing perception on the part of Augsburg's elite townsmen that a cultural division existed between

---

[75] Ibid; See also Tallett, *War and Society*, 142–3.

[76] Tlusty, *Bacchus*, 151.

[77] StadtAA, Militaria 59, 6 Aug. 1639. In the same year, Augsburg obtained guarantees from the Emperor that villages belonging to the city would also be spared further quartering of soldiers: StadtAA, Militaria 77, 5 Jan. 1639.

[78] In September 1646, Augsburg's council complained about a company of 945 soldiers in the city, which exceeded the expenses they had agreed upon. Bayerisches Hauptstaatsarchiv, Kurbayern Äußeres Archiv 2574, fol. 229r.

[79] Bayerisches Hauptstaatsarchiv, Kurbayern Äußeres Archiv 2574, fol. 278r; StadtAA, Militaria 57, Landquartierwesen, 1640, 1645. Peasants also complained about their unfair quartering burdens; Thiebault, *German Villages in Crisis*, 155.

town and country. Peasants, like soldiers, were often depicted in early modern art and literature as unruly, disorderly, even brutish. Although the bucolic pleasures of the countryside were appealing to townspeople, who were regular visitors at village festivals and country taverns, the attraction lay as much in the relative freedom from the watchful eyes of civic authorities as it did in the charm of country life.[80] The notion that the countryside was by nature less orderly made it a logical place to quarter soldiers. Civic leaders believed that the corporate identity of townspeople distinguished them from the surrounding countryside. Their increasing emphasis on respect for local power and orderly behaviour within the city's walls is reflected in the council's response to a soldier arrested towards the end of the war for drunken misconduct and resisting a local guard. Members of the council asked the soldier if he thought himself to be in 'a village, where he might defy and brutalise people at will', rather than in a locality in which 'better council' was appropriate.[81] While condemning unruly behaviour in the city, the statement comes close to condoning it in the villages. This attitude not only further encouraged a separate social identity among the soldiers, but it exacerbated the already existing antagonism between town and countryside.[82]

The sixteenth and seventeenth centuries constituted a unique phase in German military history, one that deserves more attention than just as a step on the road to national armies.[83] This was a period in which cities struggled to maintain their independent dominion and local identity was paramount. During the first half of the sixteenth century, civic defence (whether welcome or unwelcome on the part of the city) was integrated into city life, and quartering was seen as a duty of citizenship. The threat posed by such integration to individual households, however, could not be reconciled with the powerful metaphor of the orderly household as the key to a disciplined citizenship. The soldiers, perpetual 'outsiders', were moved out of the household and into public inns – and

---

[80] A. Stewart, 'Paper Festivals and Popular Entertainment: The Kermis Woodcuts of Sebald Beham in Reformation Nuremberg,' in *The Sixteenth Century Journal* 24 (1993), 301–50; R. Haftlmeier-Seiffert, *Bauerndarstellungen auf deutschen illustrierten Flugblättern des 17. Jahrhunderts* (Frankfurt, 1991), 80–97; M. Schilling, *Bildpublizistik in der frühen Neuzeit: Aufgaben und Leistungen des illustrierten Flugblatts in Deutschland bis um 1700* (Tübingen, 1990), 209–10; cf. also Stewart in this volume.

[81] 'Ob er villeicht vermain das er allhie in einem Dorff sei, allwo er die leuth nach seinem gefallen trutzen und bochen möge, oder ob er nit alberaith befinde, das er an einem sollichen orth sitze, allwo man ... bessere rath ... zuerwarten khönde', StadtAA, Urg., Hans Schwarzenberg, 13 July 1643.

[82] On increasing tension between town and country see Tallett, *War and Society*, 49–50, 154.

[83] Parrott has also made this point: D. Parrott, 'The Military Revolution in Early Modern Europe', in *History Today* 42 (Dec. 1992), 21–7.

wherever possible, out of the community entirely and into the less powerful (and, according to the opinions of many city-dwellers, less orderly) peasant villages. They were returned to private homes in the city only during periods of occupation by foreign powers, when they were utilized as punishment for confessional or political disobedience.

Financial burdens also threatened civic order. Here, too, inns played an important defence role, for the wine and beer drunk at their tables paid the bulk of the contributions that both financed local defence and kept the soldiers at bay. As recruitment centres, military quarters, and theatres for interaction with the citizenship, public houses also provided a means by which to contain and control soldiers – at least to the extent that it was possible.

The accounts of soldiers and their landlords differ significantly in their portrayal of this relationship. Soldiers report treating their hosts honourably as long as their quarters were dry, their food plentiful, and their wine of good quality. For their part, some urban innkeepers undoubtedly profited from the presence of soldiers, and most suffered less financial loss than did other members of the community. But nearly all sources from innkeepers indicate that their relationships with their unwelcome guests were strained. Multiple complaints by the beleaguered innkeepers suggest that greater social distancing of military troops from their hosts, quartering in larger groups, and the ready availability of alcohol led to an increase in the soldiers' tendency towards violence and other destructive behaviour. The inn thus had a decisive role both in the process of social segregation that set the early modern soldier apart from other citizens, and in providing the public theatre that encouraged him to live up to his reputation.

PART THREE

Regional Studies

The Pre-modern Hospitality Trade in the Central Alpine Region: The Example of Tyrol

Hans Heiss

The modern-day territories that up until 1918 made up the historical Crownland of Tyrol, namely the Austrian province of Tyrol and the Italian provinces of South Tyrol and Trentino, are currently leaders in Alpine tourism. According to a statistical study, in 1997 there were nearly fifty-three million nights spent in guest accommodations, representing nearly fifty per cent of the total of 107 million nights from ten primary Alpine regions (which in addition to the three areas mentioned include Ticino, Graubünden, St Gall, Vorarlberg, Bavaria, Sondrio, and Salzburg).[1] The successful figures do not, however, reveal that these provinces in the centre of the Alpine region are historic late-comers to international tourism. For in comparison with Switzerland and other regions in Austria, Tyrol got a relatively late start in the age of tourism – only shortly before 1900. But in spite of its delayed entry, its success has nevertheless been sustained and has had a lasting impact.

The continuity as a transit area, unbroken since antiquity, did in fact provide important preconditions for tourism in Tyrol. At the same time, however, the orientation of priorities in the nineteenth century toward through-traffic obstructed the acknowledgement of the opportunities from the new industry of real tourism for a lengthy period. Thus, a hospitality trade that was rich in tradition and deeply anchored in history simultaneously fostered and hindered the development of tourism. Even though the industry and some of its participants recognized the opportunities presented by the new tourism soon after 1800, and at times demonstrated a great dynamism, most hospitality enterprises remained bound to the traditional standards of the profession. The entrenched traditions of the trade, ingrained over the course of centuries, combined with the close ties of the hospitality industry to the inertia of local societies to allow only a very gradual approach towards tourism.

---

[1]   Autonome Provinz Bozen-Südtirol, Landesinstitut für Statistik (ed.), *Fremdenverkehr in einigen Alpengebieten 1997* (ASTAT publication series 63) (Bolzano, 1999), 12.

This paper will describe the essential features of the origins and practices of the historical hospitality trade in Tyrol. A brief view will first be offered of the geographical conditions that help provide clues about the origin of inns. Of particular interest is the typology of the various sorts of inns, which are presented according to their social and economic functions. The consideration of the social status of the innkeeping families and the division of labour within the inns brings this overview to a close. It will be shown that even in this 'land of the mountains', public houses were integrated into the local and regional economy and lay at the centre of local society. They took on important functions of facilitation as the centres of communication for local communities, and as mediators between locals and outsiders.

Tyrol lies in the middle of the main ridge of the Alps, at the widest point of this central mountain range that runs in an east-west direction. In the High Middle Ages, the region was formed as a recognizable unit under the rule of the counts of the village of Tyrol (thus providing the name); the bishops of Trent (Trient or Trento) and Brixen (Bressanone); and lords of smaller territories.[2] 1363 marked the beginning of Austrian rule with the taking over of the land by the Habsburg emperor Rudolf IV, a rule which continued until 1918. After the First World War, Tyrol was divided. As a result of the Treaty of St Germain, the southern portion of the province from Brenner down, west of the Winnebach river, and below the Reschen Pass was ceded to Italy; the northern and eastern portions remained in the new Republic of Austria.

Until 1918, the southern border of the Crownland of Tyrol reached down to the Veronese Gorge at the northern Italian lowland plain, while its northern outpost of Kufstein, which had been part of the duchy since 1503, marked the border crossing into the Bavarian foothill region of the Alps. The distance between the two points is approximately 250 km, and the area consists of mountainous territory throughout. Even though the extraordinary width of the Alps at this point does not appear to predestine Tyrol as a land of passage, the region has been the most important site of transalpine traffic since the High Middle Ages.[3]

The hospitality trade and public houses have lain at the intersection of agriculture and transit in Tyrol since the late Middle Ages. Their activity connected them with both sectors and secured them a significant function as mediator, which continued uninterrupted well into the nineteenth century, up to the point at which tourism also began to take hold in Tyrol. However, the hospitality trade functioned not only as the connecting link between rural agriculture and

---

[2]   J. Riedmann, 'Mittelalter', in *Geschichte des Landes Tirol 1* (Bolzano-Innsbruck-Vienna, 1985), 267–661.

[3]   U. Niedermayr-Loose, 'Wege über die Berge', in *Pässe, Übergänge, Hospize. Südtirol am Schnittpunkt der Alpentransversalen in Geschichte und Gegenwart* (Lana, Italy, 1999), 9–32, esp. 9.

the trans-regional traffic industry, but it also acted as facilitator between different social arenas. City, village, region, and local and trans-regional relationships and actors came into contact with one another through the mediation of the public house.

Like everywhere else in Europe, the appearance of inns and the development of a professional hospitality trade in Tyrol were part of a lengthy process that first reached an interim conclusion in the late Middle Ages. The trade underwent a process of learning and adaptation, growing out of preconditions that had roots in Christianity and in ancient times.

Influences from antiquity continued to have their effects, albeit with interruption. The area which would later be Tyrol had been under Roman rule for more than four hundred years, from 15 B.C. to shortly before 400 A.D., and thus their forms of professional hospitality were also transmitted to the Alpine area. The tradition of commercially practised hospitality survived in the collective memory of the Roman population and their successors.[4] This is indicated above all by the continuation of Roman terminology, especially the term *Wirtstaberne* (inn), which survived until the modern era. The contact with nearby northern Italy, as well, caused an eye to be kept open toward commercial forms of hospitality that were revived from the fourteenth and fifteenth centuries. Before the return to a market-oriented hospitality trade, the Christian duty to provide hospitality also had a considerable effect on Tyrol. This manifested itself beginning in the twelfth century with the establishment of hospices and hospitals along traffic routes.[5]

The territorialist policy of the Tyrolean princes, the increase in traffic, and the population expansion that was linked to these two factors led in the twelfth century to the first founding of cities.[6] Soon after 1150, Bozen, Brixen, and Trent had become fully-formed, walled cities; between 1187 and 1204, Innsbruck joined them; and a few decades later the cities of Meran (Merano, 1237–39), Lienz (1242), Sterzing (Vipiteno, after 1280), Bruneck (Brunico, around 1300), and Hall (1303) followed. This small wave of founding fostered

---

[4]   For the continuity in Italy, see G. Cherubini, 'La taverna nel basso Medioevo', in S. Cavaciocchi (ed.), *Il tempo libero, economia e società (secc. XIII–XVIII)* (Prato, 1995).

[5]   G. Mühlberger, 'Die Kultur des Reisens im Mittelalter', in L. Andergassen et al. (eds), *Pässe, Übergänge, Hospize* (Bolzano, 1999), 52–88, esp. 78–80.

[6]   For a summary, see F. H. Hye, 'Grundzüge der Wirtschaftsgeschichte Tirols im Mittelalter', in Gesellschaft für Wirtschaftsdocumentationen (ed.), *Chronik der Tiroler Wirtschaft mit Sonderteil Südtirol* (Wien 1991), pt. 1, 29–74, esp. 64–7; and idem, *Die Städte Tirols. 2. Teil. Südtirol* (Schlern-Schriften 313) (Innsbruck, 2001). As a critical balance to the research on the history of Tyrolean cities, see O. Auge, 'Stadtwerdung in Tirol. Ansätze, Erkenntnisse und Perspektiven vergleichender Stadtgeschichtsforschung', in R. Loose and S. Lorenz (eds), *König, Kirche, Adel. Herrschaftsstrukturen im mittleren Alpenraum und angrenzenden Gebieten (6.–13. Jahrhundert)* (Lana, Italy, 1999), 307–64.

commercial differentiation between the developing cities. The period marked the beginning of guild-related handicrafts, and professional innkeepers are encountered in thirteenth century sources with a certain regularity. References are to be found earlier in the southern part of Tyrol: in Trent an *Alberto tabernario da borgo nuovo* (Alberto tavern keeper in the new quarter) is mentioned in 1269, while in 1345 an *Osteria della Ruota* (Wheel Inn) followed in the northern part of the city. These were the forerunners of the increasingly developing trade in the city that served as the episcopal residence.[7] Soon after, they began to show their presence in Bozen and Meran as well, where beginning around 1300 the files of the notaries increasingly register *hosterii* (innkeepers), *tabernarii* (tavern keepers), and *caupones* (wine sellers) as witnesses and contractual partners.[8]

The position and basic conditions of the hospitality industry, as well as of the tertiary mercantile and trade sectors, were built up and strengthened through important laws beginning in the early thirteenth century. Among these was the *Niederlagsrecht* (depot law), which was granted to Innsbruck in 1239 and Hall in 1303. For Innsbruck, this meant that all merchant freight transported between the Melach (a tributary of the Inn River from the Sellrain valley) and the Ziller had first to be brought to the municipal *Niederlage* (depot) before being transported further. The compulsory channelling of traffic to this junction ensured a steady influx of merchants and coachmen to the Innsbruck hospitality trade. A logistical element of traffic organization with a similar effect was the *Bannmeile* (inviolable precincts).[9] In 1304, the city of Sterzing was granted a privilege by the prince which ordered that in the area between Brenner and the gorge at Brixen, the provision of accommodation and the serving of wine could only be practised in the city itself.[10] Therefore, the right to operate a public house within a radius of forty-five kilometres had to be concentrated in a central location, bringing a strong impetus to the city and its hospitality industry. The *Niederlagsrecht* and the *Bannmeile* were the basic elements of support for the blossoming hospitality trade in urban areas. In addition to these, there was the establishment of customs stations which the prince or other territorial lords set up at important points along the transit routes. The customs stations formed

---

[7]   E. Fox, *Storia delle osterie trentine. L'ospitalità dal XIII al XX secolo* (2nd edn, Trent, 1996), 54–6.

[8]   J. Nössing, 'Bozen in der ersten Hälfte des 13. Jahrhunderts', in *Bozen von den Anfängen bis zur Schleifung der Stadtmauern*; report on the International Study Conference held by the Bolzano Municipal Commission for Culture at Maretsch Castle, April, 1989 (Bolzano, 1991), 327–37, esp. 332; J. Riedmann, 'Das Etschtal als Verbindungslinie zwischen Süd und Nord im hohen Mittelalter', in *Bozen von den Anfängen*, 149–57, esp. 154.

[9]   See F. H. Hye, 'Das Verhältnis Stadt und Straße in Tirol von den Anfängen bis in die Frühe Neuzeit', in E. Riedenauer (ed.), *Die Erschliessung des Alpenraums für den Verkehr im Mittelalter und in der Frühen Neuzeit* (Bolzano, 1996), 197–217, esp. 210–11.

[10]   K. Schadelbauer, 'Sterzing bis zum Jahr 1363', in *Der Schlern 37* (1963), 291–6.

important points of reference for all those who passed along the open provincial road, especially in the important cities. The customs stations in Brixen, Klausen (Chiusa), and Bozen were stopping points in whose surroundings hospitality structures developed especially well.

The expansion of professionally practised hospitality in the countryside took place more laboriously. Hospitality for those passing through there did not come into existence completely voluntarily, but rather it was imposed by customary law. In most places, the community transferred the innkeeping obligation to an innkeeper who was appointed by and responsible to the community. Aside from the 'burden' of providing hospitality, the task of being the innkeeper also certainly ensured him considerable chances for profit. This feature under public law may easily be verified by viewing the *Weistümer*, the recorded established rights of some Tyrolean localities.

Between the end of the Middle Ages and the early modern era, Tyrol was under the influence of a phase of powerful economic growth that was supported by two factors: from about 1450, both mining and transit developed dynamically, bringing the beginnings of a capitalist traffic industry to the 'land in the mountains'. The hospitality trade received an impetus from both sectors. Mining and transit fostered the arrival of a monetary economy, raised the frequency of travelling, and contributed to a change in consumer behaviour, particularly in eating and drinking habits. In the sixteenth century, the improvement of the infrastructure was followed by a steady increase in traffic volume which approximately doubled during the period from 1500 to 1600, and grew even further before the effects of the Thirty Years' War also became noticeable in Tyrol.[11] The increase in traffic volume did not, however, take place evenly, but it was especially of benefit to the Brenner route. Moreover, around 1500 trade fairs on a trans-regional scale were established in Bozen and Hall, the two poles south and north of the Brenner Pass. The four fairs in Bozen especially reached the peak position in the central Alpine area and remained a fundamental point of reference for the Tyrolean transit trade until around 1800. The growing traffic volume along the north-south axis gave particular support to the numerous cities along the Brenner route.

Capabilities and weaknesses of the Tyrolean hospitality trade in the late Middle Ages are described especially vividly in a travel report from 1492. Two Venetian emissaries, Giorgio Contarini and Polo Pisani, passed through the region in the early summer of 1492 on the way to the Viennese court of Emperor Frederick III and his son, Maximilian I. A member of their entourage,

---

[11] H. Hassinger, 'Der Verkehr über Brenner und Reschen vom Ende des 13. bis in die zweite Hälfte des 18. Jahrhunderts', in E. Troger and G. Zwanowetz (eds), *Neue Beiträge zur geschichtlichen Landeskunde Tirols*, Part I (Innsbruck and Munich, 1969), 137–94, esp. 179.

the nineteen-year-old Andrea de' Franceschi, kept a diary which in some passages reads like a report of gastronomic tests.[12] The description of the inns was useful to the young writer as a cultural comparison, in order to examine his own standards of living and behaviour and those of the foreign land. The behaviour of the innkeepers, the furnishings of the rooms, the quality of the food, and the respective entertainment on offer along the route from south to north were all carefully and thoroughly scrutinized. The Rose in Trent and the *Adler* (Eagle) in St Michele were the travellers' first stops. In St Michele, de' Franceschi noted that one drank out of tin tankards and silver cups, as opposed to the glass goblets and cups that were customary in Venice. And the *Stube*, the panelled and heated central room of the building,[13] was perceived as being typically German. North of Bozen, especially in Klausen, Brixen, and Innsbruck, de' Franceschi observed with special attention the innkeepers, whom he described as self-assured and pleasant in manner and behaviour – for instance, the innkeeper Gosper at the *Lamm Gottes* (Lamb of God) in Klausen – or dismissed as arrogant and foolish, as in the case of the innkeeper of the *Lamm* (Lamb) in Brixen. Minstrels and actors appeared in nearly every inn, and their stimulating, often exotically colourful programmes were a cause for surprise and merriment. All in all, the Tyrolean hospitality industry left a good impression with the delegation, which had apparently expected more primitive conditions.

By the beginning of the sixteenth century at the latest, the hospitality trade in Tyrol had fully developed under the influence of various socio-economic impulses and was differentiated according to certain types of operations. As a result of the economic boom and public regulation, there was an improvement in what was on offer and in the qualitative standard of the public houses. No less decisive was the professionalization of the hospitality vocation, which was accompanied by an increase in social status and the public role of the publicans.

Tyrol's hospitality trade operated in three functional categories with gradations of services that accommodated the various requirements and social types

---

[12] 'Itinerario de Germania delli Magnifici Ambasciatori Veneti, M. Giorgio Contarini, Conte del Zaffo, et M. Polo Pisani a li Serenissimo Federico III. Imperator et Maximiliano, suo fiolo, Rè de Romani, facto per Andrea de Franceschi, Coadiutor del Eccellente D. Giorgio de Federicis, secretario Veneto, dell'anno 1492', ed. H. Simonsfeld, in *Miscellanea di Storia Veneta* (Venice, 1903), 275–345. For an informative summary, see J. Riedmann, 'Eine Reise durch Tirol im Jahre 1492', in *Das Fenster* 23 (1978), 2341–4.

[13] For the *Stube* within the framework of medieval home décor, see G. Fouquet, '"Annäherungen". Große Städte-Kleine Häuser. Wohnen und Lebensformen der Menschen im ausgehenden Mittelalter (ca. 1470–1600)', in U. Dirlmeier (ed.), *Geschichte des Wohnens*, vol. 2 (Stuttgart, 1998), 347–501, esp. 439.

of the guests.[14] The *Tabernwirte* (innkeepers) ranked at the top. With the provision of meals and beverages, accommodation, and stabling, their offer was the broadest. They could therefore serve travellers on foot as well as coachmen and aristocratic passengers; at the same time, they offered food and drink to local guests. Their *Wirtstabernen* (inns) were required to hang a fixed sign that could not be taken down at their discretion. The inn's sign had a double function: first, it provided an advertising signal of high symbolic force; and second, it served as proof of the bond of the establishment under public law and its duty to provide hospitality. The innkeeper had to accommodate all guests equally without distinction, whether they were from the well-paying clientele, or were manual labourers and farmers with limited liquidity. This contractual obligation placed these types of inns in the service of the local community, for which they representatively took over the Christian ideal of the obligation to provide hospitality. At the same time, they fulfilled duties that were instrumental to the transit trade of the province, which was of fundamental importance for the treasury of the princes and the economy of the duchy of Tyrol. Through many years of practising the hospitality trade, the profession and the house became inextricably linked with each other in many inns. Thus the 'rooted trades' (*radizierte Gewerbe*) formed an integral part of the house and consequently '[made] up a true part of the house and its value'.[15]

In comparison to the innkeepers, those at the level of *Baumwirte*, keepers of a kind of pedestrian inn, had more limited functions. Like the former, they offered accommodation, food, and drink, although with a slightly reduced range of services. But in contrast, they were not allowed to accommodate passengers who travelled by wagon. Thus these publicans missed a large portion of the aristocratic and wealthy public that was underway on journeys. Their primary clientele were local residents and those out-of-town guests who travelled by foot.

Finally, local needs were served by the *Buschenwirte* (winegrowers' taverns) and the *Fratschler* (beer and brandy houses). In the southern part of the land (the regions of the southern Eisack and the Etsch), winegrowers' taverns were found everywhere. Their speciality was serving wine that they had produced themselves. Under the sign of a green branch, the winegrowers' taverns proffered their guests their own goods, which offered considerable advantages to both sides – the keepers of these taverns had the benefit of the direct and swift sale of their own wine without costly procedures of marketing and delivery, while the guests had the prospect of local specialities that were at a good price

---

[14] R. Falkensteiner, *Beiträge zur Wirtschaftsgeschichte Innsbrucks im 18. Jahrhundert* (Innsbruck, 1981), 124–30; H. Heiss, 'Das Gastgewerbe der Stadt Brixen 1770–1815' (PhD University of Innsbruck, 1985), 79–80.

[15] 'einen wahren Teil des Hauses und seines Gewerbes': R. von Pelikan, *Die Realgewerbe* (Innsbruck, 1910), 13.

and, for the most part, of good quality. In this category, only cold dishes, such as bread, farmer's bacon, and cheese, were supposed to suffice as food service in order to not overly compete with the other two categories. The delimitation of the categories was further marked by seasonal prohibitions against the serving of wine by the keeper of a winegrower's tavern, who, according to local special laws in the southern part of the land, could only keep their establishments open during certain months.[16]

In the northern part of the Tyrol (primarily in the Inn valley), the function of the smaller drinking establishments, aside from the winegrowers' taverns, was filled by the beer and brandy house. Because of the absence of wine production in that region, they were still commonly unable to serve wine in the eighteenth century and thus frequently carried out their provision of beer or distilled spirits only as a secondary occupation. The serving of wine by the keeper of a beer or liquor house was for the most part forbidden in northern Tyrol. That was a privilege reserved for the innkeepers and the winegrowers' taverns. For that reason, two types of small enterprises were established in the north, concentrating their service either upon wine, or upon beer and distilled spirits. The strong spirits were especially popular among coachmen and the lower classes. These drinks, with their high levels of alcohol, were among the few consumer goods that they could allow themselves beyond the actual necessities of life. Particularly during the cold season, which they mostly had to spend outdoors, the schnapps made life easier for them. A noticeable increase in the consumption of distilled spirits apparently only took place after 1800, and by 1890 reached a disquieting level.[17]

Even though innkeepers, keepers of pedestrian inns, and keepers of winegrowers' taverns were legally separate from one another, the distinctions became blurred in practice. The everyday situation in the hospitality trade, particularly in the cities, was full of disputes between publicans as competences were exceeded and encroached on areas outside of their entitled range of activities. There were especially many keepers of winegrowers' taverns who demonstrated an uncontrolled dynamic, often hardly giving a thought to serving wines in addition to those that were self-produced and, in the place of modest, cold dishes, serving up entire guest meals. All of this was to the joy of the public, which gladly took note of the price advantages at the smaller taverns.[18]

---

[16] R. Staffler, 'Über altes Bozner-Buschenschankwesen', in *Der Schlern* 4 (1925), 387–91, esp. 388; A. Greiter, 'Beiträge zur Geschichte der Stadt Meran von 1814 bis 1860' (PhD University of Innsbruck, 1971), 194–98.

[17] L. von Hörmann, 'Genuß- und Reizmittel in den Ostalpen. Eine volkskundliche Studie', in *Zeitschrift des Deutschen und Österreichischen Alpenvereins* 43 (1912), 78–100, esp. 84–8.

[18] Greiter, 'Beiträge', 194.

The network of public houses in the cities of Tyrol was thickly woven by the early modern era. In 1775, the provincial capital of Innsbruck, with a population of five thousand, had nearly fifty publicans, of which twenty-three were innkeepers, thirteen were keepers of winegrowers' taverns, and around eleven were keepers of beer or liquor houses.[19] In the somewhat smaller city of Bozen with its market fair, there were as many as one hundred permanent establishments; and in the city of Brixen, with 2,500 residents, there were twenty-five public houses in the late eighteenth century.[20] Although not all of them were open at the same time, that comes to one establishment for every seventy to one hundred inhabitants.

The hospitality industry surpassed all other trades in topographical presence and density and helped to shape local everyday life. The varied functions of the public houses and their effects on guests, proprietors, and the social sphere generally have still not been described for Tyrol. Up until now, public houses have supplied material for cultural-historical anecdotes rather than an impetus for serious social-historical research.[21] The following framework of central tasks is structured upon the spectrum of five basic functions developed by Beat Kümin for Bern[22] and is repeated here with slight modifications.

Tyrol's public houses served guests from nearly every social stratum, and in so doing they were no different than establishments in other regions.[23] Their spectrum ranged from farmers to emperors, from peddlers to the grandest merchants. This force of integration was often felt within the briefest period of time, for instance at the Elephant (*Elephanten*) in Brixen, which hosted Emperor Joseph II (who was travelling incognito as Count von Falkenstein) on 10 March 1769,[24] while a few days later straw was spread in the corridors of the building as bedding for the farmers of the surrounding area who had come to the city for the St Joseph's Day market. No other social arena surpassed the public house's quality of encompassing all classes – not even the local church,

---

[19] Falkensteiner, *Beiträge zur Wirtschaftsgeschichte Innsbrucks*, 124–30. The exact number of the *Fratschler* is not presented for 1775. The number of active establishments in the category between 1776 and 1790 has been used here.

[20] Heiss, 'Gastgewerbe der Stadt Brixen', 84–7.

[21] See for instance H. Frass and F. H. Riedl, *Historische Gaststätten in Tirol. Nord-, Süd- und Osttirol* (Bolzano, 1978); M. Forcher, *Zu Gast im Herzen der Alpen. Eine Bildgeschichte des Tourismus in Tirol* (Innsbruck, 1989), 92–113. An important beginning to a new assessment may be found in Wolfgang Meixner, '"Tirols langer Marsch in die Gastronomie". Gastgewerbe als historischer Lernprozess', in *Tiroler Heimat 56* (1992), 143–53.

[22] B. Kümin, 'Useful to Have, but Difficult to Govern. Inns and Taverns in Early Modern Bern and Vaud', in *Journal of Early Modern History* 3 (1999), 153–75.

[23] Kümin, 'Useful to Have', 157–8.

[24] F. A. Sinnacher, *Beyträge zur Geschichte der bischöflichen Kirche Säben und Brixen in Tyrol*, vol. 9 (Brixen, 1834), 664.

which limited its pastoral care primarily to the local community of believers.[25] The house of worship and the public house practised parallel, complementary, and competing functions that clearly manifested themselves after church services, when the local men would flock from the priest to the tavern keeper. Furthermore, in the public house there was a mingling of local residents and foreigners who might also belong to non-Catholic denominations – a fact that was of particular significance to Tyrol, which was permeated by the Catholic faith and reshaped by its process of confessionalization after the Council of Trent (1549–63). [26]

The legal basis of the receptivity to all classes by public houses was the general duty to provide hospitality – the contractual obligation. No guest could be turned away without reasonable grounds.[27] Selective providing of service and open exclusion of guests were inconsistent with the Christian obligation to hospitality and the bond of the establishments under public law. The general providing of hospitality was linked, particularly in the sixteenth century, with a far-reaching relinquishment of privacy. Guests ate at the same time and at the same table, sat on benches instead of across from each other on distinct, individual chairs, and in many cases even slept together in a single bed.

Even though Tyrol's public houses were effective in encompassing all classes, they separated social strata and groups from one another through their typology and in their internal space. A primary segregation took place through the categorization in inns, pedestrian inns, and winegrowers' taverns, which appealed primarily to the upper, middle, and lower classes, respectively. The dividing lines also blurred in this area, though, since there were on the one hand inns with middle-class guests and, on the other hand, particular winegrowers' taverns for respectable carousers of the local upper class. Furthermore, the architecture and division of the rooms in the basically open, inclusive inns were pervaded by subtle dividing lines in the social realm that kept guests of different classes apart. The nobility, merchants, and travellers of means were separated from the middle-class guests, and especially from coachmen, manual labourers, and peddlers.[28] Inventories of *Wirtstabernen* indicate a vertical division according to floor, with a *Belétage* (deluxe floor) for the

---

[25] B. Kümin, 'Rathaus, Wirtshaus, Gotteshaus. Von der Zwei- zur Dreidimensionalität in der frühneuzeitlichen Gemeindeforschung', in F. Šmahel (ed.), *Geist, Gesellschaft, Kirche im 13.–16. Jahrhundert, Colloquia mediaevalia Pragensia 1* (Prague, 1999), 249–62.

[26] H. Noflatscher, 'Gehorsame Untertanen? Politik und Religion im Hochstift Brixen im 17. Jahrhundert', in H. Flachenecker, H. Heiss, and H. Obermair (eds), *Stadt und Hochstift. Brixen, Bruneck und Klausen bis zur Säkularisation 1803*, 261–89.

[27] For the general requirements, see H. C. Peyer, 'Gastfreundschaft und kommerzielle Gastlichkeit im Mittelalter', in *Historische Zeitschrift* 235 (1982), 265–88, esp. 271.

[28] H. T. Gräf and R. Pröve, *Wege ins Ungewisse. Reisen in der Frühen Neuzeit, 1500–1880* (Frankfurt am Main, 1997), 164–6.

wealthier guests, as well as a horizontal division into *ordinari Gaststuben* (ordinary guest rooms) and *Herrenzimmer* (lords' rooms.)[29] In the social arena of the inn, numerous invisible boundaries intersected simultaneously, the systematization of which was comprehended relatively quickly by most of the guests.

Thanks to the simultaneous integration and segregation of the different social groups, the guests of inns experienced tangible presentations of the social order in effect at the time, and had a view of tableaux presenting the various social communities. Thus they were witness to the structure of the various social groups and to the uniting and dividing forces of society. At the same time, the social arena of the public house not only reinforced the existing image of society, but also relieved each guest from the burden of his or her social role. Removed from the disposition and discourse of accustomed, familiar relationships, every visitor developed a little bit of new identity on the stage of the public house. The loosening and disintegration of identity elements, anthropologically designated as 'liminality', remains to this day a fundamental substratum of the hospitality sector.[30] The public house and the world of the traveller are social areas in which the norms that are valid in everyday life are suspended to a certain extent, in-between areas (*limina*) in which new experiences beyond the everyday pressure of norms intensify life experience.

The chief task of the inns, however, was tending the physical needs of the guest.[31] Hungry and thirsty visitors found sustenance, could rest, and could resume the journey with renewed energy after having spent the night. Even though what was on offer was mostly simple (and sometimes even pretty awful), it at least provided a chance to try new, often unfamiliar foods and drinks. Fish dishes, stimulating spices, and unusual side dishes were from time to time tasted with curiosity in the Alps, and in place of ordinary local wine and beer, curious locals also tippled sweet wines like Malaga or liqueurs like *rosolio*. The public house thus broke up the accustomed pattern of consumption and changed, often imperceptibly, the material culture of the local society.[32] The introduction of new standards of civilization was also encouraged by the public house, where beginning in the seventeenth century, local residents had contact with forks and knives, cloth napkins, fine table linens, pewter, and silver. From time to time, they began to use these items themselves, leading at

---

[29] Heiss, 'Gastgewerbe der Stadt Brixen', 439–58; E. Kustatscher, *Die Staffler von Siffian. Eine Rittner Familie zwischen Bauerntum und Bürgerlichkeit (1334–1914)* (Schlern-Schriften 291) (Innsbruck, 1992), 249–64, especially 260–64.

[30] V. Turner, 'Variations on a Theme of Liminality', in S. F. Moore and B. G. Myerhoff (eds), *Secular Ritual* (Assen, 1977), 36–52.

[31] Kümin, 'Useful to Have', 161–2.

[32] For a comprehensive study, see H. J. Teuteberg, G. Neumann, and A. Wierlacher (eds), *Essen und kulturelle Identität. Europäische Perspektiven* (Berlin, 1997).

least in individual cases to their introduction in private households. The improvement in furnishing standards is seen, for example, in individual inns in which, beginning in the middle of the eighteenth century, the proprietors adapted their beds (especially the mattresses) as important features of quality and increasingly placed napkins on the table. These developments were doubtless a reaction to the growing demands of travel and at the same time were further conveyed to the local area, even if to a small degree.

In addition, from the sixteenth century, conspicuous consumption also became common practice in Tyrolean taverns, against which the authorities protested more and more in the yearly issues of tavern keeping regulations.[33] *Zutrinken* (toasting), *Vollsaufen* (overdrinking), and overabundance in the *Gastereyen* (feasting) were indeed frowned upon equally by secular and church authorities, but the threat of sanctions remained for the most part without great success. In his treatise *Die Grewel der Verwüstung menschlichen Geschlechts* (The Abomination of the Devastation of the Human Race), the doctor Hippolytus Guarinonius, physician for many years in the city of Hall in northern Tyrol, castigated the tendency toward unbridled consumption that was allegedly widespread in Tyrol.[34] Through the course of more than eighty pages, he paints a picture of excessive meals at inns which he decries, providing a devastating testimonial to the Tyroleans – indicating that the norms were frequently exceeded in everyday practice.[35] Unmeasured, communicative, and ritually charged consumption of alcoholic beverages was always closely interwoven with a whole host of forms of entertainment and cultural practices.[36] Minstrels and story tellers augmented the range of attractions on offer in public houses, and especially during the evening they could hope for a thankful public that would gladly reach into their purses for an entertaining programme.

There was certainly often an ongoing rift between the entertainment wishes of the guests on one had and the police and discipline maxims of the authorities on the other. Courts and priests fought tirelessly, but often also in vain, against the exceeding of closing times, the 'raucous and reckless games, boozing, and

---

[33] R. van Dülmen, *Entstehung des frühneuzeitlichen Europa 1550–1648* (Frankfurt am Main, 1982), 206–9.

[34] H. Guarinonius, *Die Grewel der Verwüstung menschlichen Geschlechts*, in *Sieben unterschiedliche Bücher und unmeidenliche Hauptstucken abgetheilt ...* (Ingolstadt, 1610, reprinted Bolzano, 1993), especially 778–863.

[35] M. Heidegger, *Soziale Dramen und Beziehungen im Dorf. Das Gericht Laudegg in der frühen Neuzeit – eine historische Ethnographie* (Innsbruck, 1999), 241–6.

[36] M. Frank, 'Trunkene Männer und nüchterne Frauen. Zur Gefährdung von Geschlechterrollen durch Alkohol in der Frühen Neuzeit', in M. Dinges (ed.), *Hausväter, Priester, Kastraten. Zur Konstruktion von Männlichkeit in Spätmittelalter und Früher Neuzeit* (Göttingen, 1998), 187–212.

dancing until late in the night hours',[37] and against morally indecent amusement, particularly during the weeks of carnival. The ongoing tug of war between the authorities, publicans, and guests regarding the desired and allowed extent of entertainment was a part of the battle for sovereignty in the public arena. The tests of strength were seen by the adversaries as regulated conflicts that were constantly renegotiated; as necessary tests of the workability of legal norms and the manoeuvring room they provided; and as opportunities for the common reduction of tensions.

But the provision of hospitality functioned not only as an element for physical sustenance and social reproduction, introducing new and symbolic forms of consumption and comportment; it also formed a first-rate sales point for locally produced goods, some of which were flooding regional markets in overabundance. In Tyrol, this was especially true for wine, which in the subsistence economy of this relatively poor area was one of only a handful of agrarian export goods. In 1807, the wine production in the area of modern-day South Tyrol reached about 132,000 hl., or nearly a quarter of current production.[38] This was a substantial figure, because the general purchasing power was low and sales through exports were limited. And even the flourishing transit trade did not come close to providing the sales opportunities for wine that tourism later would. In good harvest years, the farmers in the Etsch Valley and environs often found themselves positively flooded with an overabundance of the juice of the vine. In the face of regular overproduction crises, the task of increasing consumption in order to keep the wine prices at an acceptable level fell to the taverns. It was primarily the keepers of winegrowers' taverns in the area of Bozen who, during that city's fairs, saw to an active wine turnover and prompt direct marketing to the thousands of visitors, particularly coachmen and craftsmen. Thus the public houses, especially the winegrowers' taverns, took on the task of stabilizing an important sector of regional agriculture and providing it with sales opportunities. They therefore functioned as a mediator between the agricultural and tertiary sector. A high level of consumption on the spot lowered transport costs, since it offered producers and guests the advantage of not having to deliver the wine along the axis over the Brenner Pass to trans-regional buyers, but rather of serving it directly on-site, often along with additional local products like chestnuts and farmer's bacon. In the city and district of Bozen in 1802, there were a total of 236 winegrowers' taverns[39]– a fantastic number which, aside from its contribution to the reduction of

---

[37] 'das starke und rauche Spielen, Zechen und Tanzen bis in die spateste Nachtzeit hinein". This complaint was made by the Court Counselor of the episcopal city of Brixen on 29 January 1785: see Diözesanarchiv Brixen, Hofratsdekrete, Dekretenbuch 1785, (no. 43), fol. 110.
[38] For production figures, see Heiss, 'Gastgewerbe der Stadt Brixen', 143–6.
[39] Ibid., 165.

the wine surplus, also underscores their role in the exchange between sectors of the economy and life in the city and countryside.

The significance of the inns as public spaces has already been touched upon. Aside from their role as a location for the representation of social orders, public houses in Tyrol also served the local society in important, basic public functions – in some villages, for instance, as a substitute for a town hall or as a venue for the court of justice.[40] Furthermore, they were spaces for doing business, best suited as a meeting point for trade in grain, livestock, wood, and victuals. Up until the sixteenth century, certain public houses in Tyrol were even 'integrated [as merchandise depots] in the economic structure of the locality, like an institutionalised market.'[41] The intensive boom in transit from around 1400, though, led to an early separation of public house and merchant site, since houses of trade quickly established themselves in the cities as independent economic facilities.

Of special significance in Tyrol was the level of military self-defence, the *Landesdefension*.[42] The *Landlibell*, a legal statute issued by Emperor Maximilian in 1511, assigned men who were fit for military service within the provincial borders the task of defending Tyrol themselves. With the organization of shooting ranges and companies, public houses served as logistical points of reference for the raising and mustering of troops, the holding of meetings, and the obligatory drink after successful shooting practice. As public areas, however, inns in the transit region of Tyrol also took on heavy public burdens. In this regard, the billeting of troops that were marching through was one of the most arduous tasks that Tyrol's innkeepers had to fulfil. From the early modern era troops had been quartered primarily at inns. Although they lodged there somewhat removed from the guestrooms and spent the night in their own 'soldier rooms' or in the corridor, the other guests, and especially the servants and innkeepers, nevertheless derived little joy from the rough and ready clientele whose aggressive behaviour and volume of noise were a great detraction. Furthermore, quarters and service were compensated at a low rate and were often paid for only after lengthy delays. In addition, many innkeepers also found themselves obliged to support military marches with extra teams of

---

[40] For a general view, see Kümin, 'Rathaus, Wirtshaus, Gotteshaus'. For the political function see C. H. Wegert, 'Wirtshaus und Cafè', in C. Dipper and U. Speck (eds), *1848. Revolution in Deutschland* (Frankfurt a.M., 1998), 170–82.

[41] 'fest in die Wirtschaftsverfassung des Ortes eingegliedert, wie ein institutionalisierter Markt'. W. Kerntke, *Taverne und Markt. Ein Beitrag zur Stadtgeschichtsforschung* (Frankfurt a. M., 1987), 82.

[42] For a summary, see O. Stolz, *Wehrverfassung und Schützenwesen in Tirol von den Anfängen bis 1918*, ed. F. Hunter (Innsbruck, 1960); L. Cole, *'Für Gott, Kaiser und Vaterland'. Nationale Identität der deutschsprachigen Bevölkerung Tirols 1860–1914* (Frankfurt a.M., 2000), 413–504.

horses, making valuable draft animals available for overcoming ascents or difficult stretches of road. The strains from the military reached a particularly horrendous level in time of war, when troops were moved between the Austrian heartland and northern Italy. The population along the roads of Tyrol suffered under endless marches during the Thirty Years' War, the War of the Spanish Succession of 1703, and the Seven Years' War, to say nothing of the 'Twenty Years' War' of the Napoleonic era (1796–1814) when Tyrol was overflowing with troops for years.[43] In 1809, the year of Tyrol's uprising against Bavarian and Napoleonic rule, publicans took on another key function – their houses served as conspiratorial meeting places for the preparation of the revolt, and they themselves organized an essential part of the rebellion against the Kingdom of Bavaria and the advancing French troops. Fourteen publicans set themselves up as the leaders of the *Schützenkompanien* (riflemen companies) that were formed against the Bavarians and French. The legendary figure of the uprising was Andreas Hofer, the 'Sandwirt' from the Passeier Valley who, as provincial commander, acted as their head for more than half a year and, through his execution in February 1810, achieved the status of national hero.[44]

Public houses in all their roles were serviced not just by individual proprietors, but by the entire household of the publican family. The issue of the division of labour within the family in the hospitality industry must be examined according to the relationship between work, family, and social reproduction. Local demand and especially the function of public houses as important public meeting places bound the proprietor families tightly to the local society of the villages, small cities, and markets of Tyrol.[45] In local life, public houses mediated between domestic-private spheres and the larger local and trans-regional 'public'. Their *Stuben* were thus fundamental social spaces for internal village communication and served to build larger circles of contact. The social and vocational profile of the landlords remained basically bound to a traditionally formed way of working and to a distribution of labour within the family, but innovative elements did enter into this.[46]

Work in the public house was always accompanied by surprises and unpredictable events. In the inns along the transit routes there was rarely any

---

[43] J. Fontana, *Das Südtiroler Unterland in der Franzosenzeit 1796 bis 1814. Voraussetzungen – Verlauf – Folgen* (Innsbruck, 1998), 356–68.

[44] See the still fundamental J. Hirn, *Tirols Erhebung im Jahre 1809* (Innsbruck, 1909); and the critical Cole, *'Für Gott, Kaiser und Vaterland'*, 225–321.

[45] Vividly protrayed in J. Weingartner, *Berühmte Wirtshäuser und Wirtsfamilien* (Innsbruck, 1956).

[46] H. Heiss, 'Selbständigkeit bis auf Widerruf? Zur Rolle der Gastwirtinnen bis 1914', in I. Bandhauer-Schöffmann and R. Bendl (eds), *Unternehmerinnen. Geschichte und Gegenwart selbständiger Erwerbsarbeit von Frauen* (Frankfurt a.M., 2000), 49–88.

question of a quiet, continuous practising of one's profession. Moreover, looking after different guests, particularly the narrow class of the travellers 'of means', required adaptability, sensitivity, and a feel for the right tone. With the arrival of better clientele, hustle and bustle and agitation were often unavoidable. The exchange with such guests must have offered a great deal of stimulation, but it was also filled with a high level of stress.[47] Because speed was of the essence, the special, at times unusual wishes of the best ladies and gentlemen for food, lodging, and other requirements needed to be fulfilled quickly. Thus kitchen and wine cellar stocks were supplemented with finer assortments, often ordered and purchased from far away by the innkeeper himself, since specialized suppliers were not always to be found within the local vicinity. Many guests expected special services, such as the preparation of coaches or horses by grooms or stable boys, or the use of servants to act as their personal cooks. The innkeepers also had to manage the sending and receiving of messages, and they took care of the entertainment of the travellers by engaging minstrels and musicians.

Therefore, unforeseeable factors played a prominent role in the everyday life of the hospitality industry – much more so than in other professions. The appearance at inns by outsiders of trans-regional origin and different social groups was inevitably linked with more exotic demands than were customary in local life. At the same time, the brevity of the stays of such guests demanded that their wishes be fulfilled immediately. A fundamental component of the life of innkeeping families was thus the constant coping with contingencies and the ability to react appropriately to the demands of guests of different social and cultural origins. Their success depended on their skills of integration, improvisation, and mediation.

The division of labour in larger enterprises, particularly in inns, took more or less the following form: The publicans had a prominent position and were for the most part local dignitaries. Although they also took on important functions in the public house as the host, as well as in the areas of procuring goods and bookkeeping, the larger part of their activity took place outside of the house. Since publicans in rural areas were among the few people with considerable monetary means, their interests were characterized by trade and speculation. At the same time, they managed agrarian cultivation areas of often considerable size in order to cover the food and feed needs of their inns, taking care of the riding and draught animals of the travellers as well as their own herds of livestock. Publicans were even classic representatives of the so-called

---

[47] For the typical work in the hospitality trade, see L. Gall, *Bürgertum in Deutschland* (Berlin, 1989), 70–5.

'in-between milieu' (*Zwischenmilieu*)[48] – mediator figures between farmers and urban dwellers, between city and country, between inertia and progress. They worked as brokers beyond their own establishment, both in the locality and in surrounding areas.[49] Tyrol's publicans often demonstrated an economic interest in several areas and readily invested in the wood trade and sawmills.

The landlords' wives occupied a remarkably strong position in the division of labour within the family. They supervised the primarily female servants and were to a large extent independently responsible for two central areas of the public house: cooking and stocking the larder. The furnishing and decorating of common areas and guest rooms as well as the cleaning of the establishment fell under the competence of the landladies. Aside from these basic functions, the proprietors' wives also took care of regular dealings with the guests. Although owners often played host, demonstratively greeting or bidding farewell to the customers, wives had at least as broad a spectrum of contacts with the guests. Business areas of the landladies and authority to make decisions were expanded as a result of the out-of-house activities of their husbands. In their function as local and regional dignitaries, but also because of their second and third business activities, publicans were frequently absent and often had to stay out of town for days at a time. Their wives would then take over the direction of the establishment and, in certain cases, also made decisions with considerable consequences.[50]

The owner and his wife introduced their children into the innkeeping business early, especially since the low technical qualifications required in many areas of work facilitated their employment. The serving of guests and simple housework and kitchen work could be easily learned, and at the same time the young people's early recruitment led to the acquisition of important professional skills even before adolescence. Many innkeeping families quickly learned, though, how necessary it was for their offspring to receive an education outside of the house. As early as the eighteenth century, therefore, proprietors of larger inns were sending their sons to out-of-town colleagues with whom they could also pick up foreign languages. Innkeepers' sons from German-speaking Tyrol often spent several months at establishments in the southern part of the province or in Northern Italy in order to learn Italian, which later made the dealings with merchants or noble travellers from cities of the peninsula easier. It was not rare for the daughters, on the other hand, to apprentice in the households of the nobility or the clergy, where they acquired

---

[48]   H. Haas, 'Postmeister, Wirt, Kramer, Brauer, Müller und Wundarzt. Trägerschichten und Organisationsformen des Liberalismus. Das Salzburger Beispiel – vom frühen Konstitutionalismus bis zum Kulturkampf', in E. Bruckmüller, U. Döcker, H. Stekl, and P. Urbanitsch (eds), *Bürgertum in der Habsburgermonarchie* (Vienna, 1990), 257–73.

[49]   Kümin, 'Rathaus, Wirtshaus, Gotteshaus', 253.

[50]   Heiss, 'Selbständigkeit', 52–7.

the fundamentals of fine cooking and rational kitchen organization. Such individual examples of observations therefore make the image of the distinct bond to the tradition of the old hospitality trade relative.[51]

After 1870, with the late expansion of the railway network through Tyrol,[52] the 'good old days' slowly came to an end. Around that time, tourism gradually moved into the province and brought with it new guests and new demands on hospitality workers. They often opened up to the demands of the modern age spontaneously and with motivation, though frequently with considerable reservations, as well. Even in 1889, a general assessment of the services of the hospitality trade turned out extremely critical:

> A prominent circumstance, which in many ways restrictively blocks the better development of the tourist industry, is the innkeepers' insufficient knowledge of the desires and needs of the guests... some inns have attached to themselves the pompous title of 'Hotel' without knowing what characteristics are necessary for it.[53]

In spite of factual objectivity, the critic missed the reasons for the sluggish change by the old hospitality trade: the connection with secular traditions, the close intertwining with the local community, and the mechanisms of a proven family economy did not allow themselves to be easily cast aside. Only the rapid increase in the numbers of guests around 1900 and especially the rapid rate of change brought about by the crises of the twentieth century were responsible for the far-reaching success of tourism and a dynamic adaptation of the industry in Tyrol.

---

[51]   Ibid., 62.

[52]   G. Zwanowetz, *Das Straßenwesen Tirols seit der Eröffnung der Eisenbahn Innsbruck – Kufstein (1858)* (Innsbruck, 1986).

[53]   'Ein hervorragender Umstand, welcher der besseren Entwicklung der Fremdenindustrie vielfach hinderlich in den Weg tritt, ist die mangelhafte Einsicht der Wirthe in die Bedürfnisse und Wünsche der Gäste ... manches Gasthaus hat sich den hochtrabenden Titel 'Hotel' beigelegt, ohne zu wissen, welche Eigenschaften hiezu nothwendig sind.' W. von Pernwerth, *Das Fremdenwesen in Tirol. Mit besonderer Berücksichtigung der Verhältnisse im deutschen Südtirol* (Meran, 1889), 7–8.

Ownership of Public Houses by the Swiss Nobility: A Regional Case-Study

Felix Müller

In 1483–84, the Swiss nobleman Kaspar Effinger acquired Wildegg castle with a number of lands and rights, which comprised among other possessions the inn at Möriken and the lower jurisdiction in the two villages Möriken and Holderbank. Wildegg belonged to the Effingers until 1912, when the family died out.[1]

During the seventeenth century the inn at Möriken brought in a small annual rent of three gulden and five batz (*Batzen*). There is no doubt that this was merely for the privilege of wine-retailing. In about 1690 Bernhard Effinger built a handsome new house on the highway outside Möriken to secure steady demand for the harvest of his vineyards, which he retailed by employing an innkeeper.[2]

In 1698 he also tried to buy another inn situated in the neighbouring village of Rupperswil, but a resident asserted his right of pre-emption, and it was not until 1705 that Bernhard Effinger succeeded in acquiring it. He had sold it again by 1720, purchasing in its place the inn at Gränichen in 1722. Another inn was acquired in 1771, at Reinach, by his grandson Niklaus Albrecht Effinger, who also opened a tavern at a crossroads outside Möriken in about 1775. The Effingers kept these houses until about 1800; they sold the inn at

---

[1]   W. Merz (ed.), *Die Urkunden des Schlossarchivs Wildegg* (Aarau, 1931), nos 67 and 68; B. Meier, *<Gott regier mein Leben>: Die Effinger von Wildegg. Landadel und ländliche Gesellschaft zwischen Spätmittelalter und Aufklärung* (Baden, 2000); F. Müller, *Aussterben oder verarmen? Die Effinger von Wildegg. Eine Berner Patrizierfamilie während Aufklärung und Revolution* (Baden, 2000). 'Inn' means here the exclusive privilege to retail wine. I should like to thank David Miller, Bristol, and Robert Krakovski, Sante Fe (New Mexico), for their help in improving my English.
[2]   Meier, *Effinger*, 145; M. Stettler and E. Maurer, *Die Kunstdenkmäler des Kantons Aargau*, vol. 2, *Bezirke Lenzburg und Brugg* (Basle, 1953), 144–6. Currency: 1 Gulden (florin) = 15 *Batzen* (batz), 1 *Batzen* = 4 *Kreuzer* (kreutzer). An agrarian worker in the mid-eighteenth century earned three to five *Batzen* a day, according to the season, along with some food. Wildegg castle, Archive Wildegg 157, e, 1, no. 36.

Reinach in 1789, the one at Gränichen in 1797 and the one at Möriken in 1807.[3]

Were the Effingers an isolated case, or did other nobles also acquire inns and taverns? Was there a connection with the lower jurisdiction? Can we identify an overall chronological trend? What are the reasons for investing in public houses? These topics – as noble economic activities in general – have received little attention in Swiss historiography.[4] This deficiency may reflect the fact that some economic activities, like manual work, were taboo for the nobility, at least in the German-speaking parts of Europe. In particular, it was inappropriate to engage in any business unconnected to agriculture.[5] One acceptable option, closely linked to the cultivation of vines, was commercial hospitality. In what follows, the importance of this business shall be assessed by means of a case study from the old Swiss Confederation.

This essay first sketches the geographical and constitutional context, in particular the administration of the Bernese Aargau. Part two examines the evidence for noble tenure of public houses and the role of jurisdictional rights. Part three investigates the financial implications for the nobility, followed by some concluding remarks about the importance of noble involvement in the hospitality trade.

The following exploration is restricted to the Bernese Aargau, i.e. the part of the present Aargau that belonged to Bern until 1798. Bern was the largest city-state north of the Alps. It extended from the gates of Geneva almost to the Rhine. Political power was in the hands of a patriciate numbering around 80 families before 1800; no new families were admitted during the eighteenth

---

[3]   Müller, *Effinger*, 263–4.

[4]   Exceptions are Meier, *Effinger*, and Müller, *Effinger*. On Lower Austria see H. Knittler, *Nutzen, Renten, Erträge: Struktur und Entwicklung frühneuzeitlicher Feudaleinkommen in Niederösterreich* (Vienna, 1989); on commercial hospitality in early modern Bern and in the Aargau region, see B. Kümin, 'Useful to have, but difficult to govern: inns and taverns in early modern Bern and Vaud', in *Journal of Early Modern History* 3 (1999), 153–75; idem, 'Rathaus, Wirtshaus, Gotteshaus: Von der Zwei- zur Dreidimensionalität in der frühneuzeitlichen Gemeindeforschung', in *Colloquia mediaevalia Pragensia* 1 (1999), 249–62; B. Kümin and A. Radeff, 'Markt-Wirtschaft: Handelsinfrastruktur und Gastgewerbe im alten Bern', in *Schweizerische Zeitschrift für Geschichte* 50 (2000), 1–19; P. Steiner, 'Die alten Gasthäuser im Wynental und seiner Umgebung', in *Jahresschrift der historischen Vereinigung Wynental* (1989/90), 1–102.

[5]   E. H. Brunner, 'Ist den bernischen Standesherren eine wirtschaftliche Tätigkeit untersagt worden?', in *Berner Zeitschrift für Geschichte und Heimatkunde* 54 (1992), 151–63; B. Stollberg-Rilinger, 'Handelsgeist und Adelsethos. Zur Diskussion um das Handelsverbot für den deutschen Adel vom 16. bis zum 18. Jahrhundert', in *Zeitschrift für Historische Forschung* 15 (1988), 273–309.

Figure 8: Johann Ludwig Aberli, The Bear at Wildegg. Drawing, ca 1760. The building on the left, partly behind a tree, is the mill, and on the hill above the vineyards is Wildegg castle. The inn is a large two-storey building; the double flight of stairs and balcony give it an even more stately appearance (Photo: author).

Figure 9: Mural painting from the Bear at Wildegg. The interior of the Bear shows some fine decoration too, as in this mural painting from the hall of the first floor (Photo: Kantonale Denkmalpflege. Used by permission).

century. The surrounding country and other towns had no voice in central government, but enjoyed a limited local autonomy.[6] This applied also to the Bernese Aargau which covered 600 square kilometres and in 1798 contained around 65,400 inhabitants.[7] It was organized in six districts (*Oberämter*), which were presided over by a Bernese governor (*Landvogt*), and four towns. These units – *Oberämter* and towns – were at the same time the districts of higher jurisdiction, trying crimes that could entail capital punishment. Lower jurisdiction dealt with civil law and smaller crimes, usually punished with a fine. Its territorial extent was much smaller and consisted of one or several villages. Bern owned most of them, but some – actually manors – belonged to institutions or noble families.[8]

The smallest unit of public administration was the commune or municipality (*Gemeinde*). It had some independence in internal matters: the assembly of male inhabitants elected a council and decided on practical issues. To carry out its responsibilities, the commune employed officials and disposed of an income deriving from taxes or communal assets.[9]

The term 'nobility' will be used rather loosely both for Bernese patricians, and for families owning rights of lower jurisdiction, the so-called *Twingherren* (or manorial lords). There were not many such families, because Bern had bought a number of manors.[10] The old family of von Hallwyl is not taken into consideration, since at this time it was economically in decline and torn by internal conflicts.[11]

In the Bernese territories there were two main types of public houses: inns, offering lodging, meals and drinks, and taverns, allowed only to serve wine (beer was practically unknown in this wine-growing region). The keepers had an almost public function, as the word 'publican' implies, and had to observe numerous regulations. Like communal officers, they had to take an oath. It

---

[6] R. Feller, *Geschichte Berns*, 4 vols (Bern, 1946–60); P. Meyer (ed.), *Berner – deine Geschichte: Landschaft und Stadt Bern von der Urzeit bis zur Gegenwart* (Bern, 1981).

[7] *150 Jahre Kanton Aargau im Lichte der Zahlen, 1803–1953* (Aarau, 1954), 17–19; B. Meier (ed.), *Revolution im Aargau: Umsturz-Aufbruch-Widerstand 1798–1803* (Aarau, 1997), CD-ROM.

[8] E. Bucher, *Die bernischen Landvogteien im Aargau* (Aarau, 1944); M. Werder, 'Die Gerichtsverfassung des aargauischen Eigenamtes bis zum Jahre 1798', in *Argovia* 54 (1942), 1–173.

[9] Bucher, *Landvogteien*, 165–81.

[10] Meyer, *Geschichte*, 138–41; Bucher, *Die bernischen Landvogteien*, 49–64; Meier, *Effinger*, 27. The term *Niedergericht* (lower jurisdiction) stands both for the rights as for the district.

[11] A. Bickel, *Die Herren von Hallwil im Mittelalter; Beitrag zur schwäbisch-schweizerischen Adelsgeschichte* (Aarau, 1975), 256–9.

aimed at strengthening the public order and at protecting the guests from being cheated or badly served.[12]

A reasonably accurate estimate of the number of public houses is possible only for the seventeenth and eighteenth centuries, when the state intensified its regulation of the trade. Four surveys (*Revisionen*) collected information on the public houses in Bernese territory in 1628, 1688, 1743 and 1786. Another survey, taken in 1581, dealt only with the district of Lenzburg in the Bernese Aargau.[13] These surveys reveal the aim of the Bernese government to restrict the number of public houses, closing those it deemed unnecessary. Moreover, the early surveys show a change in the powers of granting concessions for public houses. During the high and late Middle Ages the manorial lords (*Twingherren*) possessed the right to license taverns (*Tavernenrecht*) as part of their authority 'to enforce and to forbid' (*Twing und Bann*). This gave them the exclusive right to retail wine, which they could extend to others. With the intensification of governmental authority, especially after the Reformation, the position and rights of the manorial lords came under pressure as Bern claimed new, additional powers.[14]

The survey of 1581 mentioned almost exclusively inns and taverns in places where the lower jurisdiction belonged to Bern. Of the places where the lower jurisdiction was in private hands, the governor wrote: 'Under the manorial lords I cannot really know how many [keepers] are in your Grace's county',[15] adding a few place-names. Thus, in the court districts of the manorial lords, he did not know where public houses existed, and still less could he perform his task of closing unnecessary establishments.

The survey of 1628 was quite different: it listed inns and taverns throughout Bernese territory, noting which of them should be closed. Among the latter

---

[12] Kümin and Radeff, 'Markt-Wirtschaft', 3; Kümin, 'Useful to Have', 155; H. C. Peyer, *Von der Gastfreundschaft zum Gasthaus: Studien zur Gastlichkeit im Mittelalter* (Hannover, 1987), 220–54. The Bernese regulations are published in H. Rennefahrt (ed.), *Sammlung Schweizerischer Rechtsquellen, 2. Abteilung: Die Rechtsquellen des Kantons Bern. 1. Teil: Stadtrechte. Band 8: Wirtschaftsrecht* (Aarau, 1966), 198–255. The text of the oath is published in W. Merz (ed.), *Sammlung Schweizerischer Rechtsquellen, 16. Abteilung: Die Rechtsquellen des Kantons Aargau. 2. Teil: Rechte der Landschaft. Band 1: Amt Arburg und Grafschaft Lenzburg* (Aarau, 1923), 327–8.

[13] Staatsarchiv Bern [hereafter StA BE], B V 142–8; Staatsarchiv Aargau [hereafter StA AG], AA 1862, 349–52.

[14] Peyer, *Gastfreundschaft*, 96–112; Steiner, 'Die alten Gasthäuser im Wynental', 20; Meier, *Effinger*, 26–8 and 34–9; J. J. Siegrist, 'Beiträge zur Verfassungs- und Wirtschaftsgeschichte der Herrschaft Hallwil', in *Argovia* 64 (1952), 5–533, esp. 120–32.

[15] 'Unnder den Thwinngherren mag ich nit eygenntlich wüssen wievill dero inn Ur. G. Graffschafft synnd': StAAG 1862, S. 350.

were several in court districts of manorial lords. The survey of 1688 is even more significant in that several inns were closed that had been erected by manorial lords against the regulations of 1628.[16] A letter of the Bernese government said that the manorial lords claimed the right to grant privileges for inns and taverns, while Bern considered this to be its own prerogative. In the district of Kasteln, too, the survey of 1688 mentioned the 'right claimed by the owners of lower jurisdictions' to grant privileges for public houses.[17]

The surveys show the locations of public houses and their number. Their use for the purpose of this study is, however, limited for two reasons. First, it is sometimes not clear whether the term 'proprietor' means the owner of the building (or only of the right to keep an inn) or the person actually running the business. In Reitnau, the surveys named Hans Hunziker in 1743, but the lord of the manor (the convent of Schänis) in 1786. In this case there is no doubt that the convent of Schänis owned the right to keep an inn and Hunziker was the innkeeper, since he paid a rent to Schänis in 1743. In other cases, such additional information is lacking. Second, as this example shows, the manorial lord often merely granted the retail privilege, without a building. In those cases, the rent was small, sometimes fixed at a customary level.[18] In such a case, the manorial lord saw it as an old insignificant right and we cannot take it as evidence for the interest of a noble family in commercial hospitality. Still, it might offer a means to try and increase profits.

The four surveys at least help to define our area of examination. In the districts of Aarburg, Biberstein and Königsfelden there were no inns or taverns in the hands of nobles – nor were there any lower jurisdictions or castles as private property. In the districts of Kasteln und Schenkenberg several inns and one tavern belonged to Bern, which had acquired them (in 1732) together with the castle of Kasteln; up to then they had been the property of nobles. But, at least in the case of the two Bear Inns at Schinznach and Villnachern, all that was actually involved was the right to keep an inn.[19]

The only remaining district within the Bernese Aargau, Lenzburg, was by far the largest. Here, several manors belonged to noble families. The Effingers have been mentioned above, while members of the May family owned the

---

[16] For 1628: StA BE, B V 142 (district Lenzburg: Hard), for 1688: StA BE, B V 143 (district Lenzburg: Moosleerau, Löhren; district Kasteln: Villnachern).

[17] 'prätendierten Recht der Herrschaft, Tavernen zu bewilligen'. StA BE, B V 143, district Kasteln, Villnachern and Oberflachs; on Bern, StA AG, AA 2126, fasc. 7, a: extract from Manual der deutschen Venner Cammer der Stadt Bern, No. 39, p. 538, of 4 March 1689.

[18] StA BE, B V 144 and 145: Reitnau, Kirchleerau (rent for the inn of 2 pounds), Schinznach (*Bären*/ Bear, rent for the inn of 3 pounds).

[19] StA BE, B V 142–5.

manors of Rued (which included the Rued valley and the villages of Kirchleerau and Moosleerau) and Schöftland.[20]

The right to retail wine at Rued and Kirchleerau predates 1628 and was confirmed by the first survey. During the seventeenth century the manorial lords granted three more rights which were not accepted by Bern and earmarked for closure. This order was not carried out at Moosleerau: in 1693 the Mays still supplied the local keeper with wine. The survey of 1743 then accepted the existence of a public house in Moosleerau and discussion arose only about the question of whether it was an inn or a tavern.

The right to retail wine at Kirchleerau and Moosleerau was let out for a rent of one gulden per year during the seventeenth century and, at Kirchleerau, still in 1743. There is no indication that the May family obtained any further income from the trade.[21]

As for the inn at Rued, circumstances changed. During the seventeenth century the right was let out for a small rent of one gulden, but around 1700 a bitter dispute arose in the May family, both sides wanting to install a publican who would retail the wine of the owner as an employee. This form of lease was used throughout the eighteenth century and will be examined in detail later.[22]

The situation at Schöftland is informative. In 1628 there were three inns, of which Bern ordered two to be closed. By 1688 their number had risen again to three (if the closing-order had been observed at all), but only two were open, and the two new rights had been granted by the lords of the manor. From 1660 all public houses in Schöftland had to obtain their wine exclusively from the manorial lords – explaining perhaps why Bern did not annul the newly-granted rights. In any case, Bern rejected the claim by the innkeepers (or the May family) that no sales tax was payable on wine supplied by the manorial lords. In 1689, the Mays bought one of the inns and in 1728 a second, running it until nearly 1800.[23]

In other places, too, nobles tried to bring public houses under their control. At Teufenthal the owner of Trostburg castle had obtained the right to retail the wine of her own vineyards in 1680, whereupon the Bernese governor wanted to close the older tavern; he was overruled by Bern after protests from the commune. For several years both existed simultaneously, until the noblewoman

---

[20] W. Merz (ed.), *Rechtsquellen*, 151. For the inns and taverns of the whole district see: StA BE, B V 142–5.

[21] StA BE, B V 142 and 144; StA AG, AA 2014, fasc. 1: accounts of 1668/69 and 1693.

[22] Steiner, 'Die alten Gasthäuser im Wynental', 80–3; StA AG, AA 2001, fasc. 6.

[23] P. Kamber, 'Die Schöftler Wirtschaften', in *Jahresbericht Vereinigung für Heimatkunde des Suhrentales und Umgebung* 44 (1987), 18–22; StA AG, AA 2126, fasc. 7; StA AG, AA 797, 361–5 and register: Ohmgeld; StA BE, A II 475, 95.

managed to take over the tavern. In 1704 she sold all her possessions at
Teufenthal to a commoner.[24]

The von Graviset family had bought the manor of Liebegg in 1668 and with
it the inn (or, more precisely, the right to retail wine) at Birrwil. They let it out
for a rent of one gulden annually. In 1728 the lord of the manor intervened in a
dispute, claiming the right to choose an innkeeper and install him, whereas
hitherto the men of the commune had done so. Von Graviset wanted to raise
the rent and sell his own wine. The result of the dispute is not known, but
probably the lord of the manor secured at least part of his claim. His successor
sold the right, together with a building, in 1802.[25]

From 1731, the same Friedrich von Graviset was also in possession of the
inn at Unterkulm. But in 1741 a citizen of the village asserted his right of pre-
emption, so that Graviset lost the inn. He then opened an inn at the neighbouring village of Oberkulm, where the commune had owned the right to keep an
inn for a long time and had only a few years earlier built a new house for it. But
they could not succeed against the noble. The communal inn remained closed
until Graviset's inn shut down in about 1760.[26]

Further public houses belonging to nobles existed at Fahrwangen, Reitnau,
Schafisheim, Seengen and Tennwil. At Fahrwangen and Reitnau it was probably only the right which remained in the possession of the manorial lords; at
Schafisheim and Tennwil the nature of the manorial lords' involvement is unknown. At Seengen, Colonel von Goumoëns acquired a right in 1771 and
transferred it to his spa at Brestenberg.[27]

Most of the noble owners of public houses were manorial lords, too, so that
the lower jurisdiction might be regarded as being of great importance. But
some of the public houses were not in the manorial lords' own court district,
such as those at Oberkulm, Unterkulm, Gränichen, Reinach and Teufenthal. So
what exactly were the powers of lower jurisdiction with regard to inns and taverns?

Sometimes lower jurisdiction made it possible to terminate the lease of a
public house and to run it on behalf of the manorial lord through an employee,
as was the case at Wildegg and Rued. To be sure, the lower jurisdiction alone
was not sufficient for such a change. Otherwise, the manorial lords would
probably have tried to get control of the inns at Kirchleerau and Reitnau, too,

---

[24] Steiner, 'Die alten Gasthäuser im Wynental', 88–91.

[25] Ibid., 53–8.

[26] Ibid., 76–7, 92; J. J. Siegrist, *Die Gemeinde Unterkulm und das Kirchspiel Kulm*
(Aarau, 1957), 170–71.

[27] StA BE, B V 142–5; Siegrist, 'Beiträge', 430–34. The date of origin of the public house
at Tennwil is unknown: in the surveys it is first mentioned in 1786, but according to Siegrist it
was there as early as ca 1640. The other four rights are substantiated in 1628.

which would have brought them a considerable rise in income. Lower jurisdiction also provided a means to acquire real estate, i.e. the right of pre-emption or *Zugrecht* (the right to take over a contract of purchase on conditions already agreed upon). As we shall see, this was what the lord of Schöftland manor intended, or at least threatened. The price was then set by the 'invisible hand' of the market.

In the Bernese Aargau, then, nobles acquired, or at least gained control of, a number of public houses. In order to understand their interest in commercial hospitality the relation between owner and publican has to be examined.

In 1660 Wolfgang von Mülinen, then lord of Schöftland manor, exchanged his inn called the Lion for another inn, the Bear, plus a sum of money; in addition, the new owner of the Lion committed himself and his successors to buy wine – at an ordinary market price – only from the manorial lords. When the third inn at Schöftland came up for sale, von Mülinen wanted to exercise his right of pre-emption, but withdrew when the purchaser promised to buy wine solely from him. An exception was allowed only when von Mülinen had no wine to offer.[28]

In 1689, the lord of the manor bought back the Lion at Schöftland. The conditions of the lease now went beyond the exclusive delivery of wine; the innkeeper had to retail about 1,500 litres of wine of the owner for a fixed wage, and to buy the other wine from the vineyards of the manor. If the manorial lord did not have enough, the innkeeper could buy where he chose. Around 1740, the system was changed to the effect that the lord's two local innkeepers had to get all their wine from the manor, just like the innkeeper at Rued.[29] The lease for the inn at Rued of 1709 stipulated that the publican had to retail the wine of the owner, being allowed two kreutzer per measure (ca 1.5 litre) for doing so. On the other hand the innkeeper had to pay a rent of fifty gulden per year plus a sales tax of seven per cent. These conditions remained in force throughout most of the century.[30]

The innkeeper of the Bear at Wildegg (Figures 8 and 9) was an employee, too, with regard to the retailing of wine. The lord of the manor supplied all the wine, and the lease was very strict on this point: 'He [the innkeeper] shall not retail any other wine than that supplied by the owner, on pain of losing the lease'. He was paid only one kreutzer per measure, but had no rent and no sales

---

[28] StA AG; AA 2126, fasc. 7, b, no. 2, and c, no. 1 (however, both publicans immediately challenged this commitment: StA BE, A II 464, 360–61).

[29] StA AG; AA 2126, fasc. 7, b and c. Publicans' rate of pay: 20 *Batzen* per *Saum* = 0,8 *Kreuzer* per measure; since about 1760 1,33 *Kreuzer* per measure. Measures: 1 *Saum* = 100 *Mass* (measures) of about 1,5 litre each.

[30] StA AG, AA 2001, fasc. 6.

tax to pay. The income for the other services – meals, spirits, lodging and animal feed – went into his own pocket.[31]

Thus it seems that the nobles in a first phase sought an outlet for their own wine. Later they extended this lucrative business, and by about 1740 they were supplying all the wine to their innkeepers (whom they paid per measure retailed) even if they had to buy extra wine themselves. The profit margin is not usually known, but for Wildegg it can be calculated for 1792. It was six kreutzer per measure of wine from Vaud, and at least four kreutzer per measure of local wine (excluding the costs for maintenance of the buildings and the like). The profit per *Saum* (an old measure of about 150 litre) was thus about ten gulden – admittedly, at a time of high prices. In 1787 the Effingers reckoned on a profit of eight gulden per *Saum*, and the Mays, for their inn at Schöftland in 1760, on three kreutzer per measure, or five gulden per *Saum*.[32]

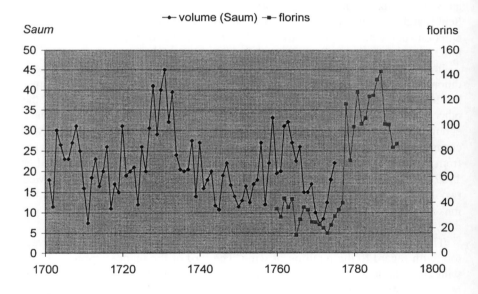

Graph 1: Wine sales at the inn at Rued according to the *Ohmgeldbuch*. Until 1775 the wine supplied in Saum per year (left scale), from 1760 on based on sales tax in florins per year (right scale). The two graphs do not correlate exactly due to the influence of the price on the sales tax, but they show clearly the strong rise in sales tax before 1780.

---

[31] Müller, *Effinger*, 267–9; Wildegg castle, Archive Wildegg 225, 55: 'so dann soll er bey Straff der Verwürkung des Lehens keinen anderen Wein verwirthen als den, so ihm von dem Lehenherrn zum Verwirthen eingemessen wird'.

[32] Wildegg castle, Archive Wildegg 175; StA AG, AA 2041, fasc. 4: Berechnung.

The quantities of wine sold are well known for some public houses. At Rued the sales from 1700–1775 fluctuated from year to year, with an average turnover of about 3,000 litres (18 *Saum*) annually (Graph 1). For the later period the figures for wine supplied are lacking, but as a substitute we can use the figures for the income from the sales tax. In the years from 1760 to 1777, it had averaged just under thirty gulden. Then it shot up, bringing in 108 gulden on average from 1778 to 1791, indicating a marked rise in volume or price (probably both).

In the public houses owned by the Effingers, the quantities were greater. In the inn at Gränichen (1749–97), wine sales varied between 6,000 and over 18,000 litres; in the inn at Reinach (1772–87), between 7,500 and 18,000 litres. The tavern near Wildegg contributed 3,750 litres on average. The figures for the Bear at Wildegg are interesting: from 1750 to 1775, sales were between 6,000 and 12,000 litres a year, rising to 27,000 litres in 1794, and then gradually falling back to about 15,000 litres. This rise is connected with the improvement of the highway which passed the inn and with the establishment of a textile factory nearby. At Schöftland from 1751 to 1759, the two inns together sold 19,200 litres on average; in the years 1782 to 1788 the keeper of the Lion bought 8,400 litres on average.[33]

The quantities of wine and potential profits were high. They affected the valuation of the public houses in the *Herrschaftsschatzungen*, the valuations of a manor. Although the accuracy of the figures found in these records is not beyond doubt, they do give a general idea of the sums involved, and of the relative importance of the inns and taverns.

In 1786, the net income from the inn at Rued was declared to be 250 gulden. The same amount was given as the income of each of the inns at Schöftland in about 1750, although 'both yield more than 1,000 gulden annually with little or no trouble' to their owner.[34] The inn at Wildegg was valued at 5,000 gulden in 1760. The inn at Reinach fetched 10,000 gulden at its sale in 1789 and the one at Gränichen sold for 13,000 gulden in 1797.[35]

The inns' share of the total income varied widely. According to a valuation of the manor of Schöftland of 1727, the two inns together brought in 252 gulden a year, which accounted for ten per cent of the total income. Another 744 gulden (28.8 per cent) came from the vineyards. The Effingers at Wildegg estimated the net income from each of their three inns as 360 gulden in 1771, or

[33] StA AG, AA 2001, fasc. 6, no. 1; Müller, *Effinger*, 265–7; StA AG, AA 2126, fasc. 7, b, no. 15; StA AG, AA 2041, fasc. 4: Berechnung.

[34] 'beyde dem besizern mit geringer, ja keiner mühe jährlich über 1000 Gulden eintragen'. StA AG, AA 2041, fasc. 4, ca 1750: Ausführliche Beschreibung; on Rued, StA AG, AA 2014, fasc. 2, 1786.

[35] Wildegg castle, archive Wildegg 157, c, 11 and 19; Müller, *Effinger*, 264.

thirteen per cent of the income of the estate. The effective income in the 1760s was between just under 3,000 and more than 5,000 gulden, which amounted to a third of the total income of the estate. For 1779 and 1795, respectively, the figures rose to 7,000 and 13,000 gulden, or about half the income. And these were accounts, not rosy estimates.[36]

Admittedly, an inn was not in every case a 'gold-mine' for the owner, as the example of Oberkulm (above) shows. Moreover, the valuations and accounts do not include the construction and maintenance of the buildings. Consider the inn at Rued, for example; in 1774, plans were made for a new building which would have cost 1,135 gulden. They were not carried out; instead, the Mays bought a house elsewhere and had it transferred to Rued, which cost almost 2,000 gulden.[37] Vineyards, too, were in some cases virtually unprofitable. Those at Schöftland already appeared to be operating at a loss in an estimate of 1760. The Effingers sold their vineyards at Auenstein in 1779, and reduced the area of vines at Wildegg around 1800.[38]

In the Bernese Aargau nobles owned an astonishingly high number of inns and taverns. Of about forty inns in the district of Lenzburg in 1743, six were run by nobles through their employees. In another five cases, nobles owned the right to keep an inn.[39] This is the result of a process that took place mainly in the years between 1680 and 1730. Earlier, around 1660, the lord of Schöftland manor had won the exclusive right to supply the inns in that village with wine. Commercial hospitality was obviously a business compatible with nobility.

This development is to be explained mainly economically. In the seventeenth century, nobles wanted to secure an outlet for the harvest of their vineyards. Selling wine to publicans proved to be lucrative, so they expanded the number of public houses they owned, as well as the right to supply wine to their innkeepers. The income from their public houses varied; but at least for one family it reached about fifty per cent of the total income from the estate in some years.

Thus the nobles took part in a larger general development. Other social groups wanted to profit from the retail sale of wine. Some of the clergy offered wine, which they had either obtained as part of the income of their benefice, or purchased for resale. In the district of Lenzburg, this applied in 1639 to the parsons of Gränichen, Seengen, Seon, Rued and Holderbank. Several sources show that Bernese officials (such as the governor or the governor's secretary)

---

[36] StA AG, AA 2041, fasc. 4: Ertrag 1727; Müller, *Effinger*, 314–16.
[37] Steiner, 'Wynental', 82–3.
[38] StA AG, AA 2041, fasc. 4: Berechnung; Müller, *Effinger*, 197 and 222–4.
[39] StA BE, B V 144.

also retailed wine. These cases date mainly from the years 1680–1730. Either they started this business then, or the competition grew sharper in this period.[40]

The number of inns and taverns rose generally over the course of the seventeenth and eighteenth centuries. For the whole territory of Bern (allowing for some uncertainty in consideration of the nature of early modern statistics) they numbered 494 in 1628, and 1,015 in 1786; thus the number of public houses had more than doubled in the course of one and a half centuries. The background to this development was the rise of the population. In about 200 years (from 1559 to 1764) the number of inhabitants of the Bernese Aargau tripled, and from 1764 to 1798 it increased by a further thirty-eight per cent to 65,400 souls.[41]

Another relevant factor is the area of vineyards, which expanded markedly in course of the seventeenth century, thanks largely to restrictions on the import of foreign wines by Bern.[42] The increase in the production of wine probably induced the noble owners of vineyards to look for secure outlets for their harvests. Details of the interplay of the various factors remain to be examined, especially for the eighteenth century.

Some other aspects, too, might be fruitfully examined, such as the function of loans to publicans. The Effingers acquired the inns at Rupperswil and Gränichen after the innkeepers had gone bankrupt. Did they lend money to publicans in order to acquire the inn more easily when the owner encountered financial difficulties? Or, conversely, did they have to take over the bankrupt's estate in order not to lose their investment? Or was lending money to keepers an 'ordinary' investment, made perhaps in the course of wine-selling?[43] Other such questions concern the geographical origins of the publicans – many of them non-residents – and the relations among the different noble families and their branches. It is very probable that they exchanged information, as some similarities in the wording of leases suggest, and that they sold wine to each

---

[40] W. Merz, *Repertorium des aargauischen Staatsarchivs*, 2 vols (Aarau, 1935), 15 (line 10), 126 (l. 1), 136 (l. 37), 153 (l. 41); StA AG, AA 797, pp 463 und 365 (clergymen: the dispute was about the sales tax). The communes, too, were involved in commercial hospitality; in 1743 they owned at least eight inns (StA BE, B V 144). See also the examples of Birrwil and Oberkulm above.

[41] Kümin, 'Rathaus', note 67; M. Mattmüller, *Bevölkerungsgeschichte der Schweiz. Teil I: Die frühe Neuzeit 1500–1700.* 2 vols (Basle, 1987), 123–4; Meier, *Revolution* (CD-ROM).

[42] Siegrist, 'Beiträge', 419–25; Meier, *Effinger*, 129–32, 156–9.

[43] H. Rennefahrt, *Grundzüge der bernischen Rechtsgeschichte*, pt 3 (Bern, 1928), 302–10; J. J. Siegrist, *Rupperswil. Ein aargauisches Bauerndorf im Mittelalter und in der früheren Neuzeit*, vol. 1 (Aarau, 1971), 251–2; W. Pfister, *Rupperswil. Die Geschichte eines Dorfes an der Aare*, vol. 2 (Rupperswil, 1966), 160; Müller, *Effinger*, 264. The Effingers took out an existing loan on the inn at Lupfig: Merz, *Urkunden*, nos 259–60.

other. Interesting, also, are the privileges of citizens of Bern itself in the wholesale wine trade.[44]

The broader context of the history of trade and economy in the Bernese territories and the economic history of the nobility has been investigated only spo-
radically. The figures mentioned above point to a boom in commercial
hospitality between about 1780 and 1795. The participation of the nobility in
trade has been examined for Lower Austria. A comparison with that study is
problematic, considering the limited information basis for the Bernese Aargau.
It seems, however, that the Bernese patricians invested more in trade or, strictly
speaking, in the real estate used for businesses like inns, mills, brickworks,
sawmills, and so forth than the nobility of Lower Austria, where such investments were contributing only a little over five per cent on average to noble
incomes around 1750.[45]

In very many respects the importance of inns and taverns in the early modern period should not be underestimated. This applies equally to their part in
the economics of the nobility. In the region examined here, an astonishing
quota of public houses belonged to nobles, with inns and taverns accounting for
a significant part – up to fifty per cent – of noble incomes.

---

[44] StA AG, AA 2001, fasc. 6; StA AG, AA 2126, fasz. 7, b and c; Müller, *Effinger*, 397–8
and 387, note 520. For trade of wine see G. Boner, 'Zur Geschichte des Weinhandels im
Unteraargau am Ausgang der Bernerzeit', in *Heimatkunde aus dem Seetal* 46 (1973), 94–107.

[45] C. Pfister, *Geschichte des Kantons Bern seit 1798,* vol. 4, *Im Strom der
Modernisierung. Bevölkerung, Wirtschaft und Umwelt 1700–1914* (Bern, 1995), 238–43;
Knittler, *Nutzen,* 182–203.

Drink Houses in Early Modern Russia

George E. Snow

In his study of the English alehouse, Peter Clark takes great care to distinguish between the types of places where alcoholic beverages were sold and, as the title of his book implies, what manner of beverages were sold there. His reasons for this careful distinction were a desire to avoid confusion between the complex types of social gathering places that existed at roughly the same times and were intended to meet the needs of quite diverse groups of people, and to avoid the oversimplification that inevitably results from lumping together disparate institutions.[1]

The same considerations hold true for any study of the drinking establishments of early modern Russia. Here, in addition to the normal social, chronological, and typological considerations, there are economic and political considerations as well. That is, in some parts of early modern Russia, most notably Muscovy as opposed to the more westerly and south-westerly Ukraine, the sale and often even the manufacture of alcoholic beverages were monopolies or near-monopolies of the state. The places that sold them were thus eminently political in nature – perhaps on a footing at least equal to if not to a far greater extent than was the case of drink houses in other parts of Europe. Moreover, the revenues of the state thus were inextricably bound up with, and increasingly dependent on, the revenues from such establishments. Hence one might argue that the state's economic viability or, at the very least, a substantial portion of its budgets and spending were tied to the financial success of drinking establishments to an extent matched by few other places in Europe.

In order to truly understand the nature of these institutions, then, the area of focus in this essay will be Muscovy and, to a limited extent, Ukraine. In the latter, as remnants of Medieval Kievan Russian practices, the major drinking establishments were the *korchmy* (sing. *korchma*, or inn). These establishments existed among many Slavic peoples, not just Ukrainians and Russians. Not unnaturally in light of the many problems attendant on early industrialization and urbanization, these institutions were the object of much Romantic speculation among members of the nineteenth-century Russian intelligentsia,

---

[1] P. Clark, *The English Alehouse: A Social History, 1200–1830* (New York, 1983), 6–14.

conservative Slavophiles and radical revolutionaries alike.[2] The *korchmy* emerge from the literature of the nineteenth century as public drinking houses where members of various groups, including *bratchiny* (general fraternal groups formed for the purpose of sharing both the costs and the enjoyment of alcoholic drinks) and specialized groups such as guilds (*tsekhy*) and workers cooperatives (*artely*) gathered, along with their wives and their children. Here they could drink and eat, have conversations and enjoy singing and music.[3] Housed in single stand-alone buildings, they were centres where local inhabitants could gather around a common table to drink and to talk about various items of local concern, business, etc. – in short, a place where all of the 'news of popular sorrows and joys' was aired. They were thus viewed as expressions of a striving for community and places where even young girls could often go without their presence being considered shameful or scandalous.[4] Indeed, according to some ethnological evidence, these early institutions were places where young men and women could meet in the courtyard or under the shed attaching to the main building in order to permit courting in a 'respectable' setting.[5] Finally, they were also centres of festive celebrations on holidays,[6] and, because of political limitations on princely power in the late Kievan period, foci of a nascent democracy, places where 'the prince had no power'.[7] Given these positive attributes, the *korchmy,* because of the absence of any additional associations of gambling and consorting with women of 'dubious virtue', represented something of a middle ground between what Clark has described in the contemporary English setting as an inn and an alehouse.[8]

Just as important as the manner in which the *korchmy* functioned, however, was the issue of what manner of beverages were sold in them. Most writers agree that only weak alcoholic beverages such as fermented honey or mead (*myed*); beer (*pivo*); ale (*braga*), kvass; and some wines were served.[9] There

---

[2]   On the shared romanticism of the Russian intelligentsia and the similarities of many of their basic assumptions and world view, see L. Schapiro, *Rationalism and Nationalism in Nineteenth-Century Political Thought* (New Haven, 1967); R. Pipes, *The Russian Intelligentsia* (New York, 1961).

[3]   I. G. Pryzhov, *Istoriia kabakov v Rossii* [A history of the taverns in Russia] (Moscow,1868), 24, 27.

[4]   'izvestiiami o narodnykh bedsviiakh i radostiiakh': D. N. Borodin, *Kabak i ego proshloe* [The tavern and its past] (St Petersburg, 1910), 29.

[5]   Pryzhov, *Istoriia kabakov*, 29–30.

[6]   Ibid.

[7]   'Kniaz ... ne imet v korchmakh nikakoi voli': Ibid., 31; Borodin, *Kabak i ego proshloe*, 30.

[8]   Clark, *The English Alehouse*, 6–22.

[9]   Pryzhov, *Istoriia kabakov*, 31. Kvass is a fermented, almost non-alcoholic beer-like beverage formerly produced through the fermentation of oatmeal, and today from malted rye,

are no indications that grain alcohol was served. Overall, this strikes one as a rather idealized picture of an earlier, more innocent age. But it should also be noted that this idyllic picture is challenged by evidence that even during these centuries the Orthodox church in Russia expressed concern about excessive drinking in the *korchmy*, and about the pagan features associated with it.[10] As Ann Tlusty has noted elsewhere, in the German context, such rhetorical expressions of disapproval of public drunkenness resulted in little real pressure to conform to social, let alone legal norms.[11] This was no less true in early modern Russia, and the situation there also serves to underscore her further point that abuses of alcohol were part of the 'traditional' drinking cultures of many peoples in this period.[12]

Institutions such as the *korchmy*, however, had no durable existence in northeastern Russia (in the frontier areas of Vladimir, Suzdal, and Moscow). In these regions drinking establishments similar to those in southwestern Russia were either prohibited or permitted only at certain times of the year by the princely authority as late as 1551.[13] Moreover, such prohibitions extended to members of the minor nobility (*dety boiarskii*) and the clergy.[14] Instead, only peasants and members of the lower social orders were allowed.[15]

Before discussing the issue of Muscovite drinking establishments further, it is necessary to address the appearance of that alcoholic beverage with which they and Russia would be inextricably linked not only in the early modern period, but in subsequent centuries as well: vodka. Its exact origins remain a

---

barley, wheat and rye, wheat or buckwheat flour, or from pastry, bread or rusks. Sugar, honey and various fruits and berries are also sometimes added to flavour it. See R. E. F. Smith and D. Christian, *Bread and Salt: A Social and Economic History of Food and Drink in Russia* (Cambridge, 1984), 74–7; I. I. Sreznevskii, *Materialy dlia slovaria drevnerusskago iazyka* [Materials for a Dictionary of the Ancient Russian Language], vol. 2 (St Petersburg, 1895), 122; W. Pokhlebkin, *A History of Vodka* (London, 1992), 19–20; G. E. Snow, 'Alcohol Production in Russia', in *Supplement to the Modern Encyclopedia of Russian, Soviet and Eurasian History* (1995), 1:192–6.

[10] Smith and Christian, *Bread and Salt*, 84.

[11] B. A. Tlusty, 'Water of Life, Water of Death: The Controversy Over Brandy and Gin in Early Modern Augsburg', in *Central European History* 31 (Fall 1998), 1–30.

[12] Ibid.

[13] S. Shakmaev and I. Kurukin, *Kabak na Russii* [The Kabak in Russia] (New York, 1996), 11; Pryzhov, *Istoriia kabakov*, 32; M. I. Smirnov, *Nizhegorodski kazennyie kabaki I kruzhechnie dvory XVII stoletiia* [The Nizhny-Novgorod state taverns and the pot-houses of the seventeenth century] (Nizhny Novgorod, 1913), 100; I. I. Ditiatin, 'Tsarskii kabak moskovgskogo gosudarstva' [The tsarist tavern of the Muscovite state], *Stat'i po istorii russkogo prava* [Article on the History of Russian Law] (St Petersburg, 1896), 472–3; Smith and Christian, *Bread and Salt*, 85.

[14] Pryzhov, *Istoriia kabakov*, 38; B. Segal, *Russian Drinking. Use and Abuse of Alcohol in Pre-Revolutionary Russia* (New Brunswick, New Jersey, 1987), 44.

[15] Pryzhov, *Istoriia kabakov*, 38.

subject of debate, but its similarity to Scandinavian aquavit and the late Medieval aqua vitae is notable. Just as both of these literally mean 'water of life', so vodka is etymologically similar: 'little water'. Two schools dominate with respect to its place of origin. One stresses that close trade contacts between Scandinavians of the Baltic via Livonia and the principalities of Kievan Rus and, later, Lord Novgorod the Great were vodka's *entrepôt* into the Russian northeast as early as the thirteenth century. The other contends that it was imported indirectly from distilled alcohol's original source in Arabic lands through Genoese merchants operating out of their port of Cafta, and thence to Periaslavl on the Dnieper, from which it spread to all of Rus in the fifteenth century.[16] More recently, a post-Soviet Russian author has tentatively advanced a third possibility: that vodka was native to Muscovy. According to this theory, it was a natural outcome over the course of 150 years of that principality's indigenous 'pot distillation' process of kvass between the mid-fourteenth and early sixteenth centuries, and was only subsequently influenced by the Genoese who, in the final analysis, introduced its consumption as a medicine (*lekarstvo*).[17] In any case, this substance, so powerful and so intoxicating, quickly overtook and surpassed mead, beer, ale, etc. in both popularity and demand — a demand that became inextricably bound up with the appearance of new types of drink establishments in Muscovy: the Tsarist *kabaki* (sing. *kabak*, tavern).[18]

The association of these new drink establishments with the principality of Moscow is further explained by the latter's close ties with and dependence on the Mongols for two-and-a-half centuries. Yet some authors argue that the establishment of the *kabaki* there must be seen as an outgrowth of the Muscovite princes' ongoing and numerous attempts to control the social life of the people, a concomitant to the stern prohibition on drink noted above.[19] The term *kabak* itself is a Tatar loan word,[20] but the fundamental difference between the establishments of the Tatars (who despite their conversion to Islam nonetheless continued to build and frequent drink houses) and those of the Muscovites was that the former served both food and alcoholic beverages in a fashion similar to the *korchmy* of southwestern Russia, whereas the Muscovite institutions served

---

[16] J. Billington, *The Icon and the Axe: An Interpretive History of Russian Culture* (Princeton, 1966); Pryzhov, *Istoriia kabakov*, 36; idem., *I. G. Pryzhov: Ocherki, stat'i, pis'ma* [I. G. Pryzhov: Sketches, Articles, Letters], ed. M. S. Alt'man (Moscow and Leningrad, 1934), 196.

[17] Pokhlebkin, *A History of Vodka*, 50–64.

[18] Pryzhov, *Istoriia kabakov*, 45–6.

[19] Smith and Christian, *Bread and Salt*, 84.

[20] Pryzhov, *Istoriia kabakov*, 45–6; Smith and Christian, *Bread and Salt*, 90.

alcoholic beverages only.[21] Whatever their origins, their conjoined destiny and the important role played by the Russian drink houses in the finances of the principality was a direct outcome of the increasing need of the new Muscovite state both for revenues to pay for its centralization of authority after the collapse of the Golden Horde, and to overtake the nations of the West.[22] In short, these new drink institutions served from the very first a redistributive function that channelled revenues from the populace to the state to a degree that would increase appreciably over the centuries, in the early twentieth century reaching over fifty per cent of all state revenues.[23]

Because of these paired needs, responsibility for the institutionalization of the *kabaki* as a means of generating revenues for the Muscovite state is generally given to Ivan IV (The Terrible, or The Dread, r. 1533–84). It was, however, only after his conquest of Kazan in 1547 and after those *kabaki* in the city that were not destroyed during its siege and sacking opened their doors to the victorious Muscovites, that Ivan's closest supporters expressed a desire that similar institutions be built on Russian soil.[24] Thus, at first, the common people were not permitted in the *kabaki*. Instead drinking there was an exclusive privilege of the *oprichniki*, the Tsar's trusted supporters in his struggle with the hereditary Russian nobles. However, the revenues generated by these state-owned and -operated establishments were so great that provincial authorities were ordered to close *korchmy* and private inns and to permit the common people to visit *kabaki* instead.[25]

From the first, Muscovite authorities made great efforts to procure agents to work in these establishments. Thus it was the state's conceit that those who were appointed for this purpose were the 'better people' of the various locales, chosen by village assemblies. They were to swear a religious oath that they would honestly serve in the *kabaki* and would not steal either from the sovereign or the people. The primary agents of the state whose task it was to operate these establishments were the *kabatskie golovy* – the *kabak* heads – and their subordinates, the men under oath. The latter were subsequently referred to collectively as *tseloval'niki* (lit. 'kissers'), or 'sworn men', so named because they all kissed the crucifix as a seal to their oath of honesty and honorable service.[26] The *kabak* heads were immediately responsible to *volost* (district) or *oblast'*

[21] Pryzhov, *Istoriia kabakov*, 45–6.

[22] Shakmaev and Kurukin, *Kabak na Russii*, 15.

[23] D. Christian, *Living Water: Vodka and Russian Society on the Eve of Emancipation* (New York, 1990), 4–5.

[24] S. Romanov, *Istoriia russkoi vodki* [A History of Russian Vodka] (Moscow, 1998), 12. Also see Borodin, *Kabak i ego proshloe*, 34: Borodin also insists that it was at this time that the term kabak replaced the older Muscovite term *postoialy dvor* (hostelry).

[25] Romanov, *Istoriia russkoi vodki*, 12.

[26] Ibid., 13; Borodin, *Kabak i ego proshlago*, 12–13.

(regional) authorities. The latter almost always were the *voevody*, or military governors appointed over the region by the Tsar. In these circumstances the *kabak* heads were required to be literate in order to complete periodical reports to these officials. In turn, however, they possessed authority over the sworn men, of whom there were two principle types: those engaged in the distillation of the liquor to be sold in the *kabak*, and those who sold the liquor.[27] The position of the *kabak* heads was problematic, however, due to their numerous responsibilities, their frequent lack of simple knowledge of arithmetic, and the short-term nature of their service. They were, for example, supposed to serve one-year terms and were subject to re-election by the village council, which could replace them, obviously, for any number of personal or economic reasons.[28] In any case, all three combined to make their tenure and hence their authority provisional and easily circumvented.[29]

This early period was also characterized by a strict insistence on conformity by both the *kabak* heads and sworn men to a prescribed set of rules and practices. For example, the latter were required to put the monies spent by patrons on drink in sealed boxes. They were strictly forbidden to make change so that there would be few opportunities for short-changing or cheating of any sort. Furthermore, they and the *kabak* heads were forbidden 'even for a short time' to put the proceeds in their own pockets or in 'other out-of-the-way places, under cups, dishes, table cloths, etc.' The earnings of each *kabak* were also to be checked weekly or monthly, according to the disposition of the ranking authority in the area.[30] Accordingly, each *kabak* was required to keep detailed records indicating the sales and transactions made by the establishment; and from time to time, the heads were summoned to Moscow to report to Tsarist authorities on their dealings. They were to be accompanied by the money boxes, all *kabak* records, a deacon, and a sworn man – the latter so that there could be little chance of deception or false swearing of one against the other.[31]

The purpose of such strictures, begun during the reign of Ivan IV and becoming yet more stringent during the brief reigns of his son Feodor Ivanovich (r. 1584–98) and his successor, Boris Godunov (r. 1598–1603) did not, of course, stem from a burning desire by the Muscovite state for moral and ethical probity in the employees of its taverns as goals in and of themselves. Rather, such measures were clearly designed to maximize the drink revenues flowing into the treasury while minimizing any embezzlement and cheating that would compromise or reduce that flow. The Englishman Giles Fletcher's detailed

---

[27] Borodin, *Kabak i ego proshlago*, 39.

[28] Romanov, *Istoriia russkoi vodki*, 13.

[29] Borodin, *Kabak i ego proshlago*, 41.

[30] 'dazhe na vremya priatat vyruchki v sobstvennyi karman'; 'potainye mesta – pod bliudstvo, charki, skaterti, i t.p.': Romanov, *Istorii russkoi vodki*, 13–14.

[31] Ibid., 14.

(but, it must be admitted, often prejudiced) account of his journey to Muscovy in 1589 recorded that a *kabak* existed in every large city he visited, where mead, beer and vodka were sold – especially the latter. The sums accruing to the Muscovite treasury from such establishments varied, he noted. One paid 800 rubles per year, another 900, a third more than 1,000 rubles, while several he recorded yielded 2,000 to 3,000 rubles per year.[32] Such figures appear inflated if not exaggerated. But the basic fact remains that the profits were immense. This situation was further exacerbated by the requirement that the *kabaki* establish an annual 'plan of earnings' for the coming year, which was to be no lower than those of previous years.[33] Food (*zakuski*, lit. snacks) was, as noted above, strictly forbidden, and those patrons who attempted to take food into the *kabaki* with them were to be quickly evicted.[34] This was the self-described system of the state-monopolized manufacture and sale of alcohol on trust (*na ver'e*).

Physically, a nineteenth-century source provides us with an idea of the appearance and lay-out of the early modern *kabaki*. According to the autodidact and revolutionary I. G. Pryzhov, they were laid out quite simply. Consisting of crude, one-storey wooden huts (*izby*), they were located in enclosed courtyards and frequently had joined to them shed-like store-rooms of comparable size that were made of unfinished wood. These sheds usually included cellars. Further, the doors and gates to the main buildings were blocked with a number of iron bars – presumably to prevent forcible entry when the *kabaki* were closed. Their interiors featured numerous iron oil lamps along the walls; the ubiquitous Russian stove for heating and cooking; and shelving along all four walls to hold vessels of various types and sizes, ranging from dippers, to large and small funnels, to containers for the serving of vodka and other alcoholic beverages. Along one wall stood a bar, behind which the sworn man would sit and from which he would serve the patrons. If the *kabak* was a state-owned enterprise – which it would have been until the beginning of the seventeenth century – one corner of the *kabak* was occupied by a clerk (*pod'iachie*), whose sole responsibility was to record how much liquor was sold and to whom for official records.

According to Pryzhov, such establishments were nearly empty in the summer, but in winter and in holiday seasons – especially in the period around Lent – they were 'full from morning until night'. Furthermore, he noted that there were two distinct types of regular denizens. There were, first of all, the common people, what he termed the 'poor of the *kabak*' (*gol' kabatskie*), which

---

[32] Giles Fletcher, *Of the Russe Commonwealth* (Ithaca, New York 1966), 55–6, 63; Shakhmatov and Kurukin, *Kabak na Rusi*, 17.

[33] 'plan' vyruchki': Shakmatov and Kurukin, *Kabak na Rusi*, 19.

[34] Romanov, *Istorii russkoi vodki*, 15.

included beggars, fugitives from the law, vagabonds, thieves, and apprentices to various craftsmen. These elements, especially the first three, also included women. The second category Pryzhov describes simply as those who came from urban society, the real 'enthusiasts of the *kabak*' (*kabatskie yarigi*). These included members of the clergy, nobles (*boyary*), and lower-ranking government officials of various descriptions. Women from these classes were, however, prohibited from even entering the *kabaki*. To all of these were added clerks and stewards on large estates.[35] In short, by the beginning of the seventeenth century, the *kabaki* had become sinks (*rakoviny*) of vice and squalor and, unlike Clark's description of the English inns of the time, definitely not centres of embryonic commercial exchange.

Certainly the monopoly manufacture and sale of alcohol and particularly of vodka on trust aided the slow but ineluctable descent of the *kabaki* to this level – and some of the abuses associated with it will be discussed below. But just as instrumental in this decline were decrees by Feodor Ivanovich and Boris Godunov introducing the 'private' ownership of *kabaki* to members of the nobility, along with the permission for them to distill vodka for sale in both state and private establishments.[36] Part of the revenues from the sale of vodka in establishments like these were owed to the state at a fixed, predetermined rate. The nobles who had been granted this right would then keep the remainder of what were quite significant sums. In this way, the state 'farmed out' the collection of its share of the vodka revenues in a system known as the *otkup*.[37] That such ownership and operation of *kabaki* existed and was seen as an attractive means of generating private income is pointed up by the fact that, during the period of succession struggles, foreign invasion and social unrest known as the Time of Troubles (1598–1613), some boyars in fact directly petitioned the Polish pretender to the throne of Muscovy for the privilege of opening *kabaki* in the towns and *volosty* that they believed were in immediate danger of coming under the pretender's control.[38]

Given this combination of factors there should be little wonder that, in addition to the conditions of exploitation created by the naked greed of the boyars

---

[35] I. G. Pryzhov, 'Gorodskie p'ianitsy' [Town Drunkards], in *Istoriia Nishchenstva, kabachestva, i Klikuchestva na Rusi* [A history of poverty, kabak-ism and deprivation in Russia] (Moscow, 1997), 175–180, here 176–7; Borodin, *Kabak i ego proshloe*, 42.

[36] Romanov, *Istoriia russkoi vodki*, 34; Segal, *Russian Drinking*, 44.

[37] Romanov, *Istoriia russkoi vodki*, 34. This system should not be confused with the later, nineteenth-century *otkup* system of collecting the tax on vodka sales. Here private individual of any class bid for the right, forwarding an agreed-upon per centage to the state and keeping whatever they accrued over and above that amount for themselves. This not only resulted in the making of considerable fortunes, but also aggravated ethnic and religious tensions in many areas of Russia. For a more complete discussion of this latter system, see Borodin, *Kabak i ego proshloe*; Pryzhov, *Istoriia kabakov.* .

[38] Romanov, *Istoriia russkoi vodki*, 46.

and the prevalence of patrons like those noted above, the hired personnel of the *kabaki* engaged in all manner of illicit practices of their own. False measuring and cutting the strength of the vodka with water were in fact among the more minor acts of dishonesty and unethical tricks aimed at turning a profit over and above the percentage owed the state. Worse yet, these people sold drink on credit to their patrons, advanced it in exchange for future crop returns, and in some instances even provided drinks in exchange for clothing.[39] Just as disturbing were the 'strengthening' of weakened vodka by foreign substances that were in themselves life-threatening and the near omnipresence of prostitution. It is not surprising then, that the term *tsel'ovalnik* came increasingly to lose its original meaning of a man under oath and began to take on the increasingly negative connotation that it had attained by the mid-nineteenth century.[40]

Aside from the shortcomings already noted, it is indisputable that the *kabaki* had become instruments of exploitation. Whether state-owned or with collection of revenues farmed out to nobles, they were extracting considerable revenues for the state by the mid-seventeenth century. This exploitation was exacerbated by the fact that it existed as an accompaniment to the state's wider effort to control the sale of strong drink to the peasantry and deprive it of the legal right to produce any domestic alcoholic beverage. All of these practices were concomitants to completing the process of popular enserfment.[41] The abuses in and of themselves – to say nothing of the drunkenness consequent to them – encouraged many peasants to petition the first two Romanov Tsars, Mikhail Feodorovich (r. 1613–45) and Alexis Mikhailovich (r. 1645–76), to close many of the *kabaki* (requests that the former ignored).[42] As several historians of this era have noted, any concern about the relation between the *kabaki,* strong drink, and questions of popular abuse of alcohol in the first half of the century focused more on the state's need for revenue from them than on perceived 'moral' or 'ethical' considerations.[43] Indeed, in the decade from 1619 to 1629 there was an increase in the number of drink houses and the revenues from them grew steadily.[44] In the final analysis it was only the endemic and increasing peasant unrest during the late 1640s that led the newly-appointed

---

[39] Ibid., 47. Also see Pryzhov, *Ocherki, stat'i, pis'ma,* 202–9.

[40] I. G. Pryzhov, 'Kabatskie tsel'ovalniki,' in *Ocherki, stat'i, pis'ma,* 209.

[41] Smith and Christian, *Bread and Salt,* 149.

[42] Romanov, *Istoriia russkoi vodki,* 55–7. Also see A. N. Nasonov (ed.), *Pskovskie letopisi* [Pskov Chronicles], 2 fascs (Moscow, 1941–1955), 2: 281 (1626–28).

[43] Smith and Christian, *Bread and Salt,* 149.

[44] *Soshnoe pis'mo: Issledovanie po istorii kadastra i pososhnago oblozhenie Moskovskago gosudarstva* [Survey book: An investigation concerning the history of property evaluation and revenue taxation of the Muscovite state], 3:538, as cited in Smith and Christian, *Bread and Salt,* 141.

Patriarch Nikon to convince Tsar Alexis that some reforms of the *kabaki* were in order on something other than fiscal grounds.

As a result of Nikon's recommendations and the work of a state commission, in 1652 Alexis Mikhailovich issued decrees abolishing the *kabaki* and replacing them with pot-houses (*kruzhechny dvory*) in towns of all sizes. All beverages were to be sold as before on trust, so that the by now infamous sworn men did not lose their positions, but efforts were made to reign in the outrageous behaviours and practices that had come to characterize *kabak* life. For example, vodka sales were henceforth to be limited to only one cup (*charka*) per customer (although the volume of the new cups were larger than that of the old ones of the *kabaki*). Moreover, priests were henceforth barred from the pot-houses, as were town drunkards, those known for profanity and violence, thieves, and vagabonds. The sale of liquor was prohibited during Lenten season as well as during the fasts of Christmas and St Peter. Greater order in these new establishments was also mandated by requiring that they operate only during specified hours in different seasons of the year. Further, the *tsel'ovalniki* were ordered to refrain from accepting clothing or goods from customers who had drunk themselves into a state of disorderly drunkenness. Failing that, they were to refuse further to serve such persons, place the proferred goods in a special closet and, when the drinkers had slept off their inebriation, scold them and return the items that had been collected from them. How an individual – even a habitual drunkard – could reach such a condition given the restrictions limiting customers to only one cup, the decree of course did not say. Additional provisions attempted to ensure that pot-house officials would not allow patrons to drink themselves to death. This stricture alone, of course, implies a frightening aspect of the pre-reform *kabak* trade.

Pot-house workers guilty of complicity in such cases, along with the drinking companions (*sobutilnikov*) of the deceased, were to be punished by being whipped with a knout and fined 20 rubles to assist the family of the victim. If the deceased had no close survivors, then the fine was to be donated to the nearest alms house (*bogadel'nia*) or church.[45] And, as before, pot-house officials were forbidden to put the monies received from drink sales anywhere but in the boxes designated for that function.[46] At the time of the enactment the number of pot-houses stood at about a thousand altogether, but within a year a number had been closed.[47]

Yet, in a recurring pattern, the exigencies and needs of the Russian state were such that these policies were reversed in little more than a decade. The introduction of pot-houses managed under the *otkup* system described above in

---

[45] Romanov, *Istoriia russkoi vodki*, 61.
[46] Smith and Christian, *Bread and Salt*, 156.
[47] Romanov, *Istoriia russkoi vodki*, 71. .

those regions where the sale of alcohol 'on trust' had not been successful – i. e., where it did not return high enough profits – clearly demonstrated that money trumped morality when it came to the drink houses.[48] Only a few of the restrictions imposed in 1652 remained in effect; for example, limits on the operation of the pot-houses during Lent and several other religious holidays. Another example of the watering down of the decrees was the significant transformation of the physical premises of the pot-houses. They became, first of all, physically much larger than the old *kabaki* ever were. Converted into durable establishments, some had their own distilling operations, cook-houses, and merchant stalls. Some pot-houses even had their own bath houses, although these were not widely used. While not specifically prohibited by the authorities, there were official prescriptions against the bath houses due to their having become scenes of 'sinful activities and naughtiness with shameful women'.[49] Added to these accusations were charges that the liquor now being sold to customers tasted bad but, at the same time, was more expensive in the pot-houses than ever before.[50]

In the decades following the introduction of pot-houses, their actual management, operation and, indeed, their function changed but little. The reintroduction of the farming-out of the sale of vodka, along with the state monopoly of its distillation, brought the treasury precisely what it had been seeking all along – immense profits. Romanov, for example, calculates that pot-house revenues and customs duties accounted for fifty-three per cent of the state's 1,222,367 rubles of income in the 1679–80 fiscal year.[51] Just as importantly, with the gradual absorption of west Russian territories under the first Romanovs, the drink institutions there underwent a transformation into the Muscovite type. So much so, in fact, that the term *korchma* (inn) now became increasingly a phrase used in connection with the illegal (that is, not state or state-farm operated) sale of alcoholic beverages by small operators.[52]

While questions might have arisen in the following decades concerning the quality of the vodka served from pot-house to pot-house, neither this nor the recurring instances of the kinds of abuses noted above influenced the organization or the culture of the pot-houses themselves. Nor, for that matter, did the efforts of some of Russia's rulers during this period. Sofia Alexeevna, for example, made only two, quite telling, changes to the matter of the administration of the pot-houses during her brief regency (1682–89). First, she mandated severe punishment for those heads and sworn men found guilty of mishandling their establishment so badly that revenues declined. And conversely, she made

---

[48] Ibid.
[49] 'zern i balovalie so sramnymi zhenkami': Ibid., 71–2.
[50] Ibid., 74.
[51] Ibid., 80.
[52] Pryzhov, 'Gorodskie p'ianitsy' [Town Drunkards], in *Ocherki, stat'i, pis'ma*, 211.

it a state policy handsomely to reward those officials who consistently forwarded large profits to the treasury.[53]

The end of the early modern period in Russian history coincides naturally enough with the beginning of the actual reign of Peter I, 'The Great' (r. 1689–1725), usually, albeit erroneously considered the first of Russia's reforming rulers. Ironically, he was also considered by some foreign observers to be one of the heaviest drinking of Russia's rulers, as witnessed by his early creation of the 'Most Drunken Sobor of Fools and Jesters', a group formed for the express purpose of providing bawdy entertainment and frequent opportunities for alcohol abuse by Peter and his closest associates. This reputation was further enhanced by his policy of forcing foreign ambassadors to join him in his bouts of binge-drinking. Nevertheless, he did attempt the introduction of some changes in the regime of the pot-houses, although again, the purpose was to better serve larger state financial needs. Few of the reforms introduced in his 1699 edicts involved their organization and management; rather, they emphasized the punishments that were to be meted out to patrons of the pot-houses who drank too heavily, rather than holding the heads and the sworn men accountable. They insisted that the function of the pot-houses not be the encouragement or promotion of drunkenness, but the serving of vodka 'moderately', requiring that patrons 'drank moderately and happily; and having their needs comfortably met and without ruining their souls'.[54] Moreover, as with other state edicts on the practices of Russia's drink establishments, they further cautioned pot-house employees against allowing patrons to drink away their last kopeck.[55] Then, too, they instructed local military governors to arrest not the pot-house employees guilty of over-serving customers, but, rather, the drinkers themselves. These unfortunates were to be put to work at hard labour in order to rid the town of them and further prevent them from flocking around the pot-houses.[56]

Thus the major thrust of the edicts had precious little to do with the organization or the administration of the drink houses themselves. The only real changes in this area were, again, purely cosmetic – changes in nomenclature. First, the former *kabaki* and *kruzhechnyi dvory* heads were now to be called *burmeisters*, while their functions remained essentially unchanged.[57] The only

[53] Pryzhov, 'Kabatskie tseloval'niki', in *Ocherki, stat'i, pis'ma*, 94.

[54] 'pili umereno i chesto v veselie i v otradu dorozhnykh pod'iatykh imi nuzhd, a ne v pagubu svoei dushi': Borodin, *Kabak i ego proshlago*, 47.

[55] Ibid.

[56] Ibid.

[57] The term *burmeister* is of German origin, an indication of Peter's continuing fascination with and affinity for the forms and institutions of that region. Beginning in 1699, Peter created the office of *burmeister* or *buriumeister*, the occupants of which were administrative officials

exception here was that greater emphasis was now to be placed on their function of overseeing the distillation of vodka, given the simultaneous general
prohibition against anyone engaging in the process other than those who possessed the 'farm' to do it.[58] Second, the former *kruzhechny dvory* were also
now to change their names to *postoialyi dvory* (literally translated as inn). This
was but one among several new terms that came to be used in connection with
Russia's official drinking establishments by the beginning of the eighteenth
century. Among these were the hostelry (*avsteriya*) and liquor shop (*fartina*).[59]
As Smith and Christian note, the distinctions between these institutions are not
clear (with the possible exception of the latter, which more nearly compares
with the practice of a 'package store' familiar to some modern readers). They
may, indeed, simply have been modish innovations for old Russian institutions
but using western models.[60]

Consideration of Russia's taverns – under whatever nomenclature adopted by
Tsarist authorities to describe them – must necessarily end with the dawn of a
new century and the transformation of Muscovy into the Russian Empire. Yet
obviously the dynamics of the Russian drink houses and the problems associated with them continued to haunt the country. Little would change in terms
of their organization and administration. Instead, efforts would continue to dis-
guise the negative connotations associated with the term *kabak* by no less than
two decrees in mid-eighteenth century. For example, one mandated that signs
on the drink establishments now bear the title *piteinyi dom* (drink house) because of the negative connotations associated with the term *kabak*. Yet, as
Smith and Christian note, internal documents continued to refer to them simply
as *kabaki*.[61] The fact remains, therefore, that in spite of the cosmetic name
changes, these establishments continued to serve the function that Russia's rulers found most agreeable – the pumping of large quantities of revenues into
state coffers. All concerns expressed about any other aspect of the drinking
houses have to be seen as the sheerest hypocrisy on the part of Russian authorities. As for the drinking establishments, Pryzhov, ever a fertile source on their
organization and operation, notes their continued existence as gathering places
for peasants in the villages, and workers and various elements of the urban un-
derclasses in the towns. It should not be assumed, however, that they had the

---

subject to the authority of the individual city halls. It is in the context of administrative official,
then, that the term was now applied to these kabak officials. See Vladimir Dal', *Tolkovyi
slovar' zhivago Velikorusskogo iazyka, V chetyrykh tomakh* [Defining dictionary of the living
great Russian language, in four volumes], vol. 1 (St Petersburg, Moscow, 1907), 352.

[58]   Pryzhov, *Istoriia kabakov*, 205–6; Romanov, *Istoriia russkoi vodki*, 100–101.
[59]   Pryzhov, *Istoriia kabakov*, 206–7.
[60]   Smith and Christian, *Bread and Salt*, 215.
[61]   Ibid.

same importance as centres of worker political consciousness and organization
as they later did for, say, German workers.[62] Nor would they change in the
coming centuries in Russia. Sometimes more elaborate, sometimes more crude,
their function in the redistribution of wealth along with their value as genera-
tors of large revenues for the state remained unchanged until the creation of the
state liquor shops in the nineteenth century. It is safe to say, then, that once
having achieved this purpose in the early modern period, Russian drink houses
would retain their essential nature and practices until late in the modern age.

---

[62] See J. S. Roberts, 'The Tavern and Politics in the German Labor Movement, c. 1870–
1914,' in S. Barrows and R. Room (eds), *Drinking. Behavior and Belief in Modern History*
(Berkeley, 1991), 98–111.

The Eighteenth-Century English Inn: A Transient 'Golden Age'?

John Chartres

Transport change played a central role in the development of the English economy during the 'long eighteenth century'. Although conventional historiography ascribed a critical position to innovation in water transport – coasting, river improvement, and canal-building – modern analysis of the long process of growth and industrialization has emphasized the contribution of roads. From the middle years of the seventeenth century to around 1800, land carriage was the primary transport medium. The world of growing commerce, of new goods and consumer tastes, and of handicraft manufacture created enormous internal and external demands for transport by waggon, cart, van, and packhorse for its relatively high-value products of modest bulk. The great age of coal, steam, and mill-based 'machinofacture', involving the large-scale movement of high-bulk, low-value minerals was emerging at the end of the century, but not yet dominant. The pace, flexibility, and relative security of road transport proved eminently suitable to the distributional needs of the protoindustrial economy.[1]

The classic 'industrial revolution' of the eighteenth century has thus been largely displaced by a historiography stressing incremental growth and the development of intensive regions of industrial activity (not necessarily characterized by factory production), and noting England's dramatic rate and intensity of urban expansion. From a modest position in the European context in the mid-seventeenth century, England rose by 1800 to challenge the Netherlands in its degree of urbanization. Its urban population, defined as those living in units of 10,000 or more, was estimated at 8.8 per cent in 1650, ranking eighth among Jan de Vries's sixteen European territories. By 1700, it had risen to 13.3 per cent (fifth); 16.7 per cent in 1750 (third); 20.3 in 1800 (second to the Netherlands); and over 40 per cent by 1850 (first), with Scotland at 32 per cent now in second place. Wrigley has estimated from these data that England alone accounted for more than half of Europe's total urban growth between

---

[1] D. H. Aldcroft and M. J. Freeman (eds), *Transport in the Industrial Revolution* (Manchester, 1983), 1–99; and D. Gerhold, *Road Transport Before the Railways: Russell's London Flying Waggons* (Cambridge, 1993), provide brief introductions to these areas.

1600 and 1800, with 70 per cent of that occurring from 1750 to 1800.[2] Rapid and intense urban growth characterized England's development during the long eighteenth century, and helped thus to differentiate Britain from its European neighbours.

Such changes interrelated with the history of the English inn. The growth of the complexity and rationality of England's urban system was a powerful force in developing road transport, which was itself heavily dependent upon the infrastructure of the inn. The industrial and commercial developments of the period required expanded transport services for both people and goods, and this too expanded the market for the inn. The outcome was the growth in number, scale, and appointment of English inns, and for much of this period of expansion, the provision of the key infrastructure for road transport by 'volunteer' innkeeper capital.

England's long eighteenth-century experience was not, however, confined to these great economic changes. A critical element of the growth of towns was that of urban society, marked by what Peter Borsay has called England's 'urban renaissance': the evolution of the provincial town as the increasingly preferred locus of at least winter residence; the development of the social stages it demanded, from public dining to club and race meeting; and the gradual emergence of a bourgeois public sphere in which more formal association took place, to create public works such as the corn exchange, infirmary, assembly room, or canal.[3]

This essay therefore explores in brief these key themes as they interacted with the history of the English inn.[4] First it assesses the numbers and distribution of inns over the long period from the later Middle Ages, before exploring their improvement from the later seventeenth century, and the intensification of fixed capital investment in them. The critical linkages with the development of road transport are then analysed, showing both passive and more active interactions, followed by an assessment of wider links with business and commerce, public administration, and new social institutions. A final section explores the vast range of leisure activities and wider social functions.

---

[2]   J. de Vries, *European Urbanization 1500–1800* (London, 1984), 85–150; E. A. Wrigley, 'Urban Growth and Agricultural Change: England and the Continent in the Early Modern Period', *Journal of Interdisciplinary History* 15 (1985), 683–728, reprinted in E. A. Wrigley, *People, Cities and Wealth* (Oxford, 1987), 157–93.

[3]   P. J. Corfield, *The Impact of English Towns 1700–1800* (Oxford, 1982) 124–45; P. Borsay, *The English Urban Renaissance: Culture and Society in the Provincial Town 1660–1770* (Oxford, 1989).

[4]   A. M. Everitt, 'The English Urban Inn, 1560–1760' in idem (ed.), *Perspectives in English Urban History* (London, 1973), 91–137, was the pioneering study of this subject.

Inns had developed as institutions from the later Middle Ages, as road transport had expanded, and commercial provision, much of it through monastic investment, had supplanted hospitality in the abbey gatehouse or *hospitium*. Unfortunately, the full history of this evolution is as yet unwritten, and while such inns as the George, Norton St Philip (Somerset), established by the Priory of Hinton Charterhouse in 1345, the Star and the Golden Cross in Oxford, the New Inn in Gloucester, or the Cardinal's Hat in Lincoln testify to this ecclesiastical promotion, its share in the early development of roadside inns cannot be evaluated. No satisfactory estimates of the numbers of inns are available before 1577, when a survey associated with the muster rolls recorded 2,163 inns among the total of over 16,700 inns, alehouses, and taverns in twenty-six counties. Extrapolating from these to England as a whole, in 1577 there were 20–24,000 premises, around 3,600 of them inns.[5]

Numbers grew during the subsequent century, with total drink outlets rising to 30,000 or more by 1630, reaching 40,000 in the 1680s, and 47,000 by 1695 – perhaps, following Peter Clark, there were as many as 60,000 around 1700. If we assume with Clark a 'fairly constant proportion' for the true inn in these global totals, then there were between 6,000 and 7,000 inns in England at the beginning of the eighteenth century. Clark's study of the alehouse suggested that numbers through the eighteenth century remained rather static, perhaps showing some decline from the 1750s to the 1820s, when numbers stood at 49,000.[6]

The share of houses performing inn functions in these totals may have risen. The true inn existed *ad hospitandos homines*, in English law a common calling, which obliged its keepers to receive all who came to seek accommodation. Burn's *Justice* defined the difference: 'Every inn is not an alehouse, nor every alehouse an inn; but if an inn uses common selling of ale, it is then also an alehouse; and if an alehouse lodges and entertains travellers, it is also an inn'.[7] Data from the War Office survey of accommodation in 1756 suggest that inns may have been rather more numerous than Clark suggests. Although evidence

---

[5]   Summarizing J. A. Chartres, 'Les Hôtelleries en Angleterre à la Fin du Moyen Age et aux Temps Modernes', in C. Higounet (ed.), *L'Homme et la Route en Europe Occidentale au Moyen Age et aux Temps Modernes* 2 (Auch, 1982), 207–28; idem, 'The English Inn and Road Transport before 1700', in H. C. Peyer (ed.), *Gastfreundschaft, Taverne und Gasthaus im Mittelalter* (Munich, 1983), 153–76; and P. Clark, *The English Alehouse: a Social History 1200–1830* (London, 1983), esp. 39–63. Clark's statistics and mine for 1577 differ in the readings of some figures, in my redistribution of borough totals to county figures, and in approaches to extrapolation for missing counties, but agree broadly on the estimation of numbers of inns in the total.

[6]   Clark, *The English Alehouse*, 41–59.

[7]   *Coke's Reports* (London, 1826) IV, 202; Lord Ellenborough's judgment in case Burgess v. Clements, Trinity 55 George III (1815), G. Maule and W. Selwyn, *Reports of Cases in the Court of King's Bench* (London, 1814–17), IV, 310–11.

comes from only the single 'Marlborough Collection', this return, covering northern and eastern Wiltshire, western Berkshire and Oxfordshire, and part of Gloucestershire, recorded the numbers of inns and alehouses in addition to the beds and stable spaces required. In the whole area of twenty-three 'divisions' and twenty-five 'out ridings', there were 814 public houses and 512 inns, the latter being thirty-nine per cent of the total.[8] Clearly, a single data set does not provide a basis for certain estimation, but, if replicated throughout the kingdom, by mid-century there would have been between 19,000 and 20,000 inns. The growth of transport needs may have combined with better quality of provision for the traveller significantly to expand the number of inns within a comparatively static population of licensed premises.

Inns were located along all the major roads, with significant clusters of inn accommodation occurring, on average, at ten to fifteen miles. An earlier War Office survey of inns, from 1686, provides a more finely-textured set of returns, and is used to document this point for the road between London and Berwick-upon-Tweed as mapped by John Ogilby in 1675, and summarized in Table 2.[9] The distribution is remarkably consistent, though deteriorating beyond Newcastle, where population was more sparse, and demand presumably lower. With some variations, similar results can be derived for all the principal main roads. More significantly, however, these listings of bed spaces and stable capacity point to routes unrecognized by Ogilby, Bowen, and other early road map makers, identifying their weaknesses, particularly in identifying the cross roads.[10] By the later seventeenth century, England's roads were extensively provided with inns, and our records of inn accommodation mapped routes in use more clearly than the more focused works of 'His Majesty's Cosmographer', whose attention was largely confined to the capital's links to the provinces, and the routes between traditional provincial capitals, such as York to Chester or Lancaster.

Unfortunately, none of the three sets of these War Office data (for 1686, 1756, and c.1780) covers London, where the locational pattern was necessarily different.[11] By the early eighteenth century, London had around two hundred major inns, besides the hundreds of taverns and coffee houses, and an estimated

---

[8]   London, Public Record Office (PRO), 'List for Billeting etc.', War Office Miscellany, WO/30/49, 96 (1756).

[9]   PRO, 'Abstract of a Particular Account of All the Inns Alehouses etc., with their Stable Room and Bedding in the Year 1686', War Office Miscellany, WO/30/48.

[10]   Based upon the comparison of the road network of West Yorkshire, 1675–1720 as mapped by the two 'national' roadbooks, John Ogilby, *Britannia* (London, 1675) and Emanuel Bowen, *Britannia Depicta* (London, 1720), with John Warburton, *Map of Yorkshire* (London, 1720), which shows a much more detailed network that maps closely onto the patterns of subsequent turnpiking.

[11]   This and subsequent comments based upon J. A. Chartres, 'The Capital's Provincial Eyes: London's Inns in the Early Eighteenth Century', *London Journal* 3 (1977), 24–39.

Table 2: Inn accommodation on the London to Berwick Road, 1686

Place	Miles	Beds	Stables	Place	Miles	Beds	Stables
Waltham Cross	13	44	64	Doncaster	155	206	453
Hoddesdon	18	71	178	Ferrybridge	170	34	95
Ware	22	n.d.		Tadcaster	183	50	72
Royston	38	n.d.		York	192	483	800
Caxton	50	37	33	Boroughbridge	209	50	60
Godmanchester	57	24	134	Topcliffe	215	24	45
Huntingdon	58	198	498	Northallerton	229	82	83
Stilton	69	63	87	Darlington	244	80	70
Wansford	77	38	106	Durham	262	290	483
Bridge							
Stamford	83	193	396	Chester-le-	268	22	87
				Street			
Coltsworth	96	34	42	Gateshead	276	54	125
Grantham	105	285	351	Newcastle-	277	634	894
				upon-Tyne			
Newark	118	231	448	Morpeth	291	143	244
Tuxford	131	21	64	Alnwick	310	95	194
Bawtry	147	57	69	Berwick	338	142	245

Sources: PRO, WO/30/48; J. Ogilby, *Britannia* (London, 1675), plates 5–9.

six thousand alehouses in the 1730s. If these London inns were of the same average size as those of Bristol, the capital would have contained around 5,100 beds in 1750; distributed proportionately to total population, there would have been more than 7,150 beds, averaging thirty-five for each of the leading 200 inns.[12] At such a scale, differentiation of inn functions was possible. London streets specialized in services to different regions, and within them, inns tended to concentrate upon coach or carrier services. Thus Fleet Street and the Strand served the West Country; Aldersgate Street, Yorkshire and the east Midlands; and Bishopsgate, East Anglia and the east Midlands. This gave London a system of inns akin to the main line railway stations of the mid-nineteenth century, and provided a series of quite specific regional loci within the rapidly growing capital, a feature to which we return later.

---

[12] Taking beds per inn at 25, the average in Bristol, noted below, Table 3. Estimating on the basis of comparative populations in 1750, London had a population of 675,000, and Bristol 50,000, and Bristol's 531 beds scale up to 7169 for London on this basis.

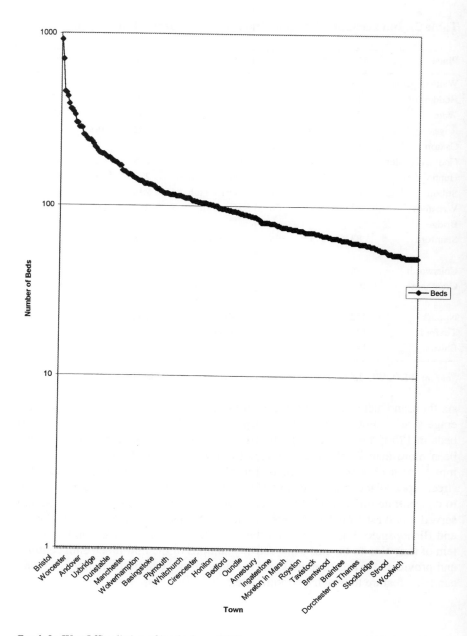

Graph 2: War Office listing of inn beds, ca 1780

Throughout the rest of England and Wales, these records of inn accommodation can be used to map the urban hierarchy, and suggest rather different patterns from those conventionally based upon population. Graph 2 plots the returns for the War Office survey of inn accommodation for ca 1780, a more aggregated listing than that for 1686 and confined to the principal centres, but with fewer of the impenetrable clusters of the 1756 list.[13] It describes in aggregate the patterns of Table 2: measured by inn bed accommodation for the leading 245 towns, the leading cadre of around thirty great towns, each with 200 beds or more, displayed a sharply curved profile. The next group in this hierarchy, approximately fifty in number with around 120 beds, curved more gently, before the remaining two thirds, running down to nine towns at fifty (the threshold adopted in this analysis) became log-linear. The leading towns of urbanizing England contained massive concentrations of inn accommodation, indicative perhaps of the most pronounced growth points; lower in the hierarchy, there was less sharp differentiation between towns, suggesting more even and more modest patterns of growth.

Urban inns were also, on average, substantially larger. The 1756 data lists the number of inns for ten English and two Welsh 'collections', as well as accommodation, and thus provides some measures of the difference. Treating the 'divisions' for each as core urban, and the 'out rides' as covering the areas lying outside the larger urban centres, the average capacity of urban inns was roughly double that of the rest of the collection – and for some great provincial capitals like Bristol, the differences were substantially greater.[14] In Wales, a largely undeveloped country where the coverage of inns was rudimentary, differences were negligible, as summarized in Table 3, and similar patterns are suggested by the returns for some of the peripheral English counties, such as Cornwall.

Along with the development of the number of inns outlined above, the seventeenth and eighteenth centuries also saw extensive re-edification and new building of inns to higher standards. It appears that growing investment took the form both of the multiplication of inns (an increase in volume), and the intensification of capital per unit. This was in part the response to increasing traffic, and partly the outcome of changing tastes and expectations from the consumer – some the outcome of relatively concrete, even economic desires for

---

[13] PRO, 'An Account of the Number of Beds and Standings for Horses which ye Publique Houses & Inns in ye Several Cities, Market Towns & Most Considerable Villages in ye Respective Countys…can & usually do accommodate guests withall', War Office Miscellany, WO/30/50 (undated, ca 1780).

[14] The 1756 listings are recorded in the 'Collections' and 'Out-Rides' of the Excise tax administration, without, in general, detailing the village communities within each; they are not conterminous with English and Welsh counties, though many approximate to county units.

Table 3: Average size of urban and other inns, England and Wales, 1756

Unit	Number of inns	Average beds	Average stables
England, non-urban	6232	2.4	3.9
England, urban	1106	4.4	7.3
Wales, non-urban	279	2.3	3.8
Wales, urban	75	3.1	4.9
Leading towns:			
Bristol	21	25.3	41.6
Bath	31	5.8	14.0
Dover	51	3.1	2.8
Grantham	31	5.4	12.2
Hereford	95	4.2	3.0
Hertford	26	8.9	20.8
Leicester	89	3.2	4.5
Coventry	122	3.2	4.4
King's Lynn	35	4.3	6.3
Marlborough	25	10.5	21.8

Source: PRO, WO/30/49

increased privacy, others essentially aesthetic in character. These developments are outlined in the following section, before assessing the capitalization of British inns in the 1770s and 1780s.

The upgrading of perhaps seven to ten thousand alehouses to perform inn functions during the period of transport expansion suggested above implied major intensification of investments, as yet not fully researched. However, architectural historians have pointed clearly to the application of galleries and

other building forms to solve the problems of passage rooms, still largely characteristic of English inns in the earlier seventeenth century. The external roofed gallery, an architectural form familiar in late medieval monastic and some urban building, was increasingly applied to circumvent the disturbance caused by the passage room. Separate access to individual chambers could be provided by one or two stories of galleries without additional land costs.[15] While these galleried chambers were by no means universal – in the small-town or rural inns, where land was at less of a premium, the block type of inn, surrounded with its yards and pastures like a substantial farmstead, was more common than the courtyard – by the later eighteenth century they had become the dominant image of the great English inn. The great galleried courtyards recorded by artists such as T. H. Shepherd in mid-nineteenth-century London became part of the iconography of the English urban inn in its maturity.

Private access to chambers provided security, and increasingly, met changing sensibility. Well into the eighteenth century, and for many travellers throughout it, beds too were shared, not just rooms. One's bedfellows could be problematic, as John Cannon recorded of his night at the Hart Inn, Stocksbridge (Hampshire) in 1726: '[I] had for my bedfellow one William Phippen of East Pennard, who in his sleep grasp'd me & cry'd out, Ah my dear Peggy, thinking he had been in bed with his wife, but I soon made him sensible of ye mistake by awaking him'.[16] Separate access to chambers permitted smaller subdivision of bedroom spaces, and thus the offering to the sensitive, or those such as salesmen with samples and goods to secure, improved quality in provision.

Even so, in times of national emergency, or for those with no pocket for better, shared beds remained part of the inn experience. Petitions of innkeepers complaining about the costs of billeting soldiers during the Napoleonic wars illustrated both inn architectural arrangements and the ultimate capacity of a bed. A petition from Wareham (Dorset) in May 1806 reflected the room and bed capacity of the town's inns: seven inns had rooms on three floors, the largest being Robert Baker's Red Lion with fifteen; the remaining eight had rooms on two floors; and in all, the town's fifteen inns had 97 bedchambers to accommodate 105 family and resident servants, and 92 billeted soldiers, more than two per bed. If the complainants were to be believed, Buckingham in 1809 produced a still more alarming press of soldiers: 26 inns contained 117 beds,

---

[15] On inn architecture, W. A. Pantin, 'Medieval Inns', in E. M. Jope (ed.), *Studies in Building History* (London, 1961), 177–87; M. W. Barley, 'Rural Building in England', in J. Thirsk (ed.), *The Agrarian History of England and Wales*, vol. 5 pt 2, 1640–1750 (Cambridge, 1985), 682–5.

[16] Taunton, Somerset Record Office, DD/SA 5 C/1193, 'Memoirs of Mr John Cannon, 1684–1742', 179.

and had 539 soldiers to billet, or an average of 4.6 per bed, raising questions about the exact meaning of 'beds' recorded by the earlier War Office surveys.[17]

Decoration of public rooms also attracted new investment, to meet the aspirational demands of the travelling public for fashionable accommodation. The New Inn, Exeter, had a fine plastered ceiling in its Appollo [*sic*] Room, created in 1689; in the 1750s, the new Antelope at Sherborne had fine wainscoting and the majority of its 'twelve handsome bedchambers ... hung with good papers'; and the George, Shaftesbury, 'enlightened' its Bull Room with '2 new Gothick windows'.[18] The growing demand for and the rising expectations of inn space reached its peak in some of the new building of the period.

The inn offered the seventeenth- and eighteenth-century landowner the opportunity to profit indirectly from the growth of both travel and association. The White Hart Inn at Scole (Norfolk), built by the Norwich merchant John Peck in 1655 at a cost of £1,500 was a notable example, but representative of a general movement that saw, along the route summarized in Table 2, new inns such as the Ram Jam near Stretton and the Eel Pie House, Elkesley. Many included assembly rooms of considerable scale, as on the first floor at Scole, and displayed architectural distinction and manner that equated to very large farmhouses, or even modest country seats. So great was the landlordly commitment to the later seventeenth- and eighteenth-century inn as an essential element of improving social fabric that they were normal features of the remodelling of villages, often on new sites, as part of landscaping.[19] 'Model' inns of this type were found in the Vernon Arms, Sudbury (Derbyshire, 1671), at Harewood (Yorkshire, WR) in John Carr's remodelling and relocation of the village (1760s), and at Edensor (Derbyshire, 1775).[20]

Insurance valuations from the 1770s and 1780s confirm these qualitative assessments. Policy values for 2,295 innkeepers derived from the records of the Sun and the Royal Exchange insurance companies are summarized in Graph 3. The range of values was enormous, and although around half of inn businesses, thus valued, lay in the range £100–500, and the next quartile lay below £900, more than 20 per cent reached £1,000 or more.[21] More than twenty exceeded

---

[17] PRO, WO/40/3, 'Innkeepers' Petitions 1759– ', 10 May 1806, 5 June 1809.

[18] W. G. Hoskins, *Two Thousand Years in Exeter* (Exeter, 1963), 128; *Western Flying Post* 316 (17 March 1755), 4, and 336 (4 August 1755), 4.

[19] Barley, 'Rural Building', 683–4.

[20] W. A. Eden, 'Harewood Village: an Eighteenth-Century "Housing Scheme"', *Town Planning Review* 13 (1929), 181–4; N. Pevsner, *Buildings of England: Derbyshire* (London, 1953), 130–31.

[21] Based upon author's database of policies from the Sun and the Royal Exchange Insurance Companies drawn from policy books in London, Guildhall Library, created from summary data deposited with the Economic & Social Research Council Data Archive, University of Essex, by Professors R. Floud and B. E. Supple, project HR4804. I am grateful to

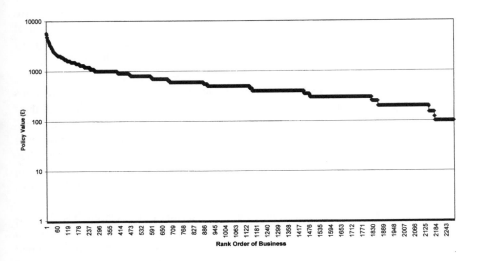

Graph 3: Insurance valuations of inn businesses, Britain, 1776-87

£3,000: the Old Ship, Brighton (£5,800 in 1777) led the list; the White Horse, Cripplegate, one of the capital's leading inns, was insured for £4,900 in 1779, and the Bull and Mouth at £4,000 (1778); and the Star, Oxford (founded as an inn by Osney Abbey in 1380) kept by Mary Stewart, was insured for £4,300 in 1783.[22] Though these policy valuations are problematic, and some London inns appear significantly undervalued by comparison with some in the provinces, they place innkeeping pretty high in the business hierarchy of the later eighteenth century.

While at the bottom end of the distribution inn businesses equated perhaps to smallholding farmers, the inn representing a specialized 'cash crop' for the modest landholder, in the top quartile they ranked with the middle ranks of the leading industrial enterprises of the period, assessed by the same sources. A normal Arkwright cotton mill or worsted spinning mill in the Midlands in the 1780s fell into the same range as the top quartile of our inn businesses; the full

the Data Archive, and to colleagues Debbie McCaffrey and Terry Screeton for their help in reorganizing this material into the current Access database.
    22   Guildhall Library, Sun Policies 385774, 393334, 484744.

range of textile trades from the same data set indicated much smaller insured values; and Peter Earle's analysis of the middle-classes of London up to 1730 produced an average value of £2,888 for the total inventoried assets of tavern-keepers, much held as investments that would not have fallen into the remit of the insured values discussed above.[23] Inns clearly reflected the entire range of business enterprise characterizing Britain in the later eighteenth century.

To this point, the inn has been treated as the passive beneficiary of exogenous transport growth. Inns as businesses gained from traffic growth, and their landlords drew rents from these booming trades. Yet in some areas of road traffic the inn was an endogenous part of that development. While few innkeeper businesses engaged extensively in the scheduled goods carrying trades, they were almost universal providers of early stagecoach services, and the critical creative force in the private-hire post-chaise system emerging from the 1740s. Inns were thus a major creative element in transport change.

Though estimates have varied considerably, modern research has demonstrated a very significant growth in public scheduled carrying services to London from the second quarter of the seventeenth century. This was sustained during the first half of the eighteenth century while extending coverage, and accelerated in the later part of the century. At the same time, provision diversified, with 'flying waggons' and vans joining waggons and packhorses on Britain's roads. Such scheduled services can only have been a part of the total traffic; interregional carriages, the internal transport services required by the 'putting-out' industry characteristic of this period, the distribution trades for manufacturers reaching ultimate markets, and the needs of merchants distributing consumer goods to Britain's rapidly developing retail trades all created goods business.[24] Inns facilitated this development by supplying critical infrastructure, and in themselves expanding flexibly as traffic grew.

In London, by the earlier eighteenth century, inns were already grouped spatially to provide support services for the carriers from specific regions. Thus the Castle and Bell inns of Wood Street, located north of the city centre, were leading servants to carriers from Shropshire, Worcester and Wales in 1715, and became the resort for those with business to transact with the region: in 1678 John Roche at Shrewsbury directed Francis Royley to the Bell to receive eight

---

[23] Sun and Royal Exchange database, passim; P. Earle, *The Making of the English Middle Class: Business, Society and Family Life in London, 1660–1730* (London, 1989), Table 4.6, 121; D. Bartlett, *London, Hub of the Industrial Revolution: A Revisionary History 1775–1825* (London, 1998), 195, compared a pooled group of victuallers, hotels, inns, and coffee and eating houses from the same sources in the 1770s and the 1820s to indicate 65 and 68 per cent of insured values lying between £101 and £500, and 6 and 14 per cent between £501 and £1000. Inns would lie towards the upper end of these distributions.

[24] Aldcroft and Freeman, *Transport*, 80–99.

pounds from the carrier to settle a bill on behalf of his brother.[25] Such inns acted on behalf of the carriers, receiving goods and commissions, and the relationship had to be one of great trust, given the unlimited liability resultant upon 'common' callings in English law.[26] When these relationships broke down, public notice was urgently given, as in 1705 when Thomas Walthew, keeper of the Swan, Holborn Bridge, advertised that he would no longer act as warehouse keeper for and receive goods on behalf of Dore, the Devizes carrier, because of the damage sustained by 'false swearing'.[27] But carrying always retained its independence, coexisting with but never taken over by innkeepers, and increasingly from the last quarter of the eighteenth century growing carrier firms like Pickford or Russell came instead to turn their London inns into their own private bases.[28] The symbiotic relationship that had so facilitated growth ultimately collapsed.

The experience of the newer stagecoach business was exactly the opposite. Services linking the provincial centres to London began only in the later seventeenth century, with the process of route development continuing into the first quarter of the eighteenth; regular services linking the provincial towns came in the second half of the century; and from its last quarter, short-stages, meeting London's suburban needs. While evidence is relatively thin, this pioneering was conducted largely by owner-drivers, who often acted within small consortia, and depended upon the inns for stabling, provender, repairs, and above all for bookings. As with the goods carriers, the inn provided essential infrastructure, without which the overhead costs of route development would have been prohibitive. The inn thus accelerated the potential for the expansion of the stagecoach system, but by the middle of the eighteenth century, it exerted effective control, and most coach services were innkeeper-owned.[29]

The process for this shift in control was primarily that of resources. While carriers appear in general to have required substantial resources, horses, waggons, and the reserves to meet unlimited liability for goods carried, the newer coach services were more vulnerable. Early practice often involved payment on arrival, as noted by William Lawrence in 1675: two of his companions were young women, in the diarist's mind clearly prostitutes, who spent their last money on breakfast at Brentford, on the run-in to London. Lawrence wickedly suggested that the coachman 'take it out in worke', but 'the

---

[25] Chartres, 'Capital's Provincial Eyes', 31; PRO, *Calendar of State Papers Domestic, Charles II*, 408 no. 53, 557.

[26] G. L. Turnbull, *Traffic and Transport: an Economic History of Pickfords* (London, 1979), 8–9: under English common law, 'common' carriers, like 'common' innkeepers, were obliged to take the business of all-comers, and could not restrict liability.

[27] *Post-Man* 1555 (20 November 1705).

[28] Turnbull, *Traffic and Transport*, 33–40; Gerhold, *Road Transport*, 34–5.

[29] Aldcroft and Freeman, *Transport*, 64–80.

wary fellow reply'd … that he had much rather have the pence than the pox', and so took clothing as surety.[30] By the 1700s, the response was to collect half the fare on booking at the inn and half on boarding, thus delivering substantial control of cash into the innkeeper's hands. William Hall's Henley stage was the object of such a take-over by Stephen Fisher, keeper of the Bear Inn, Maidenhead, in 1699 as a result of debts: two coaches, six horses, and two sets of harness, worth over £100 were attached by Fisher for debt, and while Hall ultimately gained some recompense, he had shifted by 1703 from proprietor to employee.[31] By mid-century, innkeepers were running large coaching firms, often in consortium arrangements, and were leading businessmen: Ralph Allen, innkeeper's son, made his fortune from coaching, and retired to become the squire of Prior Park, Bath, and the model for Henry Fielding's Squire Allworthy; and by later in the century men like Palmer, Horne, Chaplin were all leaders of the trade.[32] The deep resource base of the major innkeepers laid the basis for control of this new and rapidly expanding business.

A final new service, the postchaise, was almost wholly created and promoted by innkeepers from around the middle of the eighteenth century, test cases taken over their liability to Excise duty in 1748 indicating their relative novelty. It was a business of a scale that created lesser barriers to entry than the coaching trade, and which therefore permitted many to share in the revenues to be derived from personal travel. Two- or four-wheeled, the chaise was a private-hire vehicle, and those travelling in twos and threes, with aspiration for more genteel treatment at the inns en route and the capacity to determine their own rate of travel, could rent a chaise from successive inns to make their journey. On the Oxford to London road via Henley in the 1750s, at least fifteen inns located in the two termini and six intermediate towns and villages provided chaises to cover the sixty-mile journey, and shared advertising in up to five partnership arrangements.[33] As early as 1749, there were 1,362 chaises available, in addition to the 369 'official' chaises provided by the Post Office through their postmaster innkeepers; by 1754 there were 2,308 chaises described as 'for hire' paying Excise, more than two-thirds of them in London.[34] Innkeepers were thus a creative force in passenger travel.

---

[30] G. E. Aylmer (ed.), *The Diary of William Lawrence, 1662–81* (Beaminster, 1961), 27–8, August 1675.

[31] PRO, E/126/18, Exchequer Decrees and Orders, fols 385r–v, Hall v. Fisher, 15 November 1703.

[32] Aldcroft and Freeman, *Transport*, 79–80.

[33] Based on analysis of *Jackson's Oxford Journal* 153 (3 April 1756), 3; 15 (11 August 1753), 4; 12 (21 July 1753), 4; 275 (5 August 1758), 2; 112 (21 June 1755), 4; 288 (4 November 1758), 3; and 295 (23 December 1758), 2.

[34] *The Case of the Innkeepers and Keepers of Livery Stables and also of the Several Owners and Proprietors of Inns and Livery Stables, and of Hands Therewith* (London, 1749); PRO, T/4.

Inns thus covered all of the major roads of England and lowland Scotland by the early eighteenth century. They lay at the centre of the goods carrying system, represented the core entrepreneurial force in passenger carriage, and were increasingly embellished to meet rising expectations of comfort and convenience. In major towns, they remained for much of the century the sole source of large reception rooms, and were as densely distributed, and perhaps as notable as urban landmarks, as the churches. This made them the natural locus for the conduct of business and public affairs, the meetings associated with the myriad institutions of the developing public sphere.

The range of this activity was enormous, and can only be indicated briefly here. For a wide range of private businesses, the inn offered a convenient base. As middleman activity extended in the primary commodity trades, beginning long before 1650 but expanding significantly from the late seventeenth century, inns formed the resort for cornfactors and others retreating from the regulated space of the urban market. Daniel Defoe's *Complete English Tradesman* of 1725–7 explained the process: farmers exhibited samples in the market place, but adjusted the bargain in the precincts of the inn, and perhaps thereafter dealt directly with the merchant.[35] The inns of Canterbury and of Southwark became by similar processes the predominant hop markets of England.[36] Transport connections made inns the natural market for some manufactures. Most notable was the use of the George Inn, Aldersgate Street, as the London market for Chiltern lace throughout the century. Located on the street directly associated with the carrier system to Buckinghamshire and Hertfordshire, the George also had storage facilities sufficient for lace warehouses, and from as early as 1690 was advertised as the place of normal resort for the 'black and white lace men' who linked country makers and city wholesalers.[37] Dealers used the Ship and Castle, Hereford, as the wool market up to 1749, when the inn's closure led them to adopt the Greyhound, and at Worcester the Reindeer Inn was officially approved as the leather market from 1725.[38] As patterns of trading altered, the inn was the natural home for new systems of marketing.

In parallel with the expansion of the transport trades, Britain experienced significant advances in retailing in this period, and here too the inn played a role. The great urban courtyard inns often included shops beyond the normal businesses of smiths and so on, the George at Southwark containing an iron-monger, a flax warehouse, and the shop of a wholesale grocer when gutted by

---

[35]   D. Defoe, *The Complete English Tradesman* (London, 1745), vol. 2, 181.

[36]   J. A. Chartres, 'The Marketing of Agricultural Produce', in Thirsk, *Agrarian History*, vol. 5 pt 2, 491–2.

[37]   *New Observator* 2/19 (18 April 1690).

[38]   *Gloucester Journal* 1459 (12 June 1750), 3; *Weekly Worcester Journal* (30 July 1725).

fire in 1670.[39] Such inns were able to retreat into their yards for their own business, and thus free valuable street frontages for other retailers. Shops of this kind were to be found in the Hinde Head, Reading, by 1655, and the Elephant, Wantage, in 1703.[40] Protected from liability for the goods of such temporary shops by the law, innkeepers also met the retailing needs of itinerant traders, men such as Thomas Bishop of Dinton near Aylesbury. Bishop was a jobbing weaver and retailing clothier who made and retailed diaper, table and figured linen, curtains, and worsted in 1720, and traded successively on Tuesday, Thursday, and Friday at the Old Red Lion, Thame; the Turk's Head, Aylesbury; and the King's Arms, Bicester.[41] Other traders adopted inns as temporary shops during great town fairs, as at the Three Eagles, Wrexham in 1739, and the Bell, Bristol, 1747.[42] All suggest the inn's role in easing the transition to more extensive fixed retail outlets in the period.

A third example documents the function of the inn as a wider place of business, again from a new and developing trade of the eighteenth century, that of the auctioneer. While restricted usage had been made of auction for ships and trade goods before 1700, it was only in mid-century that the provincial auctioneer developed as a profession, and the inns provided a place for his sale rooms, distributing catalogues, and exhibiting goods before sale.[43] As the great nodes of the transport system, inns were a natural choice for such activities, providing the auctioneer with a convenient place of business without the overhead costs of fixed premises, and enabling him to locate the sale in the most opportune place. When in 1716 the manor of Alford, Somerset, containing the 'famous Castle Cary Waters', was offered for sale by private tender, surveys were made available at inns and shops in nine towns, with in addition, Mr Ralph Allen distributing in Bath.[44] Such practices laid the template for later auctioneers, like Way of Thame or Plummer of Reading, and for the provincial diffusion of sale by auction, such as the disposal of books, first used in London in the 1670s.[45] By the 1750s the inn was not only established as saleroom, but was also the home for the variant that melded gaming with certainty, sale by raffle, used at

---

[39] PRO, C/108/129, Chancery Masters' Exhibits, -derick v. Wall, parcel of documents relating to George, Southwark, and abstract of title, ca 1692.

[40] Reading, Berkshire RO, D/EFO T49, papers relating to the Nagg's Head, High Street, 1682–; D/EM T175, Leases etc, Elephant, Wantage, 1703–.

[41] *Northampton Mercury* 1/9 (27 June 1720), 107.

[42] *Adams's Weekly Courant* 327 (28 February 1739), 4; *Bath Journal* 153 (26 January 1747), 178.

[43] J. A. Chartres, 'Country Trades, Crafts, and Professions', in G. E. Mingay (ed.), *The Agrarian History of England and Wales*, vol. 6, 1750–1850 (Cambridge, 1989), 446–51.

[44] *Exeter Mercury* 2/60 (17 April 1716), 2.

[45] Chartres, 'Country Trades', 449–50.

the Bell, Chipping Wycombe, for the sale of a house in 100 half-guinea lots in 1758.[46]

For those retailing more personal services the inns also provided the ideal flexible place of business, and a few examples suffice to demonstrate a little of the range to be discovered in any eighteenth-century provincial town. Inns were commonplace resorts for medical men, truss-makers, tailors, and tutors, among many others. Thus Dr Shappee (physician, surgeon, and man-midwife), opting to practise as an itinerant because travel relieved his gout, took up residence at the Black Bear, Shipston-on-Stour in the spring of 1757, and practised each market day at the Crown, Faringdon and the George, Burford.[47] For those worried by the 'blackest and foulest teeth', Mr Foy of Oxford travelled to the Angel, Reading, and the George, Dorchester, also selling his preventive dentifrice powder.[48] In 1721, Dr Walpole, 'rupture master', with a modesty recalling his namesake, offered 'infallible' cures at the Spread Eagle, Northampton, each Saturday; and on his return to Ross from London in 1757, James Morgan, stay maker, offered his services to ladies at four inns where orders could be left.[49] Edward Fell of Chipping Norton, and late of London, dealt in cloth, but he would also make a suit of superfine cloth for the 'medium sized person' in a day at the Crown Inn, Cornmarket, Oxford.[50] Tutors, from the extraordinary Cornishman John Weale, blind fencing master at the Angel, backside St Clements, London (1670) to Christopher Towle, who provided dancing schools in the inns of Oxford, Coventry, Bicester, and Aynho two days a month in the 1750s from his base in Southam, also found the inn an ideal place for their itinerant business.[51]

Space, often central locations, and familiarity had long made inns the locus for much of the public administration of early modern England. With the growing significance of the Justices of the Peace and Quarter Sessions in the governance of provincial England, inns came to provide places of administrative and quasi-judicial business, perhaps spreading from the valued and prestigious ritual of the sessions dinner. In Herefordshire, the Justices vigorously debated at which house to dine before Quarter Sessions in 1722, the Ship and Castle winning on a majority vote, and in the 1740s, the Swan and Falcon,

---

[46] *Jackson's Oxford Journal* 250 (11 February 1758), 3. The house was not to be raffled unless all the tickets were sold.

[47] *Jackson's Oxford Journal* 208 (23 April 1757), 2, and 246 (14 January 1758), 2.

[48] *Reading Mercury* 623 (3 October 1757), 3.

[49] *Northampton Mercury* 1/47 (20 March 1721), 563; *Gloucester Journal* 1814 (1 March 1757), 4.

[50] *Jackson's Oxford Journal* 305 (3 March 1759), 3, and 314 (5 May 1759), 4.

[51] *London Gazette* 503 (8 September 1670); *Jackson's Oxford Journal* 295 (23 December 1758), 3.

the Redstreak Tree, and the Green Dragon all served the same purpose.[52] By extension and through convenience, sessions adjournments were frequently held at inns, and for the increasingly important Petty Sessions, inns may have been a normal venue. The Red Lion, Brentford, Middlesex was the home of the town's Petty Sessions between 1651 and 1714, apart from a brief break in 1670, when its keeper, William Parish, had caused offence: after receiving his letter of apology in 1672, the J.P.s returned from their temporary home in the Three Pigeons.[53] Rooms of a certain grandeur, certainly size, and the convenience of food, drink, and accommodation commended the inn for these purposes at a time when many towns lacked any dedicated courtrooms.

Similar use for all stages of the statutory agencies of improvement so characteristic of this period followed naturally. Inns were familiar resorts for the leading members of the county community, and were thus the natural meeting place for those considering remedy of defective bridges as at Brentford in 1687 (the Red Lion).[54] The promotion of river navigations required extensive petitioning to be organized through the inns of the major towns in order to build the necessary impetus to win empowering legislation. Turnpike trusts required promotion in similar fashion, and a heated debate over the Stratford upon Avon to Gloucester scheme took place at the White Lion, Stratford, in the summer of 1756, as part of this process.[55] Still more extensive networks were required for the successful promotion of canals: the promotion of 'one of the boldest and most magnificent projects' of 1766, the Leeds and Liverpool Canal, began with a meeting called at the Sun Inn, Bradford, and required many further inn meetings for interested parties before the trunk route was completed, more than forty years after the first navigation.[56] It presaged similar issues and inn business with the railways in the next century.

It is however in social infrastructure that the inn provided space for the processes that would lead to its replacement by more specialized institutions. As we have seen, part of the embellishment of the grander inns lay in assembly rooms, dining rooms, and ballrooms. They also provided fundamental places of entertainment, and represented a forum for displaying new standards of sensibility, emergent institutions of social and moral improvement, and the

---

[52] Hereford, Hereford RO, Quarter Sessions Order Books, Easter 1722, fol. 98; Trinity 1744, fol. 116v; Michaelmas 1743, fol. 109v; Epiphany 1748, fol. 149v.

[53] London Metropolitan Archives, M.Acc. 890, Brentford Journal, being a record of proceedings at Petty Sessions held at Brentford, 1651–1714, 26 July 1670, 130.

[54] London Metropolitan Archives, SB 443, Middlesex Sessions Book, January 1687, 39.

[55] Levi Fox (ed.), *Correspondence of the Rev. Joseph Greene of Stratford upon Avon*, Historical MSS Commission, JP8 (London, 1965), 75–6, 12 July 1756.

[56] H. F. Killick, 'Notes on the Early History of the Leeds and Liverpool Canal', *Bradford Antiquary*, n.s. I (1900), 179; J. Priestley, *Historical Account of the Navigable Rivers, Canals, and Railways of Great Britain* (London, 1831, reprinted Newton Abbot, 1969), 385–94.

development of the Habermasian 'public sphere', the epitome of bourgeois assertiveness. Numerous subscription libraries, assembly rooms, infirmaries, theatres, promenades and similar manifestations of these changing mores began with meetings and practice in provincial inns. Many of England's first voluntary hospitals, as at Northampton and Leicester in 1743 and 1766, began with meetings convened at leading inns. Subscriptions for the new Concert Room in Leeds were opened at the King's Arms in 1785, where projects for a narrow cloth hall and a library were also to be floated.[57] From the inns that had so commonly provided space for these social functions stemmed the practical processes of improvement that, in turn, created dedicated buildings that were to displace inns by the early years of the succeeding century.

Inns were closely associated with the development of commercialized leisure during the long eighteenth century. In some of these areas, as in the transport trade, they can be treated as the relatively passive beneficiaries of exogenous developments; in others, innkeeper entrepreneurship fostered development. This final substantive section explores, albeit briefly, these contrasting themes.

Within the range of new commercial leisure activities, both types can be observed. While it is hard to be certain, the general pattern visible within the great range of performance art – concerts, theatre, recitals, and exhibitions – was that of host. The reception and other public rooms offered appropriate space to the itinerant entertainer, who drew revenues from ticket sales or subscriptions, while the innkeeper gained room rents, and from the stimulus this gave to his normal trade, the sale of food, drink, accommodation, and provender. Concerts were held at the Mitre, Wells, by the musical society from the 1720s, when the old Close Hall proved inadequate; Oates and Fielding set up their theatre booth in the yard of the George at Smithfield in 1730 for a performance of *The Generous Free-mason or the Constant Lady*, and in 1760 Mr Yates of the Theatre Royal, Drury lane, moved to 'dress his dramatic turtle' at the Greyhound, Smithfield, both for the duration of Bartholomew Fair; Mr Powell, 'Celebrated Fire-Eater', toured the inns of Wiltshire and Hampshire, charcoal-grilling mutton and beef on his tongue.[58] Mr Nevill's noted mechanical model of woollen manufacture, containing an alleged 5000 moving parts, similarly

---

[57] Everitt, 'English Urban Inn', 113; K. Grady, *The Georgian Public Buildings of Leeds and the West Riding* (Leeds, 1989), 111.

[58] E. Hobhouse (ed.), *The Diary of a West Country Physician [Dr Claver Morris of Wells]* (London, 1934), 65 (11 November 1718); ibid., 133–4 (28 June and 5 July 1726); W. C. Sydney, *England and the English in the Eighteenth Century*, (Edinburgh, 1891), vol. 1, 165; *Public Advertiser* 8058 (2 September 1760), 1; *Salisbury Journal* 794 (14 May 1753), 2.

appeared at inns all through the 1750s, and could be viewed for a shilling per head.[59]

It was in areas such as competitions and sports that inns played perhaps the more creative role. It was no accident that the most significant cricketing entrepreneur of the period, John Nyren of the Hambledon Club, was keeper of the public house that was to become the Bat and Ball, and graduated to innkeeping through his cricket connections.[60] Innkeepers played major parts in the development of the provincial race-meeting in the first half of the century, organizing plates, arranging subsidiary entertainments, such as cock-fighting, ordinaries, and balls. In twenty-five provincial towns holding race-meetings prior to 1760, inns provided subsidiary entertainment in at least fifteen; in many cases owners were obliged to stable their horses at named inns, gaining business for the innkeepers from those who came to view them and proving the direct engagement of innkeepers in the floating of meetings.[61] In 1740 alone, seven provincial meetings were founded by inns, often in consortia.[62] Gentry and larger farmers may have provided the horses, as well as both birds and the team framework for the cockpit, but the inns were the creative forces. At a lesser scale, other events appearing with increasing frequency in the middle of the century were sponsored, promoted, or created by innkeepers: singing competitions, such as that at the King's Head, Wokingham, in 1754, were commonplace; wrestling or other martial events, like backsword or cudgels normally took place at inns; and other blood sports were part of the entertainment provision for towns such as Salisbury, where in 1751, a badger – 'a large and beautiful beast of its kind' – was exhibited gratis in the Fountain, prior to baiting in the inn's assembly rooms.[63]

Such events were elements in creating the new richness of provincial urban life in the period, making the towns increasingly attractive to the middling social ranks as places for residence, particularly in the winter months. As Peter Clark has recently demonstrated, the period also saw a great proliferation of new forms of social association, clubs informal and formal: freemasons' lodges or the Oddfellows; school or regional and county societies; trade clubs such as the numerous florists who 'feasted' and competed; and political associations

[59] *Jackson's Oxford Journal* 133 (15 November 1755), 3; *Gloucester Journal* 1806 (4 January 1757), 4.

[60] R. Bowen, 'Cricket in the 17th and 18th Centuries', in *Wisden, Cricketer's Almanack* (London, 1965), 137; D. Underdown, *Start of Play: Cricket and Culture in Eighteenth-Century England* (London, 2000), 114–15.

[61] R. W. Malcolmson, *Popular Recreations in English Society 1700–1850* (Cambridge, 1973), 34–51.

[62] J. A. Chartres, 'The Place of Inns in the Commercial Life of London and Western England, 1660–1760' (Ph.D. Oxford University, 1973), 403–4.

[63] *Reading Mercury* 439 (1 April 1754), 3; *Salisbury Journal* 719 (28 October 1751), 3.

ranging from the 'Old Interest', to associations for the prosecutions of felons, to artisan groups forming box clubs or simple friendly societies, or engaging in trade unionism.[64] All were part of the growth of the public sphere during the long eighteenth century, and all needed places to meet, to stay, to provide rooms for ritual decoration, and to sell them food and drink. Clark suggests that nine out of ten clubs before 1800 met in drink outlets, and it was only in the last quarter of the century, as with assembly rooms and other more formalized places of association, that dedicated premises came gradually to displace the multi-purpose inn.[65]

If clubs, balls, concerts, ordinaries, and cockfights distracted the middling sort and others from the ennui of provincial urban life in the winter months, travel and the resort town provided in spring and summer a retreat from the miasma of the towns, and a system of ritualized public resort that met widespread associational needs, not least those of courtship. Inns undoubtedly benefited from this element of the growth of travel, but in the great pleasure centre of the age, Bath, they were ancillary, not creative forces.[66] The great competitor to both after 1760 was Brighton, and it can be no accident that the most expensively-insured inn of the years 1776–87 was John Hicks's Old Ship, Brighton, carrying a policy for £5,800 with the Sun in 1777 and 1780.[67] Among later spas and resorts Scarborough and Harrogate, flourishing increasingly from the 1780s, exemplified the 'active' role for inns in the creation of commercial leisure. There inns were the centre of entertainment and the rituals of spa life, and each innkeeper his own 'master of ceremonies'. Harrogate was very much an innkeeper spa.[68]

Travel for pleasure came also to encompass the quest for the picturesque in the second half of the century, boosting the fortunes of more remote inns, and the habit of viewing great country houses en route explains the creation, outside the bounds of the park, of the lordly inn. John Peyton, keeper of the White Lion, perhaps began the Shakespeare tourist business in 1768 by organizing a feast for the jubilee. Peyton employed 300 waiters and provided 300 dozen plates, knives and forks, fifty dozen pans, and ten pipes of wine. Stratford upon Avon certainly became the most distinctive resort town of later eighteenth-century England, outside the spas and university cities.[69] Peyton symbolized the

---

[64] P. Clark, *British Clubs and Societies 1580–1800: the Origins of an Associational World* (Oxford, 2000).

[65] Ibid., 482–3.

[66] P. Hembry, *The English Spa 1560–1815: a Social History* (London, 1990), 111–58.

[67] Guildhall Library, Sun Policy 385774.

[68] Hembry, *English Spa*, 203–30.

[69] Everitt, 'Urban Inn', 102–3, indicates 'Payton' at the Red Lion; *Jackson's Oxford Journal* 5 (2 June 1753), 4, lists Peyton at the White Lion in advertising the Stage Coach and

synergy of the inn and tourism in also being the principal coach proprietor of the town.

From the middle years of the seventeenth century, inns in England, and later in Scotland enjoyed an extended period of expansion, diffusion, improvement and re-embellishment, symbolic of their central position in society and the economy. Expanding travel for business and increasingly for pleasure created their custom; the 'volunteer' provisions of extended and improved infrastructure eased the processes of development in road transport services. Central to urban space and to travel, and critical landmarks for the broad community, they naturally became key places of association, for purposes ranging from the most formal business uses to the least structured club. For tradesmen and others not yet capable of sustaining their businesses in settled premises, they provided the ideal temporary 'shop'.

Located at the commercial centres of towns, inns were also natural locations for the transaction of public business, and by association became the places in which local communities held meetings to create agencies of improvement. Directly involved, often creatively, in many forms of commercial leisure, the inn came gradually to be supplanted from the last quarter of the eighteenth century by new and more specialized provisions. By the 1830s, inns had lost many of their former associational functions, and were rapidly losing their transport trades. The golden age of the inn, peaking in the late eighteenth century, during which it met a huge range of social and economic needs with flexibility and economy, had passed. Competition for urban space, for the dense housing of the industrializing towns, crammed lean-to cottages into the decaying inn yards, notoriously in the Boot and Shoe of Leeds.[70] Like cottage manufacture, or protoindustrialization, the role of the inn in the transformation of Britain was transitional or intermediate; new scales and modes of transport, and new specialized institutions displaced it in the nineteenth century. The inn was thus consigned to an extended period of genteel decay, to be romantically recorded by artist and photographer, and only being rediscovered by the new wave of independent road travel established during the golden age of British motoring in the inter-war years.

---

the Old Stage Coach to Birmingham and Warwick. On Stratford's early tourism, see I. Ousby, *The Englishman's England: Taste, Travel and the Rise of Tourism* (Cambridge, 1990), 42–3.

    [70] M. W. Beresford, *East End, West End: the Face of Leeds During Urbanisation, 1684–1842* (Leeds, 1988), 204–5.

Index